EUREKA!

EUREKA!

50 SCIENTISTS WHO SHAPED HUMAN HISTORY

BY JOHN GRANT

ZEST
BOOKS

CONTENTS

For Bill and Kathrin DeSmedt

Connect with Zest!

- zestbooks.net/blog   - twitter.com/zestbooks
- zestbooks.net/contests   - facebook.com/BooksWithATwist

2443 Fillmore Street, Suite 340, San Francisco, CA 94115 | www.zestbooks.net

Manufactured in the U.S.A. | 4500597856 | DOC 10 9 8 7 6 5 4 3 2 1

INTRODUCTION

Once upon a time—not so very long ago, really—the world was flat and at the center of all things. The Sun and the Moon and the stars went round it, as did, in a more complicated way, the planets. All the treasures of the world had been set in place to serve human beings, more particularly male human beings, who were the pinnacle of creation. All was for the best in this best of all possible worlds.

Except that, of course, it wasn't.

We've come a long way since those days, and especially in the past few centuries. The universe that seemed so small and stable has been revealed in its vast and dynamic magnificence, with the promise that it still has plenty more secrets waiting for us. But it's not just the universe we know so much more about; it's also ourselves. We have a far clearer idea of how we function, what makes us sick, what can cure us, and how we're a part of the enormously complicated web of relationships that constitutes the environment in which we live. We recognize, too, problems our ancestors could never have dreamed of.

What has brought us out of the dark cave of ignorance into the sunshine of knowledge is science.

Technically speaking, science didn't really exist as such until the early seventeenth century, when people like Francis BACON began to systematize the best ways in which human reason could be used to acquire knowledge. We now refer to those various schemes collectively as the Scientific Method. But the scientific impulse dates back thousands of years before that, as people did their best to explain what was going on around them. Even though a lot of their efforts were misguided, it seems reasonable to refer to them as scientists.

Most of the names of those scientists have been forgotten, as is the way of things, or at most survive as footnotes in scholarly histories. In fact, one of the curiosities of the story of science is how often the work of scientists who were enormously prestigious in their own day has proven later to have had little or no lasting effect. The converse is true, too. There are plenty of examples of people whose ideas have been dismissed at the time but whom we now recognize as true groundbreakers—Ignaz SEMMELWEIS is one, Alfred WEGENER another.

There's a different reason, sadly, why some people's ideas were ignored. Science, as a human activity, is as vulnerable to social biases as any other part of society. You'll notice that men significantly outnumber women as the subjects of the essays in this book. This is because, tragically, until very recently—and, many would argue, still—both women and predominantly men have assumed the sciences aren't a fit subject for "the gentler sex." A striking example of a female scientist wrongfully ignored is Émilie DU CHÂTELET, who for two and a half centuries was widely regarded as just some mistress of Voltaire who'd done a translation job for him. Rosalind FRANKLIN was depicted as a mere hanger-on in the endeavor to decipher the structure of DNA—and as a ferocious harpy, too, just to make her seem even more peripheral.

So how do you decide whether or not a particular scientist has shaped history? It's as easy as deciding whether or not a rock band is any good—in other words, while you can bring a fair number of objective criteria to the decision (they play in tune, for example), in the end it becomes a matter of personal judgment. Although I think everyone would agree on such figures as COPERNICUS, GALILEO, NEWTON, MENDEL, DARWIN, CURIE, and, of course, EINSTEIN as history-shapers, I'm only too well aware that some of my fifty choices for inclusion and omission here might startle a few readers. *Ça va.*

All of the people I've included have helped us better understand our universe. Some have done so in very obvious ways, some far more subtly. If you removed any of them from the story of science, it'd be a different story. ■

PYTHAGORAS OF SAMOS

(ca. 570–ca. 495 BCE?)

The semi-legendary Mediterranean mystic who believed music and numbers underpinned the universe.

Nobody's entirely sure Pythagoras actually existed, since there are no surviving contemporary accounts of him, let alone any of his writings. It probably makes sense to think in terms of not so much an individual as a school of thought. In fact, some believe the Pythagoreans might have invented their spiritual and philosophical leader after the fact—creating a myth of origin, as it were—in order to bolster their own street cred. It wouldn't be the first or the last time a cult has done this sort of thing.

For the sake of convenience, though, we'll assume here that Pythagoras did indeed exist and that later Greek philosophers were right about the scanty details they recorded of his life.

Born on the island of Samos in the eastern Aegean Sea, Pythagoras may have traveled widely as a young man throughout Egypt and Babylon, learning the art of mathematics along the way. On return to his home island, he found it under the reign of a cruel tyrant, Polycrates. Soon he was forced to leave Samos as a political refugee, and settled in Croton, a Greek city in the south of Italy, where he set up a community devoted to philosophy, religion, and politics. At first this community was welcomed by the local powers, but after twenty years or so, relations soured, and sometime around 500 BCE it suffered a devastating attack. Pythagoras fled again, this time to Metapontum, also in southern Italy, where he spent the rest of his life.

We needn't spend too long on the straightforwardly religious aspects of the Pythagorean cult. Either Pythagoras or his followers thought he was semi-divine and not only had had a succession of past lives but could remember them; part of his wisdom arose because he had learning and experience from not just one but several existences.

Exercise and physical fitness were important components of the Pythagorean way of life. There were also some strange prohibitions his followers had to observe: They weren't allowed to eat beans, or to pick up anything that had fallen or been dropped, or to walk on a highway, or to use an iron poker for the fire. Equally important was that, when they got up in the morning, they should roll up their bedclothes so as to get rid of the impression their body had left. Failure to obey these rules could result in severe punishment.

The Pythagoreans thought music was the most easily accessible aspect of the harmony that underpinned the universe. This meant that, the more you knew about music, the closer you might become to the divine ideal.

It was apparent to them that, in a certain sense, music was made up of numbers. If you halve the length of a vibrating string, the note it now sounds is an octave higher than the original. In fact, all the harmonic intervals in music can be described in terms of fairly simple numerical relationships involving just the numbers 1, 2, 3, and 4. To the mystically inclined Pythagoreans, this was a clear sign that they were on the right track, because those four numbers add up to 10, a number that's sacred because it's the basis of the counting system.

But if music was a fundamental element of the cosmos and music was numerically based, this meant *everything else* should be underpinned by numbers too. And, sure enough, wherever the Pythagoreans looked they found numbers. One relationship they hit upon was the nonintuitive fact that some trios of numbers were related through their squares: $3^2 + 4^2 = 5^2$, for example, or $7^2 + 24^2 = 25^2$.

The Pythagoreans knew you could construct a right triangle with one side being 3 units long, another 4 units long, and the third (the hypotenuse) 5 units long. To put this a bit more formally, the square on the hypotenuse is equal to the sum of the squares on the other two sides. It was tempting to think this same relationship could hold true for the lengths of the sides of *all* right triangles. This is now known as the Pythagorean theorem. The ancient Egyptian architects had found this to be true through trial and error, but the Pythagoreans produced a neat geometrical proof of it.

This led them to another and much more perplexing problem. You can easily construct a right triangle whose two shorter sides are both of length 1 unit. The square on its hypotenuse must be 2 (because $1^2 + 1^2 = 2$), and so the hypotenuse itself must be of length equal to the square root of 2, or $\sqrt{2}$. But, however hard the Pythagoreans tried to calculate a precise value for $\sqrt{2}$, they couldn't: $\sqrt{2}$, they concluded (correctly), cannot be exactly represented by a fraction. There was another number they knew of that had this same quality: π, the ratio between the diameter and circumference of a circle. Since the circle was a sacred shape, π was a number that must be fundamental to the cosmos, and yet no one could give it an exact value. To use modern terminology, both √2 and π are irrational numbers.

The Pythagoreans were drawn to develop an idea called *fluxion* (flowing). No matter how close together a pair of numbers might be—like 1.999999999999 and 2—there are infinitely many *other* numbers between them. We tend to think of numbers as being partitioned off from each other, as it were, like when we count 1, 2, 3, 4, 5 . . . , but the Pythagoreans realized that numbers represented a continuous flow from the smallest to the biggest—from zero to infinity. In other words, a number like π or √2 could *theoretically* be expressed as a fraction—a ratio between two numbers—if only the subdivisions between numbers could be infinitely small.

In this they were wrong, because numbers like π and √2 really *can't* be expressed as fractions. But the idea of fluxion wasn't worthless. Imagine that you're running your finger along a calibrated rule. It doesn't matter what the units are on the rule. At one stage your finger might be on the calibration 3.1415, and soon after, it'll be on the 3.1416 mark. Somewhere in between those two, your finger will have passed over the place on the rule corresponding to π, even though you could never locate that position. The idea of numbers being a continuous stream allows for some numbers being in there that we can't precisely define.

Moreover, in pursuing this idea, the Pythagoreans came very close to the underlying notion of calculus, even though it seems not to have dawned on them that it could have any practical use. Over two thousand years later, when Isaac NEWTON devised the calculus, he called it "fluxions."

The Pythagoreans' reverence for music and numbers also led them to the concept of the Music of the Spheres. It seemed obvious the Moon was nearer to us than the Sun, and the Sun nearer than the stars and planets. Since it was assumed that everything else in the universe was centered on the (flat) Earth, it followed that the universe must consist of an outermost sphere populated by the stars and planets, with, inside it, a smaller celestial sphere defining the path of the Sun; the sphere of the Moon was smaller still. Since music was a fundamental property of the universe, these spheres must surely resonate and do so harmoniously; in other words, they must correspond to the octave, the fourth and the fifth.

After a while, the Pythagoreans realized this system of three spheres was an oversimplification, because clearly the planets moved in spheres smaller than the sphere of the stars. A later Pythagorean—probably

Philolaus—put forth a radically different view of the cosmos in which the Earth wasn't motionless at the center of everything but moved around *something else*.

This was a major conceptual breakthrough. The center of the universe was a place of fire that we could never see because we were always on the wrong side of the flat Earth from it; we could, however, see its reflected light and feel its reflected heat from the face of the Sun. There was also a counter-Earth, a hypothetical planet perpetually on the far side of the central fire. If you added up all the various spheres that were centered on the fire (Earth, counter-Earth, Moon, Sun, Mercury, Venus, Mars, Jupiter, Saturn,[1] stars) you got the mystically significant number 10.

The Pythagoreans learned lots more about the behavior of numbers and the relationships between them. Yet they didn't approach this in any sort of scientific way. The Pythagorean school wasn't some ancient equivalent of MIT but instead something far closer to a religious cult, with all of a cult's paranoid secrecy, and with numbers as its object of veneration. According to one legend, Pythagoras himself either banished or condemned to death a follower called Hippasus for having revealed to "unworthy" people the Pythagorean discovery that $\sqrt{2}$ cannot be represented by a precise fraction. And then there were all the bizarre rules of the community, like the banning of the beans.

It may seem odd to begin this book with a discussion of someone who may not even have existed, and whose supposed ideas were far more mystical than scientific. Yet we have to remember that really there was no such thing as science until about the early seventeenth century, and that what the Pythagoreans were doing was pursuing knowledge using the best tools they had. One way or another, they stirred up a revolution of sorts in ancient Greek civilization, and much later we're still reaping the benefits. ■

BUT THERE'S MORE . . .

- *The Music of Pythagoras* (2008) by Kitty Ferguson is a very entertaining account of the importance of the Pythagoreans.
- Carol Goodman's novel *The Night Villa* (2008) involves a modern-day Pythagorean cult.
- There's a crater on the Moon named for Pythagoras, as well as the asteroid 6143 Pythagoras.

---

1. The ancients didn't know about Uranus, Neptune, etc.

HIPPOCRATES
(ca. 460–ca. 370 BCE)

The "Father of Medicine" who, with his followers, established some of the health care principles by which we still abide today.

Hippocrates, along with his followers, established a rational approach to health and sickness in a world ruled by superstition and primitive medicine. Hippocrates dismissed supernatural explanations for illness—such as that epileptic seizures represented demonic possession—in favor of physical ones. He was not the "first physician," although he's sometimes mistakenly called that; there were certainly others before him.

The only source we have for his biography is *The Life of Hippocrates*, written by Soranus of Ephesus several hundred years later, around the end of the first century CE, so the details of his life may be fanciful.

Hippocrates was born on the island of Cos (or Kos), which, although Greek, is just a few miles off the coast of Turkey. According to legend, his family was descended from Asclepios, the Greek god of medicine. He supposedly traveled widely around the Mediterranean in his youth, learning the art of medicine wherever he went. He may have studied with Democritus, who developed the idea in Greek culture that matter was made of indivisible atoms.

Finally—and this part at least seems true—he returned to Cos, where he set up a medical school. What we know of Hippocrates's ideas derives from the seventy-two manuscripts of the *Corpus Hippocraticum* (Hippocratic Collection); they seem to have come from the library of a later physician. How many, if any, of these treatises were by Hippocrates himself is uncertain.

In Hippocrates's time, it was believed health was governed by four bodily humors, corresponding to the four elements (earth, air, fire, water) of which everything was supposedly made. The four humors were melancholy (black bile), blood, choler (yellow bile), and phlegm (the term meant something quite different from our modern word *phlegm*).

In a healthy person, the humors were in balance. Illness was caused by an imbalance among them, or by a corruption of one or more humors.

In a strong individual, the natural course of a disease was that it would reach a crisis and then wane. What was happening was that the body was, in effect, "cooking" the relevant humors to make them "digestible" once more.

The Cos physicians also had the idea of the "deposit," a symptom initially confined to just a single part of the body but capable of migrating, in a process called metastasis, to other parts. The effect was that one disease could seem to turn into another. We still use the word *metastasis* to describe how cancers spread through the body.

Hippocratic ideas of physiology were way wide of the mark—like those of the physicians of the rival school at Cnidas, at the southwestern tip of Asia Minor—but this needn't have hampered them too much. In fact, the Cos and Cnidas physicians seem to have focused less on curing diseases and more on what we'd today call preventive medicine (diet, exercise, hygiene, etc.), on keeping patients comfortable, and on observing the progress of diseases in much the same way modern physicians keep case histories.

Simply knowing what's likely to happen next in a sickness is really quite a useful medical tool; for example, if you know that patients displaying certain symptoms are likely next to have a fever, then you can wrap them up warmly beforehand. Moreover, the medical ideas then prevalent elsewhere were so primitive that patients were actually far more likely to recover if their physicians *didn't* try to cure them! Although it's not stated explicitly by the Hippocratic writers, the principle of "first do no harm" was clearly important to them: the idea that it's better to do nothing at all than something that makes matters worse.

The Cos physicians thus achieved better recovery rates than their rivals, though this would also have been helped by the placebo effect. If patients believe the physician is doing the right thing, a surprisingly high percentage—up to about one-third—will recover of their own volition. Since patients knew the Cos and Cnidas physicians achieved better recovery rates than their rivals, this likely boosted the placebo effect.

Alas, the idea of medicine as something to be approached rationally rather than mystically didn't survive in the ancient world for too much longer, as various mystical ideas became more popular. It wasn't really until midway through the nineteenth century that the doctrine of the four humors disappeared from European medicine. Other, better, Hippocratic ideas were largely lost.

A further reason for the long hiatus in medical progress was the popularity of the ideas of Galen. Galen was born around 130 BCE in Pergamum (now the Turkish city of Bergama), and for a time served as physician to the Pergamum gladiators. Oddly enough, dissection of human cadavers for scientific study was at the time taboo, but watching people hack each other to bits in the arena was okay. Galen was thus able to gain considerable anatomical knowledge that was denied other physicians.

He also dissected animals. This led him to some correct conclusions about human anatomy and physiology, but also to some disastrously wrong ones. He believed blood was formed in the liver and passed from the right to the left chamber of the heart through minute holes in the intervening wall. In the left half of the heart the blood mixed with air from the lungs, which gave it vitality. When it reached a (nonexistent) network of arteries under the brain it gained an "animal spirit" responsible for, among other things, consciousness. It wasn't until 1628, when William HARVEY worked out the true nature of the blood's circulation, that these ideas were discarded.

Galen shared with the Hippocratic physicians the idea that health was governed by the four humors, but he didn't share their pragmatic "first do no harm" approach to treatment. Since he saw the universe, including its occupants, as something designed by a divine creator, his teachings became especially popular among Christians, and thus spread all through Europe.

Hippocrates is perhaps best known for the famous Hippocratic oath, which was probably written in its original form either by Hippocrates himself or by one of his disciples. Traditionally taken by medical students as they complete their course of training, the oath consists of a statement of medical ethics and a promise to abide by them. Interestingly, in Nazi Germany the practice of taking the Hippocratic oath was abolished. Similarly, in several US states today it's regarded as not in breach of the Hippocratic oath for physicians to take part in executions by lethal injection. ■

BUT THERE'S MORE . . .

■ There are various editions of the Hippocratic Collection in print. An interesting if somewhat dry analysis of the more important essays is *Hippocrates* (1971) by Edwin Burton Levine. *Hippocrates in a World of Pagans and Christians* (1991) by Owsei Temkin describes how the scientific Hippocratic ideals competed with beliefs in faith healing in the ancient world. Jacques Jouanna's vast *Hippocrates* (1998) isn't a biography but an account of Hippocratic medicine and its historical influence.

■ Hippocrates, played by Charles Coburn, appears as a character in the 1957 movie *The Story of Mankind*, in which the Spirit of Man (played by Ronald Colman) argues with the Devil (played by who else but Vincent Price) over humanity's potential for good and evil. The French movie *Hippocrate* (2014; aka *Hippocrates: Diary of a French Doctor*) uses the name of the great physician wryly; the story is in fact about a modern trainee doctor with ambitions higher than his current skills.

■ There's a crater on the Moon called Hippocrates, and an asteroid called 14367 Hippokrates.

■ In 2009 Donald Singer and Michael Hulse inaugurated the Hippocrates Society to provide "an international forum for people from anywhere in the world interested in the interface between poetry and medicine"; its annual Hippocrates Prize is open to submissions of poems on medical subjects.

EUCLID OF ALEXANDRIA

(ca. 325–ca. 270 BCE)

The mathematician who set down a way of looking at the universe that survived for over two millennia.

Almost nothing is known about the life of this great mathematician, and some have suggested there was no such individual—that the name *Euclid*, meaning "glorious," was adopted by a group of mathematicians working together. However, scientists like ARCHIMEDES, who lived and worked in Alexandria not long after we think Euclid did, clearly regarded him as having been a real person. Often called the "Father of Geometry," Euclid made huge contributions to mathematics and logic.

After the death of Alexander the Great in 323 BCE, the great conqueror's huge empire fell apart, with his generals squabbling among each other to seize bits of it. The general who grabbed Egypt, Ptolemy I Soter, decided to build up his capital, Alexandria, as a great center of knowledge, and set about attracting the best scholars of the known world. Among the first to join this enterprise was Euclid. Euclid may have studied in Athens under the philosopher Plato, and certainly he seems to have had the same notion that Plato did of "ideal forms." For example, in the real world, no matter how carefully you draw a straight line and no matter how sharp your pencil, the line still has tiny wobbles and still has a thickness. Yet we can conceive of lines that are perfectly straight and have zero thickness. Likewise, in nature there's no such thing as a perfect sphere, yet we can conceive of a perfect—"ideal"—sphere. And it's with these ideal forms that geometry deals.

Euclid wrote several treatises on mathematics and science. *Phaenomena* is about astronomy, but its real concern is with what we'd now call spherical geometry. *Optics* is mainly about perspective—in other words, geometry again. While that part of the treatise is fine, his discussion of physiological optics suffers from his bizarre error (inherited again from Plato) that our vision works because we emit rays from our eyes that bounce off things in front of us.

By far his most important book—one that has shaped the whole course of Western civilization—is *Elements*. In thirteen volumes, *Elements* collected much of what was then known about math, especially (yet again) geometry. It was so comprehensive that, with minor revisions, it was still being used as a textbook over two thousand years later.

His real breakthrough was the way in which he presented all this information.

He began with five axioms and, more importantly, five postulates (really just five more axioms). An axiom is something that seems self-evidently true and that we can use as a starting point for further reasoning. Here (in edited form) are the five postulates:

1. You can draw a straight line between any two points.
2. You can extend a straight line infinitely in either direction.
3. You can choose any center and any radius to construct a circle.
4. All right angles are equal.
5. Two parallel lines, extended infinitely, will never either meet or grow farther apart.[1]

From relatively simple assumptions like these, Euclid was able to create a grand scheme of geometry, with each of his geometrical proofs and demonstrations following on logically from what had gone before. This meant the book wasn't just a treatise on mathematics but was also, in a sense, a description of the way the universe works, because central to it was the idea that these mathematical truths were valid not just here and now but *anywhere* and *always*.

Even just from the postulates above we can glean a couple of the profound statements Euclid was making about the universe. From postulates 2 and 3 it's evident he thought the universe was infinite in all directions. From postulate 3 we can infer that he thought space was infinitely subdivisible, because he was saying a circle could be not just as big as you wanted but also as tiny.

Postulate 5, however, seemed less self-evident than the others, and by the nineteenth century this was beginning to trouble some mathematicians. What if the postulate was actually *wrong*? The most significant

---

1. More formally: If two straight lines are intersected by a third straight line, and if the two internal angles on one side of this third line add up to less than 180°, when the other two lines meet it will be on that side of the third line.

investigation of this possibility was that done by the German mathematician Bernhard RIEMANN, who constructed a geometry based on the notion that parallel lines *do* eventually meet.

The almost certainly apocryphal tale is told that Euclid's sponsor, Ptolemy I, found math pretty hard going, and asked the mathematician if there weren't some quicker and easier way he could get his head round it. "No," said Euclid. "There's no such thing as a royal road to geometry." ∎

BUT THERE'S MORE . . .

- There are several bands named for the great mathematician, and a surprising number of albums titled *Euclid*.
- The small lunar crater Euclides is named for the mathematician, as are several places in the US.
- A computer program and a programming language bear his name, as does one of the annual math competitions held by the Centre for Education in Mathematics and Computing at the University of Waterloo in Ontario.
- The Euclid space mission, scheduled for launch in 2020, will, it's hoped, substantially increase our knowledge of dark energy and dark matter, the invisible entities thought to make up some 95 percent of our universe.

ARCHIMEDES OF SYRACUSE

(ca. 287–212 BCE)

The single most important scientist of the ancient world.

Probably the greatest genius of the ancient world, Archimedes was born into an aristocratic family in Syracuse, on the island of Sicily. His father was an astronomer called Phidias. The family was likely related to that of Syracuse's ruler, Hieron II, and this may well be why, after receiving his education in mathematics in Alexandria, Archimedes returned to Syracuse rather than stay on in that great city of learning. His friend Heracleides wrote a biography of him, but this has been lost, and so we have to rely on later writers for our knowledge of Archimedes. We have no idea how much those later writers embellished their accounts.

One of the most frequently repeated stories about Archimedes concerns his discovery of the famous Archimedean principle. Supposedly Hieron had recently had a gold crown made, and was suspicious the craftsman might have cheated him by alloying some silver into the gold. He asked Archimedes to find out the truth, at the same time stressing that the crown shouldn't be in any way damaged. Archimedes was puzzled as to how to do this until one day, climbing into his bath, he sloshed some water over the side. He immediately realized that he could fill a container to the brim with water, carefully lower the crown into it, and then, by measuring the volume of the water that spilled over the container's sides, establish the volume of even such a complicated structure as the crown. Since gold and silver have different densities, by weighing the crown he could find out if it was solid gold or not.

According to the legend, he was so excited by this brain wave that he ran naked and dripping all the way to Hieron's palace to tell him about it, shouting, "Eureka!" ("I've got it!") as he did so.[1]

Allied to this realization was his discovery of the principle of buoyancy (or principle of flotation). If something is floating in water, the

---

1. The ancient Greeks weren't as worried about public nudity as we are, so the "naked" part of the story is unremarkable.

water it displaces has the same weight as the floating object. If you float a plastic duck in your bath, very little of the duck is below the waterline; in other words, the duck has displaced very little water. This is because it has a very low average density, being made up mainly of the air inside it. Try the same with a piece of wood, and a much higher proportion will be underwater.

Archimedes did a lot of work on the principles of the lever. It was well known that if you put the fulcrum of your lever close to a heavy object, you need apply relatively little effort to the other end in order to move the object. On the other hand, you have to move the lever's far end quite a distance in order to move the object just a little. Archimedes worked out the mathematics of this, and made the boast that, given a place to stand and a lever long enough, he could move the world.

Hieron supposedly questioned this and challenged Archimedes to move, if not the world, something impressively heavy. The story goes that Archimedes, having realized that the block-and-pulley is really a specialized system of levers, even if it doesn't look like it, was able to single-handedly pull a ship out of the water and up the beach.

In the field of math, he calculated a very precise value for π; he proved it must lie between (translated into decimals) 3.14085 and 3.14286. Since its actual value (to five decimal places) is 3.14159, you can see how close Archimedes got.

But the way in which he derived his estimate is actually more interesting than the estimate itself. He approached the problem by imagining a circle with a polygon circumscribed around it and another polygon inscribed within it. The greater the number of sides those polygons had, the closer they would approximate to the circle. In fact, if either of those polygons had an *infinite* number of sides, it would actually *be* the circle. Although the idea of infinity was known to the Greeks before Archimedes's time, no one had worked out how to handle it mathematically. Even so, Archimedes came tantalizingly close, here and in other calculations, to discovering the principles of calculus nearly two millennia before Isaac Newton and Gottfried Leibniz.

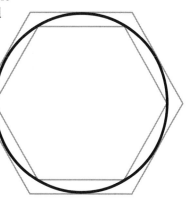

Archimedes wasn't without a sense of humor. He was in the habit of sending the scholars at Alexandria the results of his calculations, but without the workings. After a while, he noticed that some of the Alexandrian scholars were claiming his results as their own. After that, with each batch of conclusions he sent he'd slip in one or two that were completely bogus, and then wait with delight for the fraudulent scholars to solemnly repeat them.

He was reputed to have invented the Archimedean screw, a device for raising water, but in fact this trick had been known to the Egyptians long before. It's possible he worked out the math of it, just as he did with the lever.

In 215 BCE Hieron died. Years earlier he'd made a treaty with the Romans to take their side in their seemingly interminable war with Carthage. His heir, a grandson called Hieronymus, soon after taking the throne reckoned the Carthaginians were winning, and so switched sides. Hieronymus was assassinated before he could learn quite how disastrous a decision he'd made. In 214 BCE the Romans, back in the ascendant over the Carthaginians, sent a navy to suppress Syracuse.

The resulting siege lasted nearly three years, resistance being offered by, it's said, just one man, Archimedes. Supposedly he used giant lenses to set the Roman ships on fire, deployed elaborate systems of pulleys to capsize them in the water, and so on. Probably most of this was fabrication by later Greek writers eager to show a smart Greek making the dumb Romans look stupid. However, three years was an unusually long time for a siege to last, so there may be some kernel of truth in the tale.

There's far less doubt about the manner of Archimedes's death. He was widely known and respected as an inventor (his theoretical work, though far more important, impressed people less), and the Roman general in charge of the siege, Marcus Claudius Marcellus, issued orders that he was to be well treated when the city fell, as inevitably it must. However, when a Roman soldier came across Archimedes—reportedly studying a geometrical figure he'd drawn in the sand—the soldier acted as invading soldiers generally do, killing the man on the spot and asking questions afterward.

Marcellus professed to be horrified. He arranged a lavish funeral, and Archimedes was given the tombstone he'd said he wanted. The mathematical achievement of which he was proudest was his calculation of the relationship between the volume of a sphere and that of the cylinder circumscribing it. Apparently either a diagram representing this relationship was carved onto the stone, or a structure comprising a sphere and a cylinder was erected over the grave. Much later, in 75 BCE, Cicero claimed actually to have seen the grave, but thereafter it was lost.

As with so much of the scientific and mathematical work of the ancient world, the writings of Archimedes were eventually lost to Europe and survived only among the Arabian scholars who translated them and annotated them. (Some of the Islamic scholars, hoping to give themselves greater authority, claimed their own works were actually translations from his originals.) In 1544, however, Archimedes's works were translated from Arabic into Latin. The appearance of that translation was one of the events that sparked the Scientific Revolution, spearheaded by figures like KEPLER and GALILEO.

More recently, in 1906, the Danish historian Johan Ludvig Heiberg was investigating a Christian text in Constantinople when he discovered it was a palimpsest.[1] The text that had been overwritten proved to consist of scientific treatises, including several by Archimedes, one of which had been thought irretrievably lost. The palimpsest is now at Baltimore's Walters Art Museum. ■

BUT THERE'S MORE . . .

■ In T. H. White's novel *The Sword in the Stone* (1938), the wizard Merlin's highly intelligent owl is called Archimedes in honor of the great scholar.

■ On the Moon there's not just a crater named for Archimedes but a mountain range. Also, there's an asteroid called 3600 Archimedes. A long list of mathematical and physical entities are named for Archimedes, some rightly so but others having nothing to do with him.

■ For obvious reasons, there are no straight biographies of Archimedes (aside from a few short ones for children), but you might enjoy Alan Hirshfeld's *Eureka Man: The Life and Legacy of Archimedes* (2009). It gives as much of a biography as is sensible and then explains some of Archimedes's scientific ideas before supplying an account of the Archimedes Palimpsest. Sir Thomas Heath's brief account of the man and his work, *Archimedes* (1920), is clearly dated but worth a read; you can find it on Project Gutenberg.

---

1. In the Middle Ages vellum was expensive, and so scribes often scraped older texts off vellum scrolls and wrote new texts on the surface. Such documents are called palimpsests.

PTOLEMY
(CLAUDIUS PTOLEMAEUS)
(ca. 90–ca. 168)

An Alexandrian astronomer and geographer whose encyclopedic works guided Western thought for many centuries.

I t'd be easy to make the case that Ptolemy was the most significant astronomer the world has ever known. His ideas of how the universe worked dominated scientific thought, at least in the West, for something like 1,300 years.

Which was a pity, because he got just about everything wrong.

Except for the fact that he lived and worked in Alexandria, in Egypt, very few details of Ptolemy's life are known. His earliest astronomical observation, as recorded in his major astronomical treatise, dates from 127 and his latest from 141; since he wrote other major books after that, it's reasonable to suppose he lived a couple of decades longer. Because of his name, some historians think he might have been born in Ptolemais Hermiou, a city on the west bank of the Nile, but they're really just guessing.

In Alexandria, Ptolemy built himself a rooftop observatory so that, far above the optical interference of the city's lights (meager by today's standards, of course), he could see the skies more clearly.[1] More important, the city contained the greatest repository of knowledge in the ancient world, its famous library.

Among the works to which Ptolemy had access there were the writings of Hipparchus, arguably the greatest of all the Greek astronomers. Working in the second century BCE, Hipparchus made an accurate calculation of the Moon's distance from the Earth, constructed the first major star atlas, invented the concept of celestial latitude and longitude (and, as a by-product, formalized the system of terrestrial latitude and

---

1. Remember, all of his observations were by naked eye; the telescope wouldn't be invented for centuries.

longitude into something much like the one we use today), saw the first recorded nova (although he had no way of knowing it was an exploding star), was the first to classify stars according to their brightness, discovered the famous precession of the equinoxes, and much more.

Hipparchus also developed a cosmology that was to be hugely influential. Although Aristarchus of Samos and others had correctly deduced that the Earth and the planets went around the Sun, not the Sun around the Earth, the majority scientific view was that the Earth was the center of the universe and everything else circled it. Hipparchus subscribed to the Pythagorean notion of celestial spheres. In his scheme there were eight of these, the outermost being that of the stars, with the other seven corresponding to the five known planets, plus the Moon and Sun. He thought all the spheres were centered on a position in space, the *eccentric*, that was close to the Earth and circled it.

The planets were not actually fixed to their spheres (*deferents*) as if by some sort of celestial glue. They were, rather, fixed onto the outsides of smaller spheres (*epicycles*). For each planet, as the deferent circled the eccentric, the epicycle, bearing the planet, rotated around a fixed point on the deferent. By tampering with this Rube Goldberg system appropriately, astronomers could produce a good match to the actual observed motions of the planets. With Aristarchus's system, by contrast, because of the assumption that the planets must move in circles, the calculations very soon slipped out of kilter with the observations.

How much of Hipparchus's work Ptolemy "borrowed" is debatable, but it seems clear that some of it he just stole. Analysis of many of the observations Ptolemy said he'd made himself in Alexandria shows they were much more likely made from the latitude of the island of Rhodes, which just happens to be where Hipparchus lived and worked! In one instance that puzzled historians for a long time, Ptolemy claimed to have observed the 132 CE autumnal equinox about twenty-eight hours after it actually happened. The solution to the mystery proved to be that Ptolemy took Hipparchus's observation for the autumnal equinox of 146 BCE and based his own "measure-

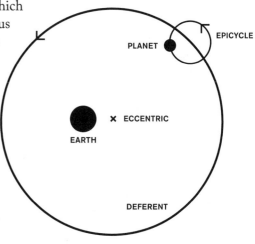

ment" on the assumption that exactly 278 years had passed. The figure he used for the length of the year was the one calculated by Hipparchus. Unfortunately for him, Hipparchus's calculation was slightly adrift.

Ptolemy swallowed Hipparchus's geocentric ("Earth-centered") cosmology more or less hook, line, and sinker, although he simplified it a little. He put all this, as well as much further astronomical lore, into what we could think of as a grand encyclopedia of his era's knowledge of astronomy. He called it the *Mathematike Syntaxis* (Mathematical Treatise), a title his successors often modified to *Megale Mathematike Syntaxis* (Great Mathematical Treatise) or even *Megiste Mathematike Syntaxis* (Great*est* Mathematical Treatise). As European intellectual culture collapsed, Ptolemy's great work was preserved by Arab scholars, who referred to it as *Almagest* (The Greatest). It's as the *Almagest* that it's universally known today.

Forgotten in Europe for centuries, the *Almagest* was translated from Arabic into Latin in about 1175 by Gerard of Cremona, and thereafter was regarded almost universally as the last word on astronomy until COPERNICUS showed that geocentrism was a fallacy.

Ptolemy's other major work, the *Geographia*, was likewise a compilation of all that was then known and understood about a topic, this time geography. Really it was more a sort of annotated atlas, the maps being revised versions of those in an atlas compiled earlier by Marinus of Tyre, with additional information from other sources. Again, this was lost to the West for centuries but preserved by Arab scholars.

The *Geographia* was translated from Arabic into Latin in 1406, and had a profound effect on the thinking of Christopher Columbus. Unfortunately for Columbus, in deciding on a figure for the Earth's diameter, Ptolemy chose the estimate produced by Posedonius, about 5,725 miles (about 9,210 km), rather than the far more accurate one derived a century or so earlier by Eratosthenes, about 7,960 miles (about 12,800 km). Thus Columbus thought the westward distance from Europe to the Indies was a lot shorter than it actually was; had he realized the true figure, he'd probably never have set off, because he'd have known he couldn't take sufficient supplies to last the voyage. Luckily for him and his crew, he discovered the West Indies instead.

Ptolemy wrote further treatises. One, on optics, was, in its Arabic translation, very influential on the work of ALHAZEN; the latter considerably revised it. Then there was the *Tetrabiblos* (Four Books), on astrology. He also wrote about music, math and other topics.

Ptolemy's great contribution to the world of his time was to gather existing knowledge and present it in works of encyclopedic scope. Today we accept that human knowledge is in a constant state of flux, with old ideas being revised in favor of better ones. Our ancestors didn't have that attitude. Ptolemy's countless errors were the errors of his era. The blame for the fact that his works misled Western thought for so very long lies with the human tendency to regard ancient texts as sacrosanct just because of their ancientness. Centuries after Ptolemy's time, people could face persecution or even death if they disagreed with his version of the way the universe operated—GALILEO was one to bear the brunt of this. The lesson to be learned from the centuries-long Ptolemy fiasco is that we must recognize that, while the ancients very often had wisdom, they grievously lacked information, and their ideas were limited accordingly. It's thus foolhardy to see them as unchallengeable authorities on any aspect of knowledge. ■

BUT THERE'S MORE . . .

- Craters called Ptolemaeus on both the Moon and Mars honor the astronomer, as does asteroid 4001 Ptolemaeus.
- A star cluster he observed in the constellation Scorpius is still called the Ptolemy Cluster.
- You can listen to work by the experimental band Ptolemy at ptolemy1. bandcamp.com.

HYPATIA OF ALEXANDRIA

(ca. 355–415)

*Victim of a lynch mob, the greatest female mathematician/
philosopher of the ancient world.*

A young pagan woman of extraordinary beauty, Hypatia taught her
philosophy to adoring students at what was then the greatest seat of
learning in the world. However, she got caught in the midst of religious
strife, and one day a mob of Christian monks cruelly murdered her.

This is the legend rather than the reality concerning Hypatia of
Alexandria, but its gist is true.

Hypatia can be regarded as the first female mathematician of importance; she was also, for centuries, the last. Her death is often taken
as marking the start of the Dark Ages, that long period during which
Europe suffered intellectual stagnation; the heirs to Hypatia and all the
other philosophers in the Greek tradition were to flourish in the Arab
countries until they, too, suffered their own dark ages.

She was the daughter of a mathematician/philo-sopher called Theon.
He was no great innovator, but he produced revised editions of some of
the most important scientific books of antiquity. His version of EUCLID's
Elements, containing minor amendments (not all for the better!), was so
influential that it wasn't until the nineteenth century that a copy of Euclid's
original was rediscovered. Theon also revised PTOLEMY's *Almagest*.

Hypatia seems to have helped her father in these projects and also,
after his death, to have prepared her own edition of the *Almagest*, now
lost to us. In fact, all of her works have been lost. They're believed to have
included commentaries on Euclid's *Elements*, Apollonius's *Conics*, and
Diophantus's *Arithmetica*, as well as an astronomy textbook of her own
called *The Astronomical Canon*. We obviously have no way of evaluating
how significant her written contributions were, but we can deduce they
weren't trivial from the very high regard in which she was held as a teacher.

Lecturing on the natural sciences, primarily astronomy and math,
Hypatia was by about 400 regarded as *the* key figure in the school of
religious philosophy known as Neoplatonism. We know a fair amount

about her as a lecturer because the writings of a couple of her students survive, most importantly 156 letters by Synesius of Cyrene, some of them written to Hypatia herself. Synesius seems to have been a pagan who eventually converted to Christianity. From what he tells us about other students, it's patent that Hypatia exercised no religious discrimination in her selection of pupils; some were pagan, others were Jewish, and yet others were Christian, and they were all expected to get along. What was important in Hypatia's worldview was the pursuit of knowledge, and this she imparted very firmly to her students. For decades Synesius corresponded with some of his fellow ex-students, and it's clear they continued to strive toward her ideals.

Our modern picture of Hypatia as a beautiful young woman—"the incarnation of beauty and wisdom"—derives originally from a 1720 tract by the Protestant zealot John Toland. By now the Enlightenment had dawned, and it was realized how much had been lost during those centuries when Europe had been dominated by superstition and ignorance rather than reason. Hypatia was the perfect heroine for this new climate of thought. Even better, so far as Toland was concerned, was that the tale of her life and death gave him an opportunity to bash the Catholics. His version of events was essentially repeated by Voltaire and by Edward Gibbon in his historical epic *The History of the Decline and Fall of the Roman Empire* (1776–88).

But the legend really came into full flower with Charles Kingsley's novel *Hypatia* (1853). Like Toland before him, Kingsley was keen to discredit the Catholics; the novel has a definite touch of eroticism, too, presumably with the intention of making the reader yet more shocked by the horrific murder at the end. The novel, and thus this somewhat skewed version of Hypatia's legend, was hugely popular for some decades. Most readers remained blissfully ignorant of the fact that, at the time of her murder, the "glamorous young heroine" was about sixty.

Hypatia lived during what were turbulent times for Alexandria. Earlier in the fourth century, Constantine the Great had decreed that Christianity was to be tolerated throughout the Roman Empire. By the time Hypatia became active, Christianity had reached a dominant position in the empire and was moving to stamp out its rivals.

In 384 one Theophilus took over as Patriarch of Alexandria; he persecuted not just pagans and Jews but also members of Christian sects whose views he regarded as heretical—in one of his campaigns he is reported to have slaughtered some ten thousand monks of a rival Christian sect. He was responsible also for the destruction of Alexandria's temple of Serapis in the year 391; since the Serapeum housed many of the books belonging to Alexandria's great library, who knows how much knowledge was lost to us.[1] He recruited an army of some five hundred monks, the *parabolans*, as a sort of Rent-a-Mob to intimidate and, if need be, lynch anyone who opposed him.

Hypatia somehow managed to stand clear of Alexandria's battle between Christianity and pagan polytheism—at least during Theophilus's reign. In part this may have been because she had influential Christians among her students, individuals whom even Theophilus might have thought twice about antagonizing. Another of her supporters (and possibly a student) was the Roman prefect Orestes.

When Theophilus died, his position as patriarch was taken by his nephew Cyril, now known as Saint Cyril and by nicknames such as "Pillar of Faith" and "Seal of All the Fathers" but at the time regarded by many, inside as well as outside the Church, as a monster. He stepped up the persecutions. Orestes did his best to defend Alexandria's pagan institutions, but Cyril was not to be thwarted. Since Hypatia was the figurehead in the city for paganism, freethinking, and reason, Cyril sent in the *parabolans* as a lynch mob. According to some accounts she was flayed alive with sharpened oyster shells or broken crockery; according to others she was torn to pieces. Whatever the truth, there seems little doubt that her death was a brutal one. Almost immediately a cover-up began, an attempt to absolve Christian leaders of involvement in what was realized to be a shameful deed.

For the next one thousand years or so, Europe would pay the price for that extinction of scholarship. ∎

BUT THERE'S MORE . . .

- Maria Dzielska's *Hypatia of Alexandria* (1995) gives a useful overview of what little is known about Hypatia's life and ideas, as does Michael A. B. Deakin's *Hypatia of Alexandria* (2007); the latter gives more information on her math. Kingsley's *Hypatia* is available at Project Gutenberg.
- Well worth a watch is the movie *Agora* (2009), starring Rachel Weisz as Hypatia. Although largely fictional, it does give a sense of the conflict between reason and superstition.

---

1. The Christian mob's attack on the Serapeum was not entirely unprovoked. Some of the pagans were behaving pretty violently too.

- Hypatia's place in the history of science is honored by the naming of a crater on the Moon; oddly, Theophilus and Cyril have been similarly honored. A large asteroid is named for her: 238 Hypatia. A stone found in Libya in 1996 and believed to be the first fragment of a cometary nucleus ever discovered is known as the Hypatia Stone.
- Also named for her are the typeface Hypatia Sans Pro, designed in 2007 by Thomas Phinney, and the scholarly journal *Hypatia: A Journal of Feminist Philosophy*, founded in 1986. The progressive rock band Telergy released its (excellent) album *Hypatia*, inspired by her life, in 2015.

ALHAZEN
(ABU ALI AL-HASAN IBN AL-HAYTHAM)
(ca. 965–ca. 1040)

Perhaps the greatest of those Muslim scientists who kept the light of reason burning when it had been snuffed out in Europe.

For a full six centuries, from roughly 750 to 1350, the cultural lights were off in Europe. Outside Asia, the cradle of human knowledge was the Arab world. Funded by various beneficent rulers, Arab scholars translated and transcribed texts on science, mathematics, medicine, and philosophy from Greek, Egyptian, Babylonian, Persian, and Indian sources, and did a fair amount of original research and theorizing. Major libraries at Baghdad and at Córdoba, Spain, reportedly contained tens of thousands of volumes; by way of comparison, in Christian Europe at the time, the biggest libraries might have a few *hundred* books.

Arguably the greatest of the Arabic scientists was the man whom the Western world came to know as Alhazen. He was born in Basra (and so was sometimes known as al-Basri). He seems to have trained as a public servant, while at the same time studying religion. He became increasingly dissatisfied with what he learned from his religious studies and decided to focus instead on what we'd now call science. He was particularly intrigued by the ideas of the Greek philosopher Aristotle.

In due course he earned a reputation in the Basra region for his scientific prowess. Hoping to latch onto a permanent patron, he went to Egypt, where the caliph al-Hakim bi-Amr Allah ruled. Al-Hakim was a curious mixture of sadistic tyrant and man of culture, with a special interest in science; he built up a major library and made many astronomical observations himself, probably for astrological purposes. Hearing that Alhazen had devised a scheme for regulating the flow of rivers, al-Hakim summoned him to Cairo and hired him to regulate the flow of the Nile.

Alhazen took a team of engineers up and down the river and slowly realized his scheme wouldn't work; even worse, he couldn't think up any alternative way of tackling the job.

He must have found al-Hakim in a good mood when he confessed this failure, because, rather than have him executed in a slow and interesting way, the tyrant gave him some kind of administrative post. Alhazen likely realized this might represent merely a temporary stay of execution, and so in self-defense he pretended he'd gone mad. Confined to a form of house arrest, he was able to keep away from the tyrant's attention and carry on his scientific studies in peace. Unfortunately for him, he had to keep up this pretense for many years, until al-Hakim's death. He then had the sticky task of persuading *everyone else* that he wasn't really mad after all!

Alhazen's scientific interests ranged widely, but his main concern was physics, in particular optics. He realized the Greek account of how vision worked—that the eyes emitted rays—was nonsensical. He was very interested in refraction and, centuries before NEWTON, discovered how lenses worked. As for reflection, the Greeks had investigated the properties of flat mirrors but hadn't really gotten very far with curved ones. Alhazen constructed various curved mirrors, both concave and convex and both spherical and parabolic,[1] and worked out the geometry involved in reflections from them.

He discovered the principles of the camera obscura. From observing the effects of atmospheric refraction on the images of the Sun, Moon, and stars, he reckoned the atmosphere must be about ten miles (16 km) thick. In fact, this isn't too bad an estimate for the depth of the troposphere (about 7.5 miles/12 km), which is the lowest layer of the atmosphere; since the upper reaches of the atmosphere, beyond the top of the troposphere, become progressively more rarefied,[2] it's not unreasonable to credit Alhazen's estimate as a hit.

His magnum opus was a seven-volume treatise on optics called *Kitab al-Manazir*. In 1270 this was translated into Latin as *Opticae Thesaurus Alhazeni*, and in 1572 a printed edition was published, so the work could be studied far and wide. Since at the time European scholars were still relying for their understanding of optics on PTOLEMY's *Almagest*, dating from the second century, the impact of Alhazen's work was major—at least, among scholars who chose not to ignore it. Among

---

1.   A spherical mirror is one whose surface represents part of the surface of a sphere. A parabolic mirror is one whose surface represents part of the surface of the figure you'd get if you took a parabola and spun it on its axis. Parabolic mirrors are used in, for example, astronomical telescopes and car headlights.

2.   For example, the International Space Station, which we'd think of as orbiting in outer space, is technically speaking still within the Earth's atmosphere.

those who seized upon it and put it to good use was the astronomer Johannes KEPLER.

All told, Alhazen wrote nearly a hundred books, of which over half survive. It's clear he was a sort of Isaac Newton of his era and environment, with an astonishing ability to see to the root of problems and a refreshingly pragmatic approach to scientific investigation, founded on experimentation rather than baseless theorizing—in effect, he developed a version of the Scientific Method a couple of centuries before European philosophers like BACON.

After al-Hakim's death and once Alhazen was free to return to normal life, he continued his scientific studies but was unable to make a living out of them. He therefore worked as a tutor and as a copyist—i.e., making written copies of other people's manuscripts. It's disheartening to think that this genius ended up being a sort of human photocopier. ■

BUT THERE'S MORE . . .

■ The small lunar crater Alhazen commemorates him, as does the name of the asteroid 59239 Alhazen. He has been featured on Iraqi banknotes: on the 10-dinar bill issued in 1932, and on the 10,000-dinar bill issued in 2003. He has appeared on postage stamps from various nations, including Malawi, Pakistan, and Qatar.

■ Although written for younger people, Bradley Steffens's *Ibn al-Haytham: First Scientist* (2006) is a surprisingly good short biography.

NICOLAUS COPERNICUS
(1473–1543)

The timid Polish cleric whose theory that the Earth goes round the Sun ushered in the Scientific Revolution.

For over a millennium and a half the Judeo-Christian world believed the Earth was motionless at the center of the universe, with all the other celestial bodies—Moon, Sun, stars, and planets—revolving around it. This was a cosmology based upon the one expounded by PTOLEMY.

The problem in this scheme was the motions of the planets. The system devised to explain these, involving deferents and epicycles, had by the end of the fifteenth century been revised and further revised to the point where it had become infernally complicated. Any dispassionate viewpoint would have made clear that this system couldn't possibly represent the physical reality. Unfortunately, the Church taught that it did, and at the time, if you disagreed with the Church on scientific matters, you were liable to face the Inquisition. Even as late as 1600, the Italian priest Giordano Bruno was burned at the stake for heresies including the claim that the Earth went round the Sun.

The Polish priest Nicolaus Copernicus (or Mikolaj Kopernigk) showed few signs of brilliance in early life. His father died when he was young, and the boy was taken under the wing of his uncle, the important prelate Lukasz Watzenrode. Nicolaus made slow progress at school and later at university; it seems likely he was doing a lot of bunking off. In due course his uncle sent him to Italy to study canon law at the university in Bologna. After some years there, Copernicus got a job on his uncle's staff, where he trod water for a while before becoming a Roman Catholic canon.

His interest in astronomy seems to have been sparked around 1496–97, while he was living in Bologna. Despite his field of study at the university being canon law, he took rooms with Domenico Maria di Novara, an astronomy/astrology professor.[1] Soon he was acting as Novara's

---

1. In those days astronomy and astrology were essentially the same thing.

assistant, and it was possibly from Novara that he gained his skepticism about the Ptolemaic system.

Sometime before 1514 he laid out the bones of his heliocentric (Sun-at-the-center) theory in a short essay that would become known as the *Commentariolus*. He made handwritten copies of this and sent them to friends, who then made further copies to send on to *their* friends, and so on; it was the sixteenth-century version of going viral. Luckily for Copernicus, the essay was anonymous; only a few people knew who'd written it, and they weren't telling.

The starting point of his new theory was that the Sun, not the Earth, was at the center of the universe, with everything else—including the stars—going round it in perfect circles. (The insistence on perfect circles was essentially a mystical one. Copernicus couldn't commit himself entirely to reason.) The Moon was the only celestial object that circled the Earth. The reason other celestial objects *seemed* to circle the Earth was that the Earth was spinning, making one full rotation every day.

The profound philosophical breakthrough was the recognition that, rather than being motionless at the center of the universe, the Earth was *moving*. At the time this seemed to fly right in the face of common sense—surely we'd all zoom off into space! But of course Copernicus was right, and he knew he *had* to be right because this was a logical deduction from a conclusion he'd reached through the application of reason. It was this stunning breakthrough to which GALILEO referred decades later when he (reportedly) said, in the face of the Vatican's clampdown, *"Eppur, si muove"* ("Still, it *does* move").

In his essay, Copernicus explained that he'd done the necessary observations and math to back up his notions, but that he'd leave those for a book, which he implied would be soon forthcoming.

Yet for decades that book didn't appear. During the many years Copernicus labored over it, he began to realize that publishing might not be the best plan in terms of personal welfare. At best he might be mocked as an idiot; at worst he might be condemned by the Catholic Church for heresy. Even though the Reformation was spreading through Europe, it had yet to take hold in Poland, and anyway there was no guarantee the newer form of Christianity would look any more kindly upon a moving Earth than the old. Once he'd completed his manuscript he did the equivalent of stuffing it away in a drawer. It's a worrying thought that, had he died without publishing it, some executor of his might have looked at the manuscript, assumed it was worthless, and chucked it on the fire.

The book, written in Latin, was *De Revolutionibus Orbium Coelestium* (On the Revolutions of the Celestial Spheres), and was finally published in 1543, shortly before Copernicus's death; in the English-speaking world it's generally known today as *De Revolutionibus* or *On the Revolutions*.

That it was published at all is due to the arrival on Copernicus's scene of a much younger scholar, the mathematician Georg Joachim Rheticus. Rheticus had been sent on a two-year expedition to meet and learn from Europe's greatest astronomers as part of a post-Reformation effort to reorganize the German educational system. It was during his travels that he first learned about this obscure Polish cleric with the revolutionary (no pun intended) ideas. He spent two years studying with Copernicus, and eventually persuaded him to publish *De Revolutionibus*.

Rheticus oversaw the early stages of the publication, but unfortunately had to depart Poland before the book appeared. He left the completion of the task to the Lutheran theologian Andreas Osiander. Osiander took it upon himself to add an anonymous preface saying the theory was a mathematical exercise dedicated to increasing astronomical accuracy rather than a depiction of physical reality. This was exactly the opposite of what Copernicus's theory was about, but presumably Osiander was concerned with not rocking the boat too much. Of course, the book *did* rock the boat—so much so that the ripples are still spreading today.

Copernicus himself could not know this. Within at most weeks of the book's publication, he was dead, probably of a stroke.

For decades after his death the heliocentric system struggled for acceptance. The resistance came not just from the Church. Because of Copernicus's insistence that the paths of the planets were perfect circles, his system was actually less accurate for navigation and astrology purposes than the revised versions of Ptolemy's geocentric system. Sailors and astrologers weren't interested in the physical realities of the universe; they just wanted a good way to calculate celestial positions. It wasn't until KEPLER and then NEWTON refined the system, correctly identifying planetary orbits as ellipses rather than circles, that the Copernican hypothesis became irrefutable. ■

BUT THERE'S MORE . . .

- A good short biography of Copernicus and explanation of the Copernican Revolution is Jack Repcheck's *Copernicus' Secret* (2007). The section on Copernicus in Arthur Koestler's *The Sleepwalkers* (1959) covers similar territory. Dava Sobel's *A More Perfect Heaven* (2011), examining Copernicus's life and the consequences of his theory, is interesting but odd—its central third is an unproduced two-act play![1] John Banville's novel *Doctor Copernicus* (1976) is an intriguing reconstruction of the man.
- Copernicus's image was featured on the Polish 1,000-złoty banknote in 1962 and again (a different portrayal) in 1975. Both bills are now long since out of circulation. His image has appeared on the 10-złoty coin.
- Chemical element no. 112, copernicium, discovered in 2009, is named in his honor, as are craters on the Moon and Mars, the star 55 Cancri, the highest peak of California's Mount Hamilton, Warsaw's Copernicus Science Centre, the European Space Agency's Copernicus Programme, and the asteroid 1322 Coppernicus (*sic*).

---

1. Eventually staged a few years later, in March 2014, in Boulder, Colorado.

TYCHO BRAHE
(1546–1601)

An astronomer with a metal nose and a passion for meticulous observation of the heavens.

The preeminent observational astronomer of his day, Tycho Brahe—usually known just as Tycho—was born to an aristocratic Danish family and intended for politics. However, having witnessed the solar eclipse of 1560, he changed his plans entirely, and instead turned his attentions to math and astronomy, alongside astrology and an occasional digression into alchemy.

In 1565, while still a student at the university in Rostock, in what is now Germany, he got into a duel because of his own arrogance—a personality trait that caused him trouble throughout his life—and his opponent cut Tycho's nose off. Thereafter he had to wear an artificial nose made out of metal.

In 1572 he noticed a "new star" in the heavens, one that hadn't been there before. He carefully observed it for the next eighteen months or so as it grew to be brighter in the sky than the planet Venus, then faded into invisibility. We now know that what he saw was a supernova, the explosion of a large star toward the end of its life span.

Frederick II of Denmark was so impressed by Tycho's observations of the nova (Tycho's term) that he paid for a great new observatory, Uraniborg, built for the young astronomer on the island of Hven, between Sweden and Denmark. Tycho fitted this out with the best astronomical instruments Frederick's money could buy—none of which were lensed devices, for the telescope was still an instrument of the (then very near) future.

The great comet of 1577 offered Tycho another chance to display his observational prowess. He showed that it was more distant than the Moon, contrary to the prevailing view—nurtured by Aristotle millennia ago and endorsed even by GALILEO—that comets were phenomena of the atmosphere, like clouds. But the comet presented Tycho with problems of his own, because he still refused to accept the heliocentric

(Sun-centered) system proposed by COPERNICUS and clung to the notion, as per PTOLEMY, that the Earth was at the center of the universe. How then to explain that the path of the comet was clearly not a circle and didn't appear to be taking the object around the Earth? Moreover, the path of the comet was obviously taking it *through* the planets' supposed crystalline spheres, which led to the nasty conclusion that those spheres were imaginary.

In a desperate attempt at compromise, Tycho proposed a cosmology of his own. In terms of scientific cosmologies—as opposed to religious ones—Tycho's stands as among the odder. In it, the spheres were abandoned. All the other planets except the Earth went round the Sun. The Sun and the Moon revolved around the Earth. It's easy enough to see how Tycho's own observations might be read so as to agree with this model for the two planets closer to the Sun than we are, Mercury and Venus, but far harder to make things work for the other planets.

All went well for Tycho while Frederick II remained alive, but in 1588 Frederick died, and his successor, Christian IV, was less interested in astronomy and less willing to put up with Tycho's tantrums. Eventually Christian shut Uraniborg down, and Tycho sought the patronage instead of the Holy Roman Emperor Rudolf II. From 1599 he was established at Prague, setting up a new observatory nearby (although he used it for just a few months). He also hired an assistant: Johannes KEPLER.

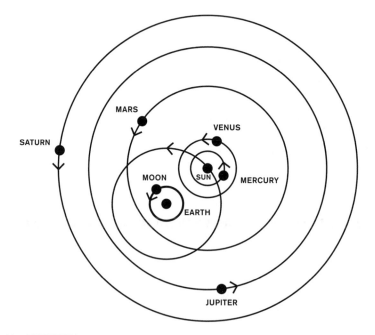

While no great theoretician, Tycho was a tremendous observer. Despite having no telescope, he increased the accuracy of observational astronomy to such an extent that, by 1582, it became clear the calendar was in urgent need of reform: the year was longer by a few minutes than for centuries it had been assumed to be. Thanks to this reform we now have the correctional system whereby "century years" (like 1800 and 1900) aren't leap years unless they're divisible by 400 (like 2000).

More important in terms of astronomy was the enormous bank of painstakingly recorded observations Tycho made over the years—and the fact that he passed them on to Kepler.

Tycho was an eager bon vivant, and it was this that by all accounts killed him. On the night of October 13, 1601, he attended a party in the home of a friend and, presumably because he was enjoying himself so much, failed to leave the table despite the urgent pleadings of his bladder. He still hadn't peed by the time he got home, finding it now impossible to do so. He died about ten days later, probably of uremia. There's a lesson here for us all.[1] ∎

BUT THERE'S MORE . . .

■ Two of Tycho's cousins, Frederik Rosenkrantz and Knud Gyldenstierne, have a place in literary history. In 1592 they visited London on a diplomatic mission, and there it's believed they encountered Shakespeare. Some years later the Bard incorporated them, at least by name, into *Hamlet* (ca. 1600).

■ In 1651 the Italian astronomer Giovanni Battista Riccioli published a book called *Almagestum Novum* (New Almagest), the title referencing PTOLEMY's great work. For religious reasons, Riccioli rejected COPERNICUS's heliocentric cosmology and was one of the few to favor Tycho's "compromise" scheme. In his book he published the best maps to date of the lunar surface and introduced the naming system for its features (i.e., celebrating great astronomers) that we still use today. He gave the non-Copernican astronomers all the best craters, and Tycho the biggest of the lot. Much later, Tycho was also awarded a crater on Mars, as well as the asteroid 1677 Tycho Brahe. The Tycho Brahe Planetarium opened in Copenhagen in 1989.

---

1. There have been suggestions that Tycho was instead murdered by poison, Kepler being fingered as the villain. In 2012 a team of scientists who'd examined Tycho's exhumed remains specifically in search of poisons declared this theory untenable.

- The Danish crowdfunded amateur space organization Copenhagen Suborbitals has been naming its manned space capsules *Tycho Brahe* in honor of the astronomer. As yet, none of these capsules has either borne an astronaut or made it into space, but there are ambitious plans for the next few years.
- Inaugurated in 2008 by the European Astronomical Society, the Tycho Brahe Prize honors achievements in observational astronomy and astronomical instrumentation.
- In some parts of Scandinavia various days of the year are regarded as unlucky, and these are traditionally called Tycho Brahe's days; if you can't blame the loss of your homework on the dog, you merely shrug it off as the fault of today's being one of Tycho Brahe's days. No one knows where the tradition originated.

FRANCIS BACON

(1561–1626)

The philosopher and twister who gave the world the modern method of doing science.

Francis Bacon—ennobled as Baron Verulam of Verulam and as First Viscount St. Albans—was a devious politician who sucked up to power and readily betrayed friends, was a judge convicted of taking bribes (his defense was that, yes, he took the bribes, but it made no difference to his judgments!), blithely switched sides whenever the political wind changed direction, and was always quite happy to do the dirty work of his political masters. He was, in other words, a totally unscrupulous toad.

But he also left us with the basis for perhaps the most valuable of all tools for the acquisition of knowledge: the Scientific Method.

Bacon first entered the English court during the reign of Elizabeth I and became an aide to Robert Devereux, Second Earl of Essex ... whose friendship he later sold out, even serving as one of the judges who condemned Essex to death. Soon afterward, Elizabeth died, but Bacon had had the foresight to suck up to James VI of Scotland, who succeeded Elizabeth as James I of England. Under James he served in various important government posts before finally being caught in corruption. By 1621 his political career was over.

By then he had published the two books that would have so much influence on Western culture. *Of the Proficience and Advancement of Learning, Divine and Human* (1605)—more usually called just *The Advancement of Learning*—explained why human beings *should* try to learn more about the world and the nature of existence, then set out a scheme for achieving this. In this scheme Bacon distinguished between the study of the natural, physical world and the study of the divine, stressing the former as the domain of what today we'd call the sciences.

The other was *Novum Organum* (1620).[1] In this he demolished Aristotle's ideas on reasoning, ideas that had been accepted for nearly two thousand years. Bacon said that Aristotle's deductive method of reasoning was fine for mathematical proofs but not for studying the real world. If you wanted to find out a truth about the real world, you needed to go through a process of gathering as many facts about it as you could and then drawing conclusions from those facts. Bacon's method has since been considerably honed until it looks something like this:

- Get rid of your preconceptions.
- Make lots of relevant observations.
- On the basis of these observations, make a hypothesis.
- Make a prediction based on your hypothesis.
- Carry out an experiment.
- If your experiment seems to support your hypothesis, make a few more predictions and carry out a few more experiments to test them. And so on.

These two books were part of a grander project of Bacon's, the *Instauratio Magna* (Great Instauration). It was intended to revolutionize our ways of thinking. He also wrote countless other works on many subjects, including an influential treatise on medicine, and a novel, *New Atlantis* (1627), which envisaged a future utopia. In this utopia there was an institution called Salomon's House, a college of philosophers and scientists that can be seen as prefiguring the modern university. After Bacon's death, a group of amateur experimental scientists in London began, in imitation of Salomon's House, to hold meetings at which they shared their ideas and results. That group eventually evolved into the Royal Society.

Bacon supposedly died as a result of a scientific experiment. He was riding in his carriage on a snowy day when it occurred to him that chilling or freezing might delay the rotting of meat. He jumped out, bought a chicken, stuffed it with snow . . . and came down with pneumonia.

Francis Bacon wasn't the first person to promote the scientific way of discovering the truth about the universe. Among his contemporaries and near contemporaries, people like HARVEY and GALILEO advocated

---

1.   Aristotle's major works on logic are collectively called the *Organon*, or "Method [of Acquiring Knowledge]." *Organum* is the Latin form of the Greek *organon*, so the title of Bacon's book meant "The New Method."

ANOTHER SLICE

Centuries before Francis Bacon advocated a forerunner of the Scientific Method, the thirteenth-century English monk and alchemist Roger Bacon tried to do much the same. (Despite the coincidence of names, the two men seem to have been unrelated.) Roger Bacon investigated optics and astronomy, claimed the Earth was spherical and people should be able to sail right round it, and made an estimate as to the size of the universe (which he believed was centered on the Earth) that is laughably small in terms of current knowledge but was recklessly huge for the time. He also investigated alchemy and astrology, which back then were seen as sciences.

Roger Bacon urged that the quest for knowledge ignore such considerations as magic and superstition and focus instead on experiments and calculations. In this he was centuries ahead of his time. He was also by all accounts an incredibly abrasive man who didn't suffer fools gladly. This wasn't appreciated by his superiors in the Church, and so he spent considerable time in jail—despite being on good terms with Pope Clement IV.

observation and experimentation as the way to do science. But, because he was highly placed in society and respected as a philosopher, his version had much greater influence. ∎

BUT THERE'S MORE . . .

- Various other notable people have borne the name Francis Bacon, among them the Irish artist Francis Bacon and the UK engineer Francis Thomas Bacon, who was responsible for the first practical hydrogen-oxygen fuel cell. The former Bacon was supposedly a descendant of Sir Francis's elder half-brother Sir Nicholas Bacon while the latter was actually a descendant of *the* Francis Bacon.
- A forest of conspiracy theories surrounds the authorship of the plays most of us attribute to Shakespeare. The first and still one of the most popular is that Bacon was the author but, in order not to embarrass himself as he ascended the political ladder, persuaded the theatrical impresario Shakespeare to claim the authorship of the Baconian plays he staged. The idea was first promoted by Delia Bacon, seemingly an-

other nonrelation! Her book *The Philosophy of the Plays of Shakespeare Unfolded* (1857) is available at Project Gutenberg.

- Daphne du Maurier's *The Winding Stair* (1976) tells Bacon's story with all the readability you'd expect from the author of *Rebecca* (1938), although its promotion of the "Bacon as Shakespeare" theory is a bit of a bummer. Rather meatier, but very well worth the effort, is Paolo Rossi's *Francis Bacon: From Magic to Science* (1968).

GALILEO GALILEI

(1564–1642)

A brilliant multidisciplinary physicist whose obstreperous nature and tangles with the Vatican got him into deep trouble.

The great twentieth-century philosopher Bertrand Russell remarked in his book *The Scientific Outlook* (1962): "I believe that if a hundred of the men of the seventeenth century had been killed in infancy, the modern world would not exist. And, of these hundred, Galileo is the chief."

What everyone knows about Galileo is that he fell foul of the Inquisition for insisting the Earth goes round the Sun. Most people also know that he discovered the moons of Jupiter using the newly invented telescope. What people tend to forget is that he was a bold thinker and a devoted experimenter who made fundamental contributions to many branches of science.

He was born in Pisa, Italy. His father, Vincenzio Galilei, was a musician whose interest extended to the mathematics of music; it's likely that Vincenzio's experiments on vibrating strings seeded Galileo's later focus on experimentation as the core of what science was all about. Like his father, Galileo also became a very fine lute player—and remained one for the rest of his life.

In 1581 Galileo entered the University of Pisa to study medicine, but he soon switched to mathematics and physics. It was during this time that he made his first major scientific discovery, reportedly during a service at Pisa Cathedral. The person lighting the candles on one of the chandeliers had inadvertently set it swinging. Using his pulse to keep time, Galileo discovered that, even as the angle of the swing became smaller and smaller, the time taken for each swing stayed the same. He realized that this principle might be used to make mechanical timepieces—i.e., clocks, which hadn't yet been invented. Later in life he'd demonstrate that the time a pendulum takes to go through a full swing depends on the length of the arm and not at all, as had earlier been assumed, on the weight of the bob.

In 1585 Galileo left the University of Pisa without receiving a degree, but a few years later he returned as the university's Professor of

Mathematics. (He would leave again in 1592 to take up the same position at the University of Padua, where he would invent the thermometer, or a very primitive version of it.) It was while at Pisa that Galileo shook up the science community in a big way. He demonstrated that Aristotle's claim that heavy objects fall to the ground faster than lighter ones was nonsense—even though European scholars had accepted this to be fact for over a thousand years.[1]

One problem for Galileo and all the other experimenters of his time was the lack of accurate timepieces. Galileo had to use his pulse in order to time the swing of the cathedral chandelier because there were no proper clocks then. Without an accurate way of measuring time, the timing of falling objects represented a real challenge. By a great leap of the imagination, Galileo was able to make the problem simpler. He realized that if, rather than dropping objects, he rolled them down sloping surfaces (inclined planes), he could make everything happen in, in effect, slow motion. It was through the use of inclined planes that he was eventually able to show that falling objects accelerate in a uniform way. A body falling under the influence of Earth's gravity near to the surface does so at the rate of approximately 32 feet per second per second (32 ft/s^2; about 9.8 m/s^2); in other words, it drops 32 feet in the first second, 64 feet in the next, 96 feet in the third, and so on.

Galileo's emphasis on experiment was transformational, so far as physics was concerned. The Greeks had worked out that the "immutable" heavens were governed by mathematical laws, but they tended to be on much more uncertain ground when they tried to work out the science of our own world. In large part this was because their approach was subjective: they thought of the world in terms of *why* things might happen without pausing to realize that, first of all, it's a good idea to find out what actually *is* happening.

Galileo reckoned the same mathematics that governs the heavens can be found here on Earth: God, or Nature, was a mathematician. The way to approach reality is through observation, experiment, and measurement. Only once you know what's really going on can you start investigating *why* things are the way they are.

Scientists like NEWTON would expand upon Galileo's observations of the behavior of gravity, while philosophers like BACON would more comprehensively formalize the basics of what we now call the Scientific

---

1. The legend that he did so by dropping a cannonball and a bullet off the Leaning Tower of Pisa and observing that they both reached the ground at the same time is just that: a legend.

Method. But science still, for the most part, follows Galileo's guiding principle: find out what the facts are before you start theorizing.

In 1609 Galileo learned of the discovery of the refracting telescope, and he promptly built himself one. His first telescope was capable of a magnification of only x3, but he soon improved that to gain a magnification of roughly x32.[1] The astronomical discoveries he made with his telescopes came thick and fast, and they radically altered our knowledge of the heavens. He published his findings in the pamphlet *Sidereus Nuncius* (Starry Messenger; 1610), which propagated like a shock wave across Europe.

Some of these observations seem obvious to us today, but at the time they were revolutionary. Galileo discovered that the Milky Way is made up of millions of stars rather than being just a sort of smear of light. He observed that Venus showed phases, similar to those of the Moon—clear evidence that it traveled in a simple orbit round the Sun, not in a complicated one round the Earth. He saw that the surface of the Moon wasn't smooth, as had previously been thought, but was marked by mountains.[2] By using his telescope to project an image of the solar disk, he also observed that there were spots on the surface of the Sun.[3] His findings reached even as far as Saturn: he noticed it had an oval shape, although he was unable to explain this. A few decades later, in the 1650s, the Dutch telescopist Christiaan Huygens finally discovered that Saturn was ringed.

Arguably all of these observations were eclipsed (no pun intended) by his discovery that Jupiter had moons. Galileo was able to discern the four largest of these, and immediately he realized that, if Jupiter could have a retinue of moons, the Sun could likewise have a retinue of planets—of which the Earth was surely one.

In 1613 Galileo came out publicly (and loudly) in favor of the helio-

---

1. The design he used differs a little from that of modern refracting telescopes, in that the eyepiece was a concave rather than a convex lens; this meant that the image he saw was the right way up. Soon astronomers realized that it didn't much matter to their observations if the image was the right way up or not, and that they were better off with convex eyepieces.

2. It's surprising that no one had deduced this before. Just before and just after the Sun completely disappears behind the Moon during a total solar eclipse, there's a moment during which the Sun's light appears as a curved line of discrete spots—now called Baily's Beads for the UK astronomer, Francis Baily, who first described them in 1836. The effect is created by sunlight shining through the gaps between the Moon's mountains.

3. DO NOT, UNDER ANY CIRCUMSTANCES, LOOK AT THE SUN, EVEN FOR A MOMENT, THROUGH A TELESCOPE. You'll immediately and permanently blind yourself in that eye if you try it.

centric theory of the solar system as proposed by Copernicus. This was embarrassing for the Roman Catholic Church, which was fence-sitting on the subject. It was all very well for somebody suitably distant from the Vatican like Copernicus, far away in Poland, to espouse a heliocentric hypothesis, but Galileo was nearby, in Padua; moreover, he was a celebrity. In 1616 the Church warned him that the heliocentric cosmology was heretical and told him to quiet down. For the time being he obeyed, keeping his opinions to himself.

In 1623, however, the relatively liberal Urban VIII became pope. Urban had followed Galileo's work with friendly interest, and he now gave the scientist permission to set out the arguments for and against heliocentrism and geocentrism. Galileo did this in the form of a dialogue, published as *Dialogo Sopra i Due Massimi Sistemi del Mondo* (Dialogue Concerning the Two Chief World Systems; 1632). There was no real way to argue against all the evidence Galileo amassed in the book in favor of Copernicanism, so he might just about have gotten away with it . . . except the debater he invented to support geocentrism, a nitwit called Simplicio, was quite clearly intended as a caricature of Urban VIII! It's hard to know what was going through Galileo's head here. Surely he must have realized that was a stupid move.

The Vatican banned the book throughout the Roman Catholic world, and Galileo was brought to Rome to face charges of heresy that could well incur the death penalty. However, he managed to avoid that through following the advice of the court to lie, revoking the Copernican theory. It's said that, even as he was doing so, he added a muttered aside: *"Eppur, si muove"* ("Still, it *does* move"). He was sentenced to house arrest for the remainder of his life; the conditions eventually were relaxed a little though, especially after he went blind in 1638.

Johannes KEPLER was the first prominent astronomer publicly to express support for Galileo, and at a very important time for the Italian. In an ideal world the two men would have become great allies, for both believed firmly in the concept that astronomy should try to explain physical reality—should focus on the physics—rather than be just about compiling navigational tables. Yet, although Kepler and Galileo exchanged letters several times, eventually Kepler found himself ignored. Galileo's boorishness cost him; his own astronomy would have been much improved had his ego allowed him to take Kepler's theories on board.

The problem with Galileo's astronomy—the problem that Kepler could have helped him fix—was that, like so many before him (Copernicus included), Galileo was wedded to the idea that the planetary orbits must be circles. He had partly formulated the concept of inertia, and he saw this as being the factor that kept the planets moving in their orbits. Had he realized that the orbits were not circular but elliptical and put this together with his notions on inertia, it's possible he might have made the conceptual leap that NEWTON would later make and discovered the principle of universal gravitation.

While under house arrest, Galileo wrote his last great book, *Discorsi e Dimostrazioni Matematiche Intorno a Due Nuove Scienze* (Discourses and Mathematical Demonstrations Relating to Two New Sciences, often called just "Two New Sciences"; 1638). Part of Galileo's sentencing had been the banning of not just the "Dialogue" but of all his other works. The manuscript of *Due Nuove Scienze*, smuggled out of Italy, was eventually published in Leiden, in the Netherlands, in 1638. Again, it takes the form of a dialogue. In this book Galileo, surely aware his life was nearing its end, summarized his scientific work and, in effect, made a statement of himself for the benefit of future generations; he was, after all, never one to underestimate his own importance.

Appropriately enough, the bones from the middle finger of Galileo's right hand, removed from his remains in 1737 when his grave was being relocated, have been publicly displayed in various museums of science. ■

BUT THERE'S MORE . . .

- James MacLachlan's *Galileo Galilei: First Physicist* (1999) is a good short biography. David Wootton's *Galileo: Watcher of the Skies* (2010) goes into much greater depth. In *What Galileo Saw* (2014), Lawrence Lipking uses Galileo as the springboard for his argument that the Scientific Revolution of the seventeenth century was really a revolution that extended throughout European culture. In her best-selling *Galileo's Daughter* (1999), Dava Sobel uses the letters of Galileo's elder daughter, Virginia Galilei, as the basis for a depiction of the relationship between the two.
- Joseph Losey's movie *Galileo* (1975), starring Topol as Galileo and with John Gielgud, Edward Fox, and Patrick Magee as cardinals, was based on Bertolt Brecht's play *Leben des Galilei* (1945), adapted for the English-language stage as *Life of Galileo* by Brecht and Charles Laughton.
- Galileo is honored by the naming of one of the Moon's craters, Galilaei. Also named for Galileo was the asteroid 697 Galilea, discovered in 1910.
- NASA's *Galileo* probe was launched in 1989 to investigate Jupiter and its moons; it got there in 1995. It's to this probe that we owe the knowledge that Europa, Callisto, and Ganymede have subsurface oceans of liquid water while Io has an extraordinary level of volcanism; the probe was also the first to make a (relatively) close encounter with an asteroid. For more on the project, see Daniel Fischer's *Mission Jupiter* (2001).
- You can find an interesting podcast about Galileo the lutanist at the *365 Days of Astronomy* site (cosmoquest.org/x/365daysofastronomy/ 2009/06/22/june-22nd-galileo-and-his-lute/).

JOHANNES KEPLER

(1571–1630)

The German astronomer who established the basis for planetary motions . . . and also had to defend his mother on charges of witchcraft.

Perhaps more than any other figure, the German astronomer and mathematician Johannes Kepler can be seen as straddling the divide between the old, dogma- and superstition-ridden way of looking at the universe and the new method of inferring the workings of the world from the evidence of the senses and the construction of mathematical models.

At first, though, as with COPERNICUS, Kepler was to a great extent misled by notions of how the cosmos *ought* to be—Copernicus thought the circle was the divinely ordained geometrical figure (as had thinkers before him all the way back to PYTHAGORAS), while Kepler thought the distances of the planets from the Sun should reflect harmonic intervals.

Kepler was born in Weil der Stadt, near Stuttgart. His father, Heinrich, was a mercenary who was frequently off fighting in far-off wars. In 1588, when Johannes was sixteen, Heinrich left one day and never returned, presumably killed in battle. Johannes himself was a sickly child, and so the family concluded the best career for him was in the Church. Most of his school education was conducted in Latin, the language used by scholars throughout Europe, and for the rest of his life he would write very well in Latin but only rather clumsily in his native German.

As a child, he saw the Great Comet of 1577, an experience he apparently never forgot; it's probably from this that his lifetime passion for astronomy stemmed.

At the University of Tübingen his studies focused on theology and mathematics; in those days math included astronomy and, by extension, astrology. For the rest of his life he'd supplement his income by casting astrological tables—in fact, it was because of his perceived skill as an astrologer, not as a scientist, that he gained important sponsorship from powerful figures like the Holy Roman Emperor Rudolf II. This must have been particularly galling for him because, so far as we can tell, he thought astrology was nonsense. Still, it paid the bills.

After graduating from Tübingen in 1591 he taught mathematics and astronomy at the University of Graz, in Austria. By this time he'd become a convert to the Copernican cosmology, with the Sun, rather than the Earth, at the center of the universe. This isn't to say, though, that he'd abandoned the mystical views of the ancients. His first major attempt, in 1595, while he was still teaching in Graz, was to add to Copernicanism by establishing some rules for the orbits of the planets. Believing that God, the great master of math, including geometry, must have arranged the solar system accordingly, Kepler theorized that the planetary orbits must be defined by the five regular convex polyhedra (see sidebar).

In Kepler's day just six planets were known, and it was assumed these were all the planets that existed: Mercury, Venus, Earth, Mars, Jupiter, Saturn. Kepler envisaged a sort of nest of polyhedra centered on the Sun. Mercury's orbit was defined by the inside of an octahedron whose outside points defined the orbit of Venus, and so on, all the way out to a cube that defined the orbits of Jupiter and Saturn. He didn't believe there were actually physical polyhedra there, just that God had used the "special" polyhedra to give the solar system a pleasing mathematical basis.

The bizarre aspect is that, in an era when astronomical observations were pretty rudimentary (no telescopes yet, for example), Kepler's system yielded roughly the right values for the planetary orbits. As the years passed, however, Kepler realized the construct didn't match the reality, and he abandoned it.

Even so, Kepler's scheme was at the time regarded as possibly a significant contribution to astronomy, and it attracted the attention of prominent scientists like Tycho Brahe and Galileo.

Kepler's Europe was riven by the aftermath of the Protestant Reformation, and his life would be

THE REGULAR CONVEX POLYHEDRA

In two dimensions, a polygon is a geometrical figure with straight sides: a triangle, a rectangle, a pentagon (or pentangle), and so on.

A *regular* polygon is one in which all the sides are of equal length and all the angles are equal; for example, a regular rectangle is a square.

A *convex* polygon is one in which all the points are the same distance from the polygon's center: a star shape, for example, isn't convex, because some of its angles are closer to the center than others.

A property of regular convex polygons is that you can draw a circle inside them, so that the circle just touches the centers of the sides. And you can draw another, larger circle *outside* them, so that the points of the polygon just touch the circle.

Polyhedra (or polyhedrons) are solid geometrical shapes made up of flat faces. A regular polyhedron is one in which all the faces are identical and all have equal sides, and the definition of convexity is the same as for polygons.

Only five regular convex polyhedra can be constructed; this "specialness" was recognized by the ancient Greeks, which is why these polyhedra are sometimes called platonic solids. Five of the six dice used in the game Dungeons & Dragons take the form of the platonic solids.[1] And, just as you can create circles both inside and outside regular convex polygons, so you can create spheres that neatly go inside and outside the five platonic solids.

---

1. They are d4, d6, d8, d12 and d20. The ten-sided d10 die isn't a regular polyhedron, because its triangular faces aren't equilateral. There are also four regular *stellate*, or *star*, polyhedra, so named because they're the three-dimensional equivalent of the star-shaped polygons. Kepler discovered two of them.

molded by the ebbing and flowing of power between Protestant and Catholic rulers. In 1598, as a Protestant, Kepler was forced out of Graz and went to live in Prague. In 1600 he got a job there as Tycho's assistant. Although Tycho died less than a year later, he was obviously mightily impressed by his young protégé, entrusting to him a lifetime's worth of astronomical observations and the task of completing what came to be called the *Tabulae Rudolphinae* (Rudolfine Tables). Rudolf II had commissioned Tycho to construct a new set of tables of planetary positions, and Tycho hadn't finished it by the time of his death. What with the religious upheaval and his own researches, it took Kepler upward of a quarter century to complete the job. When the Rudolfine Tables were finally published in 1626–27, they represented only the third such compilation in history. The two predecessors were those produced by PTOLEMY and Copernicus; Kepler's effort is reckoned to be some fifty times more accurate than either. In terms of improvement of accuracy over what had gone before, it was, as it were, the Hubble Space Telescope of its day.

In 1604 there was a "new star" in the sky—in fact, as we now know, a supernova. This wasn't as bright as the one that Tycho had painstakingly observed back in 1572 (see page 39), but Kepler was able to confirm much of what Tycho had recorded.

In 1609 Kepler published a massive treatise called *Astronomia Nova* (New Astronomy), embedded within which were the first two of his three "laws" of planetary motion. Back in the mid-1590s Kepler had realized the planetary orbits really didn't match up to his scheme of regular convex polyhedra. At the same time, though, neither did they match up to the Copernican scheme, which had the planets moving in circles. Kepler's great conceptual breakthrough, based on his calculations of planetary motions using Tycho's painstaking observations, was that the planetary paths were *ellipses*. His First Law states, then, that a planet traces out an ellipse as it goes round the Sun, which sits at one of the two foci of the ellipse.

His Second Law—which he in fact worked out first—states that an imaginary line drawn between the Sun and a planet sweeps out equal areas in equal times. What this means is that the closer the planet gets to the Sun during its orbit, the faster it moves.

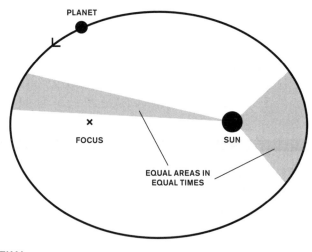

His Third Law had to wait until the publication of another book, *Harmonices Mundi* (The Harmony of the World; 1619). As you might guess from the title, much of his densely packed, nigh-unreadable text harked back to the preconception of the ancients that music was integral to the workings of the universe. Toward the end, though, came Kepler's mathematical conclusion that the cube of a planet's mean distance from the Sun is proportional to the square of the time it takes to complete a full orbit. This may seem pretty abstruse, but it laid a piece of the groundwork for NEWTON's work on universal gravitation.

Another proposal Kepler made that would impact Newton's work was that the Sun rotates, a prediction soon confirmed when people became able to observe sunspots. Kepler also thought that the Sun exerted some kind of magnetic influence on its surroundings, and that it was this magnetic influence that drove the planets in their orbits. It's tempting—perhaps too tempting—to see this as a sort of fumble toward gravitational theory.

In 1610 the Elector of Cologne lent Kepler a telescope, and this rekindled his interest in optics, on which he'd earlier done important work (see sidebar on next page). He devised a better form of telescope than the one Galileo was using, and also did some work on curved mirrors that in due course would help Newton devise the reflecting telescope.

Kepler's access to a telescope, which allowed him for the first time to observe the craters on the Moon and the moons of Jupiter, led him to conjecture about life on other worlds. He wondered if the lunar craters might not be circular walls built by that world's inhabitants so they could enjoy some shade during the long lunar day. And the fact that Jupiter had moons surely implied that the giant planet had intelligent inhabitants. After all, God wouldn't go to the effort of giving Jupiter moons if there weren't people there to admire them!

This interest in the idea of extraterrestrial life led Kepler to write an early work of science fiction. While still a student, Kepler had produced an essay proposing that to an observer on the Moon, the fact that the Earth was moving through space rather than remaining motionless would be obvious; moreover, the observer would see the Earth go through phases, just as we see the Moon do. Over the decades this developed into a fictitious tale of Kepler falling asleep and dreaming of a man being transported by "daemons" to the Moon, meeting lunar inhabitants, and so on. Kepler tinkered with the tale over decades; it was eventually published as *Somnium* (The Dream) in 1634, some years after Kepler's death.

NOT JUST AN ASTRONOMER

We tend to think about Kepler's feats in astronomy, but there were other areas of science in which he made significant contributions.

In his book *Astronomia Pars Optica* (The Optical Part of Astronomy; 1604), he tackled optics, correctly deducing—as NEWTON would prove later—that the brightness with which we see an object drops off with our distance from it according to an inverse-square law: double the distance and the brightness diminishes to a quarter, treble it and the diminution is to one-ninth, and so on. But his real breakthrough in that book was his explanation of how the eye works. Before him, people thought images were somehow trapped by the eye's aqueous humor (the fluid within the eye). Kepler realized that the lens of the eye captures light rays and projects them onto the retina. He knew the image thereby formed would be upside-down and back-to-front; he could offer no explanation as to how the brain reconstitutes the image so that we see things the way they really are.

In his 1615 book *Nova Steriometria Doliorum Vinariorum* (A New Way of Measuring the Volume of Wine Casks), he laid the groundwork for the integral calculus, although it's likely neither Newton nor Gottfried LEIBNIZ knew this.

It's possible that an early, leaked version of *Somnium* contributed to the accusation of witchcraft lodged against Kepler's mother, Katharina, in 1615 by one Ursula Reinbold, who was in financial dispute with the Kepler family.[1] The charges could very well have resulted in Katharina being burned at the stake had they not been roundly defeated. As it was, after years of mental stress and a term of imprisonment, possibly with some physical torture, she died within months of the case's finally being thrown out, in 1621.

When Copernicus presented his new model of the solar system, his publisher timorously stated that he wasn't describing how things actually *were*, just offering a better way of calculating navigational tables.

---

1. Accusations of witchcraft were a fairly standard means of settling financial and other scores at the time. Since it was extremely difficult for the accused to prove their innocence, chances were they'd be put to death and you'd be able to enjoy your ill-gotten gains in peace.

This was the general attitude of other astronomers in the decades after Copernicus's death, and it was the compromise forced upon Galileo by the Vatican. Kepler was made of sterner stuff. He was adamant that astronomy was of no use without physics to back it up. He therefore offered theories of physics in order to explain how things *really were*. Some of his theories were complete nonsense, but his three laws of planetary motion, for example, were more or less spot-on, even though it would take Newton with his theories of gravitation to prove why they *had* to be so.

Kepler remains a giant in the story of science, his reputation if anything increasing as time goes on. And yet his burial place is unknown, the graveyard in Regensburg where he was laid to rest having been completely destroyed by one or another faction during the Thirty Years' War. ■

BUT THERE'S MORE . . .

■ A crater on the Moon is named after Kepler, as is asteroid 1134 Kepler. First launched in 2011 by the European Space Agency, one of the cargo ships used to supply the International Space Station is called *Johannes Kepler ATV*. But undoubtedly the circumstance that makes Kepler such a household name today is that in 2009 NASA launched the spacecraft *Kepler* bearing a telescope of the same name whose task is to search for exoplanets, the planets of other stars. This quest has been immensely successful, and we now know that planets are commonplace in the Milky Way galaxy.

■ Philip Glass's opera *Kepler*, with libretto by Martina Winkel, premiered in 2009 in the Austrian city that was Kepler's home for large parts of his life, Linz. The Mannheim Steamroller album *Fresh Aire V* (1983) was based on Kepler's *Somnium*, and Kim Stanley Robinson's *Galileo's Dream* (2009) borrows the notion.

■ A good short biography is James R. Voelkel's *Johannes Kepler and the New Astronomy* (1999). David Love's *Kepler and the Universe* (2015) is well worth a read, as is the long section on Kepler in Arthur Koestler's *The Sleepwalkers* (1959). In *Heavenly Intrigue* (2004), Joshua and Anne-Lee Gilder claim Kepler murdered Tycho BRAHE in order to lay hands on his boss's invaluable observational data. John Banville's novel *Kepler* (1981) re-creates Kepler and his world in absorbing fashion.

WILLIAM HARVEY

(1578–1657)

The English physician who discovered the circulation of the blood.

Harvey's discovery that the blood circulates around the body in a system powered by the pumping of the heart spelled the end for the medical theories of Galen (see page 15), which had for nearly 1,500 years stifled progress in medicine.

William Harvey was born in Folkestone, Kent, at the southeastern tip of England. He took a first degree at Cambridge University, then studied medicine in Italy at the University of Padua under such tutors as the physiologist Fabricius of Aquapendente. Fabricius's specialty was study of the veins, and in a book published in 1603, *De Venarum Ostiolis* (On the Valves of the Veins), he announced his discovery that the veins had little valves in them. This discovery was to provide a major clue to Harvey.

Another scientist at work in Italy during the time Harvey was there was GALILEO. There's no proof that the two men ever met, but certainly Harvey seems to have picked up the great Italian's ideas about how to do science—through experiment and conclusion rather than through empty theorizing.

Back in England, Harvey became chief physician at St. Bartholomew's Hospital in 1609, and in 1618 he was appointed "physician extraordinary" to James VI and I; among his other patients at court was Francis BACON, whose ideas about the method of science may have been influenced by conversation with his doctor. Harvey continued to serve James and then his son and heir, Charles I, until the beheading of the latter in 1649 at the end of the English Civil War. In 1654 Harvey was elected president of the College of Physicians but declined the honor on the grounds that, at age seventy-six, he was too old. He was right; he died just three years later.

In the second century, Galen taught that the liver manufactured blood from digested food and sent it around the body through the veins. Much of it was turned into flesh at the body's peripheries; some went to the heart's right side, then passed through minute pores in the heart's dividing wall to the left side before being launched, now laden with a sort of vital spirit, to refresh the muscles, nerves, and brain. Through observing the actions of the heart, Harvey realized that Galen's model would require the liver to manufacture some 540 pounds (200 kg) of blood daily—clearly an absurdity.

The only credible alternative was that the body contained a limited amount of blood that was constantly being circulated around the body by the pulsings of the heart. Harvey realized the valves Fabricius had discovered in the veins controlled the flow in those vessels: the blood in them could flow only toward the heart. He concluded that the heart must pump blood around the body through the arteries; the veins served as vessels to bring the blood back to the heart.

To demonstrate this point, he devised an experiment that took advantage of the fact that the arteries are buried much deeper in the flesh than the veins. He applied a tourniquet to a patient's arm and saw how the arteries to the heart side of the tourniquet bulged as the blood backed up in them. When the tourniquet was loosened a little, so that blood was free to flow through the arteries, the veins in the arm were still constricted, and now it was in *them* that the blood backed up, on the side of the tourniquet *away* from the heart.

Through dissection, Harvey showed that Galen's idea of microscopic pores letting blood pass from one side of the heart to the other was a fantasy. He correctly deduced that the blood circulates via two "loops": a smaller one that passes through the lungs, and a larger one that consists of a system of arteries spreading all through the body, getting ever smaller, and a complementary system of veins that returns the blood to the heart.

He published his conclusions in book form in 1628. Harvey's little book—just seventy-two pages long—appalled the medical establishment because it dared to challenge Galen, a revered authority for centuries. Distinguished physicians published sturdy rebuttals, and Harvey's medical practice suffered grievously. Harvey just let them bluster, sure the truth would triumph sooner rather than later—as indeed it did.

Harvey also did important work on reproduction. Starting with the development of chicks in the egg, he went on to discover that the females of other animals, humans included, have eggs, and he was able to study how the embryo develops from those eggs. He was also pretty certain it was the male's semen that initiated that development but, lacking a microscope (it wasn't until after Harvey's death that Antonie van Leeuwenhoek began to explore biology's microscopic world), he couldn't establish a mechanism for this.

It's too easy to think of the great scientists of the past as possessed of boundless objectivity, and to forget they were part of the world they lived in. In Harvey's day, witchcraft was accepted as a genuine phenomenon. One of the widely known "facts" about witches was that they often had one or more "familiars"—a black cat, perhaps, or a warty toad—which were avatars of the Devil and assisted in the doing of the witch's evil deeds. The same William Harvey who discovered the circulation of the blood somehow got hold of a witch's toad and, in all seriousness, dissected it in search of the supernatural bits. To be fair, he did so in expectation he'd find nothing; he regularly debunked witchcraft, and his efforts saved the lives of a number of people accused of dark practices. ■

BUT THERE'S MORE . . .

■ D'Arcy Power's 1897 biography *William Harvey* is available at Project Gutenberg, as are the text of T. H. Huxley's lecture "William Harvey and the Discovery of the Circulation of the Blood" (1878) and a collection of images by various artists put together in 1913 by the Royal Society of Medicine, *Portraits of Dr. William Harvey*. Geoffrey Keynes's *The Life of William Harvey* (1966) is a solid biography that I enjoyed a lot. For a (much!) more recent account, try Andrew Gregory's *Harvey's Heart* (2001). Lisa Yount's *William Harvey* (2008) is a good short biography for younger readers. Helen Rapson's *The Circulation of Blood* (1982) is also recommended.

■ There's a medium-size crater on the Moon named for Harvey.

ISAAC NEWTON
(1642–1727)

The English scientist who brought the Scientific Revolution to its glorious crescendo—while at the same time studying such pseudosciences as alchemy.

Nature and nature's laws lay hid in night;
God said Let Newton be! *and All was* Light.
—ALEXANDER POPE, EPITAPH FOR NEWTON

Isaac Newton was perhaps the greatest scientific genius of all time. In *Principia Mathematica* (1687) and *Opticks* (1704) he gave us two treatises that laid the groundwork for modern science. At the same time he conducted bitter feuds with scientific contemporaries like John Flamsteed, Gottfried LEIBNIZ, and Robert Hooke, and wasn't averse to abusing any positions of power he held. And yet he was personally very generous. He gave money not just to family members but also to complete strangers in need.

There were plenty of other contradictions in his character. Although he worked out why the tides ebbed and flowed, a mystery so far as earlier scientists had been concerned, he never bothered to travel the few score miles to the North Sea or the English Channel to see a tide for himself. This most dedicated of hands-on experimenters just took other people's word for it as to what the tides did.

Newton was born in rural Lincolnshire in the early hours of Christmas Day, 1642, the year that saw the start of the English Civil War; his father had died four months earlier. When he was three, his mother remarried to a much older man who wanted nothing to do with the child. For the next eight years, Isaac was raised by his grandmother. After her second husband's death, Isaac's mother came home, but within a couple of years he was separated from her again and being sent off to school. By now, the Civil War was over, and Oliver Cromwell ruled the country.

To attend school, Isaac boarded with an apothecary, and it seems that his landlord—and his landlord's books!—kindled the boy's interest in science. He didn't do particularly well at school, but outside it he soon earned a reputation as an inventor.

In 1661 he was admitted to Cambridge University's Trinity College. Cambridge was at the time not the hallowed place of academia it would later become; "study" there seems to have been, for most of the dons and students, one long drunken party. Young Newton ignored the orgifying —no party animal he!—but otherwise the situation was ideal for him because it meant that instead of being forced by a don to adhere to a prescribed course of study, he could follow his own instincts and educate himself . . . which is really what he'd been doing all along. His interest soon focused on math; he read EUCLID's *Elements*, although he found it so simple he was bored, and René Descartes's *La Géométrie* (1637), which gave him a far tougher time. He also supplemented his income by lending money at interest to other students.

Newton did find one don who took his responsibilities seriously though: Isaac Barrow, who in 1663 became the university's first Lucasian Professor of Mathematics (he'd eventually pass the position on to Newton in 1669). Barrow took the young man under his wing and much later, in 1671, would be the one to personally transport Newton's newly invented reflecting telescope to the Royal Society when the inventor himself was too much of a recluse to do so.

In 1664 Newton bought himself a prism and started the research that he would much later publish as *Opticks*. He discovered the spectrum; he worked out the rules of reflection, refraction, and diffraction; and he showed that white light is a mixture of colors, thereby disproving the belief that had survived since the time of Aristotle that colors arise from the mixture of white light with darkness. That year, 1664, represented the start of a three-year period that would later be referred to as Newton's *anni mirabiles* (miracle years). Aside from his work on optics, he discovered integral and differential calculus (although he delayed publication on this for decades), and he worked out the basics of his theory of universal gravitation. Any one of these achievements would have earned him a place in this book; to restate, he did all this in *just three years*. To cap it all off, in 1668 he built the first reflecting telescope, a device that improved the light-gathering and optical efficiencies of telescopes by a factor of something like forty!

In 1665, in the middle of this amazingly productive period, Newton had to leave Cambridge for a while for the family home in Lincolnshire because the Great Plague had arrived in the city. It was in the family orchard during this enforced hiatus that he saw an apple falling from a tree. Of course, this was something he'd seen often enough before, but on this occasion it sparked an idea. The reason the apple fell from the lofty tree was that the Earth's gravity extended that far from the ground. If the pull of gravity could reach the treetops, could it not reach much farther—as far as the Moon, perhaps?

But if Earth's gravity is pulling on the Moon, how come the Moon doesn't fall to the ground but instead continues serenely going round the planet? Here Newton made a sudden cognitive leap. Because of the Earth's gravitational pull, the Moon is indeed falling toward the planet—constantly so. But, because of its angular momentum, it never actually gets there.

You can gain an idea of what's going on if you tie a weight to a piece of cord and whirl it round your head. (For safety's sake, do this outside and well away from other people.) To keep the weight "in orbit," you need to keep pulling on the cord. If you let go of the cord or it breaks, the weight keeps moving in a straight line in whatever direction it was going at the moment of release. This is the basis for the first of Newton's three celebrated laws of motion:

1. Unless acted on by a force, a body either remains at rest or, if already moving, continues to move at the same velocity and in a straight line.
2. A force F that's exerted upon a body of mass m will give it an acceleration of a, the three quantities being related through the simple formula $F = ma$. The bigger the mass, the smaller the acceleration, and vice versa.
3. Every action has an equal and opposite reaction—for example, if you push against a wall, the wall pushes back with the same force.

Newton also deduced that the Earth's gravitational pull drops off with distance according to an inverse-square law. This may have been an idea suggested to him by Robert Hooke, whose guts he hated. Newton initially thought the path of the orbiting Moon was a circular spiral, but Hooke publicly pointed out this could not be and threw out the idea that the path might be better represented as an ellipse. In both cases, Hooke's instincts were right, but they were no more than instincts—he did nothing to back them up. It was Newton who took these hunches and, with

DON'T TRY THIS AT HOME

Newton was an absolutely relentless experimenter. In his studies of optics he stared at the Sun with one eye shut, just to see what would happen; what *did* happen was that he had to spend three days in darkness to recover his vision. Even more imperiling to his eyesight was the experiment he conducted to test Descartes's theory that light was, like sound, a sort of pressure wave, but one operating in the luminiferous aether (the intangible substance that was for a long time believed to fill empty space) rather than the air. If that were the case, Newton reasoned, then altering the shape of the retina should produce an interesting effect.[1] So he stuck a needle over the top of one of his eyes and as far as he could round the back of it in order to distort his retina.

To repeat: DON'T TRY THIS!

---

1. Don't read the next sentence if you've just eaten.

---

mathematical rigor, demonstrated the reality of them.

Let's take a look back here. One of the reasons it was difficult for people to accept COPERNICUS's new theory that the planets went around the Sun was that it didn't work very well: the preexisting Ptolemaic construct of cycles and epicycles, while increasingly difficult to reconcile with physics, was actually a better predictor of planetary positions. Then KEPLER came along and, after many years of work, resolved this discrepancy: the planetary paths were ellipses, not circles. And now came Newton. Forget "many years": in a matter of at most *weeks* he showed why the planetary orbits *had* to be ellipses.

He never did completely solve the problem of the motion of the Moon, however, and in later years this would lead to one of his several bitter feuds with fellow scientists. In 1704 he approached the Astronomer Royal, John Flamsteed, who was using the observatory at Greenwich to compile a catalogue of the precise positions and apparent brightnesses of the stars. Newton needed that positional data to help him work out his theory of the lunar orbit, but Flamsteed refused to release it until it was finished to his satisfaction. Eventually, of course, Newton got his hands on the catalogue, but not until after years of unnecessary rancor and some extremely scurrilous behavior on the part of the more celebrated scientist.

Newton was able to analyze how the universe operated under the command of gravity, but he could do no more than speculate about what gravity actually *was*. The best conclusion he could manage was that God had endowed every particle of matter with a gravitational influence upon every other particle of matter. Were the universe finite, that would have led to everything collapsing in on itself; but the universe was infinite, and so we could expect to find concentrations of matter, the product of local collapses, scattered hither and thither across the cosmos. In this act of conceptualization Newton was far ahead of his time, because bits of his picture bear an uncanny resemblance to that painted by modern cosmology.

Newton published his work on gravity in 1687 in *Philosophiae Naturalis Principia Mathematica* (The Mathematical Principles of Natural Philosophy), usually called simply the *Principia*. The book was in Latin—the first edition in English didn't come along until 1729[1]—and that wasn't the only way in which Newton did his best to ensure that as few people as possible could understand it. He made things this difficult for his readers because he didn't want the purity of his scientific thinking sullied by its being accessible to second-rate minds. Even so, there were soon popularizations on sale, notably one by Voltaire (with much help, as the tactful saying goes, from Émilie DU CHÂTELET), called *Eléments de la Philosophie de Newton* (Elements of Newton's Philosophy; 1745).

That the *Principia* was published at all was largely thanks to the influence of Edmond Halley, who managed to persuade Newton to part with his precious manuscript and the Royal Society to publish it. Before the *Principia*, the Royal Society had published exactly one book, the previous year's *De Historia Piscium* (The History of Fishes; 1686) by Francis Willughby. This was a commercial disaster and nearly bankrupted the society. Halley, the society's clerk, offered to finance the publication of the *Principia* himself. After the book had appeared, the society announced that it was in even worse financial shape than thought, and so in the future Halley's salary as clerk would be paid in the form of unsold copies of *De Historia Piscium*!

There's gratitude for you.

BORN TO FEUD

Newton's feud with Flamsteed was just one of many. The most celebrated was with the German mathematician Gottfried LEIBNIZ. Leibniz and Newton weren't initially foes. On the contrary, when asked by the Queen

---

1. The hugely influential French translation, done by Émilie DU CHÂTELET, appeared in 1759.

of Prussia what he thought of the *Principia*, Leibniz replied: "Taking mathematics from the start of the world to the time of Sir Isaac, what he has done is much the greater part." The two men published their work on calculus at about the same time; Newton had in fact developed it earlier, but in his usual obsessive way had withheld publication for years. At first he and Leibniz seem to have been quite happy to share credit, but over time zealous "patriots"—both English and German—fomented trouble over which of the two could rightfully claim precedence.

Like a fool, Newton allowed himself to be dragged into this manufactured feud, and in time Leibniz had little choice but to start retaliating. Eventually Newton used his position as president of the Royal Society to effectively write Leibniz out of mathematical history, so far as the English were concerned.

As if Newton's feud with Leibniz weren't bitter enough, there was also his dispute with Robert Hooke. Hooke was in many ways a genius too, devising countless experiments and gadgets for the edification and entertainment of his fellow members of the Royal Society. Among these were telescopes. In those days the only telescopes known were refractors: long tubes with a big lens at one end (the objective lens) that refracts the light coming through it to a focus near a smaller but more powerful eyepiece lens. For the kind of light-gathering capability you really want in astronomy, however, refractors tend to be big and cumbersome.

By 1671 Hooke had established himself as the nation's foremost telescope maker and expert on optics. Suddenly, out of nowhere, a young unknown from Cambridge called Isaac Newton presented the Royal Society with a new telescope he'd invented—one that used a curved mirror rather than a big lens. For the same light-gathering abilities, the reflecting telescope was a fraction the size of a refractor, and the images you saw through it were less susceptible to distortion.

Hooke was still reeling from this "insult" when Newton passed on to the Royal Society his discovery that white light is made up of a spectrum of different colors—something Hooke, after all his experiments in optics, might reasonably have been expected to have discovered himself. In fact, Hooke claimed he *had* done the relevant experiments with prisms and that Newton had merely interpreted the results wrongly.

Newton had concluded that light was made up of streams of tiny particles (corpuscles); Hooke was convinced light was made up of waves. The rivalry between the wave and corpuscular theories of light continued for centuries. (We now know that light has both wave and particle properties.)

Years later, after Newton had delivered the first two volumes of the

Principia to Halley and thereby to the Royal Society, Hooke rather peremptorily requested some acknowledgment in the book of his having suggested the inverse-square law to Newton. Newton's reaction was to go all the way through his text seeking out every mention he could find of Hooke's name and deleting it.

There are no known contemporary portraits of Robert Hooke. The Royal Society possessed one during his lifetime but, after Hooke's death and Newton's accession to the society's presidency, it mysteriously vanished.

BREAKDOWN

In the latter part of 1693 Newton suffered a brief nervous breakdown, as revealed in some odd letters he wrote to friends like the diarist Samuel Pepys and the philosopher John Locke. It's not certain what the cause was, but one suggestion is that his breakdown may have been born of his infatuation with the much younger Swiss mathematician Nicolas Fatio de Duillier. Fatio was by all accounts a very charming and cocksure young man. The pair met in 1691; in 1692 Newton offered Fatio an allowance if he'd agree to live in Cambridge, near Newton. They talked of taking lodgings together.

The relationship was probably regarded by Newton himself as being entirely platonic. It's conceivable, though, that in 1693 he found himself forced to confront the fact that there was a physical component to the attraction—which was extremely bad news in the 1690s, especially to someone so devout as Newton. It's worth noting that, just a few months after Newton's breakdown, the friendship between him and Fatio, so fervent at its height, was dead.

Another explanation that has been put forward for the breakdown is that Newton was suffering from mercury poisoning as a result of his many years of alchemical experimentation. Modern analysis of locks of his hair has shown that his body did indeed harbor what by today's standards are alarmingly large amounts of mercury and lead. Yet most of his symptoms were wrong for mercury poisoning, and his condition cleared up in a matter of months at most, whereas flushing the effects of mercury out of the system typically takes years. It's tempting, though, to wonder if some of his aggressive bullying and frequent paroxysmic rages might have had something to do with the amount of lead he'd absorbed.

ALCHEMY

Alongside his scientific, mathematical, and theological studies, Newton investigated alchemy. He carried on his alchemical experiments obsessively for decades, and at his death left as much as a million words of manuscript recording his results and speculations. All of it was, of course, wasted labor. We can only begin to imagine what else he might have achieved had he devoted that monumental effort to something more productive.

EXTRA STRONG FOR THE MINT

While at Cambridge, Newton befriended Charles Montagu, later to become Lord Halifax. In 1694, Montagu was made Chancellor of the Exchequer. This was a period in which the nation was plagued by forgery of the coinage. It's estimated that about 95 percent of the coinage in use was either counterfeited or had been "clipped"—i.e., some of the silver had been slyly removed.

In 1696 Montagu offered his old friend Newton the position of warden of the Royal Mint. This was the second-top job there; Newton would be serving under the command of the master of the Mint, Thomas Neale. However, since Neale regarded the job as a sinecure, Newton was essentially the man in charge. And on Christmas Day, 1698—his birthday!—he was promoted to master in Neale's place. He continued his pursuit and ruthless prosecution of counterfeiters and vastly improved the Mint's manufacture of coins so that they were harder to fake or clip.

Some while after Newton moved to London, his attractive, free-spirited niece Catherine Barton joined him as housekeeper. She soon turned heads in London, among them that of the satirist Jonathan Swift. Uncle and niece seem to have grown fond of each other; she was the daughter Newton had never had. In 1698, however, Montagu's wife died, and after a while the widower hired Catherine to be his housekeeper. It was widely believed that she became a lot more than his housekeeper. Newton's enemies—such as Flamsteed—had a field day when, on Montagu's death in 1715, it emerged that he'd left Catherine a tidy sum "as a small recompense for the pleasure and happiness I have had in her conversation." The story began to be put about that Newton had earned his public distinction—and his job at the Mint—not because of his prowess in the sciences but through trading his niece's favors to a powerful man. The fact that Newton started work at the Mint some time before Montagu so much as met Barton was ignored in the interests of tasty gossip.

In 1705, Newton was knighted by Queen Anne, but it wasn't for his scientific achievements or even for his accomplishments at the Mint; it was for his service as a loyal Whig backbencher in Parliament, as the intermittent MP for Cambridge University. Just about all he'd done as an MP was vote as instructed exactly once for something the ruling party wanted.

DISCOVERY OR REDISCOVERY?

To a great extent Newton thought he was merely rediscovering wisdom that the ancients—whether Greek or biblical, but notably PYTHAGORAS—had known before him. He somehow persuaded himself that sages like Solomon had understood not just that the Earth and the other planets orbited the Sun but that the orbital paths were ellipses—that these ancients, in other words, knew about his very own law of universal gravitation. It's feasible Newton was worried his discoveries might be judged contrary to religion and so was setting up the safely dead ancients as culprits, but it's more likely that, a deeply religious man himself, he was too modest to claim his discoveries as his own. Bearing in mind how arrogant he was in almost every other respect, this can be hard to believe; and yet, as we saw at the outset, Newton was nothing if not a contradictory character.

The narrative poem *Lamia* (1820) by John Keats contains a fragment that's often regarded as a barb directed at Newton:

> *Philosophy will clip an Angel's wings,*
> *Conquer all mysteries by rule and line,*
> *Empty the haunted air, and gnoméd mine—*
> *Unweave a rainbow . . .*

In this Keats was echoing the views of all the Romantic poets, notably including William Blake, who felt that Newton's reduction of the universe to mathematics and laws had written God out of the equation and had somehow destroyed beauty. The first charge is manifestly nonsensical; Newton's intent was to *reveal* the hand of the Creator.

Approaching two centuries later, the biologist Richard Dawkins confronted the latter part of this calumny head-on in *Unweaving the Rainbow* (1998). There's a far greater beauty to be discovered in *understanding* the rainbow than can ever be gained by simply staring at it in dumb incomprehension. Of course, the rainbow is very beautiful just to look at, and no one would ever dispute that. But the beauty isn't diminished through knowledge of refraction. In his studies of optics Newton didn't so much unweave the rainbow as weave something new and exciting and exquisitely lovely. ∎

BUT THERE'S MORE . . .

- *Dark Matter* (2002) by Philip Kerr is a mystery novel in which Newton plays a sort of late-seventeenth-century Sherlock Holmes during his time as warden of the Royal Mint. The Newton depicted by Kerr doesn't bear much relation to the real one, but the book's a lot of fun. A nonfiction account of this period in Newton's life is Thomas Levenson's *Newton and the Counterfeiter* (2009); it reads almost like a thriller.
- A very entertaining account of Newton, his discoveries, his contemporaries at the Royal Society, and his relevant predecessors is Edward Dolnick's *The Clockwork Universe* (2011). A good short biography is Peter Ackroyd's *Newton* (2006). For something a bit more in-depth, try James Gleick's *Isaac Newton* (2003). The text of William Stukeley's *Memoirs of Sir Isaac Newton's Life* (1752) is available online at the Newton Project website (www.newtonproject.sussex.ac.uk/), a "nonprofit organization dedicated to publishing in full an online edition of all of Sir Isaac Newton's . . . writings—whether they were printed or not." A good short biography of Edmond Halley, who played such an important role in bringing Newton's work to the world, is *Scheduling the Heavens* (2007) by Mary Virginia Fox.
- In Spring 2015 a "lost" manuscript of Newton's was discovered in a private collection that had been bought by the Chemical Heritage Foundation. Alas, there were no great new scientific insights to be found within it. It was one of his alchemical studies, and described the preparation of a component of the hypothetical Philosophers' Stone!
- Meeting Queen's Brian May during an episode of BBC TV's long-running TV show *The Sky at Night*, Astronomer Royal Sir Martin Ryle told him, "I don't know a scientist who looks as much like Isaac Newton as you do." Newton wasn't as good a guitarist, though.
- Between 1978 and 1988 Newton's image appeared on the UK £1 note, now long since replaced by a coin.
- The desktop toy Newton's Balls is not at all what you might think.

GOTTFRIED LEIBNIZ
(1646–1716)

A brilliant German polymath who gave us the form of
the calculus we use today, but who also made the mistake
of getting into a feud with Isaac Newton.

Gottfried Wilhelm Freiherr von Leibniz was born in Leipzig, an important German trading center and university city. His father, Friedrich, a professor of philosophy at the university, died when Gottfried was just six; we don't know much about his mother except that she was called Katherine Schmuck.

The boy inherited his father's library and intellectual enthusiasms, and soon proved a prodigy. Leibniz taught himself to read Latin by the time he was eight years old and Greek by the time he was fourteen. At fifteen he entered the University of Leipzig to study law, earning his degree in 1663. After receiving his doctorate in 1666 from the University of Altdorf, near Nuremberg, he decided his best chance of a financially successful career was to latch onto someone powerful and wealthy. In 1667 he entered the service of Johann Philipp von Schönborn, elector of Mainz. For the next few years he was occupied on various diplomatic missions, including a visit to Paris in 1671 in an (unsuccessful) attempt to dissuade Louis XIV from invading the Rhineland. While there he met the Dutch physicist/astronomer Christiaan Huygens, and the two remained lifelong friends.

In between diplomatic activities, Leibniz carried out research into mathematics and science. Not only did he have seemingly boundless energy, he was from childhood a voracious reader and could cram more intellectual activity into a day than most people could manage in a week. Being a genius was helpful too, of course—and there's little doubt that Leibniz was a genius.

While in von Schönborn's service, Leibniz devised a system of symbols for use in expressing logic, rather like the one created by English mathematician George Boole about 180 years later. He also worked for years on a calculating machine that could not just add and subtract, like the one invented by French mathematician Blaise Pascal in the 1640s, but multiply and divide.

About a century and a half before the work of Charles Babbage and Ada LOVELACE, Leibniz worked out the basics of the digital computer. Although he wasn't the first to investigate binary numbers,[1] he was the first to publish on the subject. He envisaged a device in which rolling marbles could be either obstructed (a 0) or allowed to pass (a 1) in such a way that the machine could do calculations. Of course, a machine like this would be so monumentally slow you'd be better off just doing the calculation yourself, but, with the advent centuries later of electronics, the principle became practicable.

In 1673 Leibniz visited London, where he was elected to the Royal Society and fraternized with scientists like Isaac Barrow and Robert Boyle. It's possible someone leaked a few hints about the new mathematical tool, calculus, that Isaac NEWTON had developed. Whatever the case, it was around this time that Leibniz began to have thoughts of his own along such lines.

Leibniz published his version of the calculus in 1684, which was by chance roughly the same time that Newton went public with his own system. Initially the two men showed no rivalry over this, but eventually other people stirred up trouble between them and thereby generated one of the great feuds of Newton's feud-filled life. Matters weren't much helped by Leibniz's lifelong habit of writing up his results in fairly slapdash fashion, focusing on the results and hurrying carelessly through the workings.

Spurred on by faux-patriotic hangers-on, Newton decided to declare war with Leibniz over who had precedence on the discovery and used his position of power in the Royal Society to destroy—quite dishonestly —Leibniz's claim. The fly in the ointment for the Royal Society was that Leibniz's nomenclature for the calculus was extraordinarily easier to use than Newton's "fluxions." So, while the mathematics of continental Europe forged ahead using Leibniz's version, math in Britain floundered for the best part of two centuries until the country's mathematicians saw sense. It's Leibniz's version that's used universally today.

In the 1690s Leibniz hit upon the concept of the conservation of mechanical energy, showing that kinetic energy (energy of motion) and potential energy (latent energy that an object has through its position)

---

1.   That was Thomas Harriot, although Harriot's work wasn't published until long after—in some cases centuries after—his death.

are equivalent.[1] He also published some ideas that seem uncannily prescient of those that EINSTEIN more systematically developed in the early twentieth century. These ideas of Leibniz's—that space, time, and motion must all be considered in relative rather than absolute terms—were in direct conflict with the prevailing Newtonian orthodoxy.

It's been said that Leibniz was the last major scientific figure not to have gotten the telegram about specialization. So far as he was concerned, the whole area of knowledge was his territory, to roam through as he pleased. He thus made contributions in all sorts of unrelated fields, throwing around brilliant ideas whenever they occurred to him, whether the subject be psychology or math or physics or geology. The idea that the Earth must have a molten core was one of his, and a measure of its sophistication for the time is that Leibniz's approximate contemporary, the astronomer and physicist Edmond Halley, thought it possible the Earth was hollow.

In 1700 Leibniz persuaded the elector Frederick III of Brandenburg to set up the Kurfürstlich Brandenburgische Societät der Wissenschaften (Electorate of Brandenburg Society of Sciences), a learned organization to rival the Royal Society in England and the French Académie des Sciences. Today it's known as the Königlich-Preußische Akademie der Wissenschaften (Royal Prussian Academy of Sciences), and is still a major international center of scientific learning. Leibniz was its first president, and retained the position until his death.

By the time of his death, however, this witty, manipulative, hugely intelligent man had fallen far out of favor in both scientific and civil society. Neither the Royal Society nor the Brandenburg Society of Sciences did anything to commemorate his passing (the French Academy did), and he was committed to an unmarked grave. ∎

BUT THERE'S MORE ...

∎ There's a very large crater on the far side of the Moon named Leibnitz (*sic*) in his honor, with three small associated craters named Leibnitz R, S, and X, respectively. The asteroid 5149 Leibniz was discovered in 1960.

∎ A quick and cheery introduction to Leibniz is offered by Paul Strathern

---

1. To demonstrate this equivalence, hold something out in front of you and drop it on your foot. You'll realize that the potential energy the object had through being held higher in a gravitational field than the floor was translated into the kinetic energy the object had by the time it collided with your foot.

in *Leibniz in 90 Minutes* (2000). Another recommended short account is George MacDonald Ross's *Leibniz* (1984). John Dewey's *Leibniz's New Essays Concerning the Human Understanding* (1888) is a scholarly examination of much of Leibniz's thought; rather more readable than it sounds to be, it's available at Project Gutenberg.

- The Gottfried Wilhelm Leibniz Prize is the most important award given by the Deutsche Forschungsgemeinschaft (German Research Foundation), in Bonn; and there's a federation of German research institutes called the Wissenschaftsgemeinschaft Gottfried Wilhelm Leibniz—usually referred to, outside Germany, as the Leibniz Association (which, lemme tell you, is a whole lot easier to type).

- While studying at the University of Hannover, more correctly called Gottfried Wilhelm Leibniz Universität Hannover, you could survive on Leibniz-Keks—cookies named for the great man and available in various flavors, notably the Choco Leibniz.

ÉMILIE DU CHÂTELET
(1706–1749)

Ignored for over two centuries, the brilliant scholar who defied her era's sexism and brought Newton's Principia *to the French.*

For over two centuries Émilie du Châtelet was treated as the merest footnote in the history of science; she was a mistress of Voltaire's who had, under his direction, translated Isaac NEWTON's mighty *Principia Mathematica* (1687) into French. It's only relatively recently that we've come to appreciate that, so far as science was concerned, she was, as it were, the more important member of the partnership.

Du Châtelet (or du Chastellet) was born as Gabrielle Émilie Le Tonnelier de Breteuil, daughter to one of Louis XIV's chiefs of protocol. It seems her father was eager to see his daughter excel in all areas of life, because he brought in tutors for her in various of the sciences, and did not neglect her sporting and artistic talents. She grew up to be a tall, beautiful, free-spirited and freethinking woman.

When she was eighteen she was married off to the much older Marquis Florent-Claude du Châtelet-Lomont. The couple soon had three children. The du Châtelet line thus adequately preserved, the marriage was effectively over, although the pair remained fast friends. In her midtwenties, with the support of the marquis, du Châtelet resumed her studies in science. In 1733 she began a relationship with the playwright and satirist Voltaire (you could say he was Lady Châtelet's lover), and soon they were living together at her country château in Cirey, where they welcomed intellectuals of all kinds.

In 1726 Voltaire had gone to the UK, where he'd spent a few years and mixed with some of the brightest people in society, including followers of Newton; he even attended Newton's funeral. By the time he returned to France he was convinced that in Newton's works lay true science, as opposed to some of the ideas championed by the French intelligentsia.

In particular, there was the debate over what kept the planets moving in their courses around the Sun. Newton explained this via his theory of universal gravitation. In France, philosophers like René Descartes had proposed the idea that the planets were embedded in a sort of vortex in the aether,[1] so that they swirled around the Sun rather like bits of grit swirl around a plughole. What impressed Voltaire was that Newton had produced rigorous mathematical demonstrations of his theory; by contrast, the French thinkers were merely theorizing without a solid basis.

Although Voltaire backed Newton, his own knowledge of math wasn't up to understanding Newton's work. When he published his book *Éléments de la Philosophie de Newton* (Elements of Newton's Philosophy; 1738), which popularized Newton's ideas, the bits of the book covering the more difficult math and science were in fact written by du Châtelet.

By that time, she had already written an essay called "Dissertation sur la Nature et la Propagation du Feu" (Dissertation about the Nature and Propagation of Fire) for a 1737 scientific competition; among other things, it predicted the existence of the infrared. And in 1740 she produced her own first book, *Institutions de Physique* (Lessons in Physics), a summary of the latest ideas in the sciences with contributions of her own. She'd originally intended it as an aid in teaching her teenage son but soon realized it had a wider application.

Meanwhile, the French intellectual establishment had for some years been growing increasingly horrified by Émilie du Châtelet. Not only was she openly flaunting her ideas of free love but she had the impertinence to regard women as potentially the intellectual equals of men. The fact that she was living proof of her contention simply rubbed salt in the wound!

Such resentments culminated in an extended essay by Jean-Jacques d'Ortous de Mairan, secretary of the Académie Royale des Sciences. In the essay, he rebutted the points in *Institutions de Physique* one by one, explaining in effect that women couldn't be expected to understand science and physics. Silly move. Du Châtelet's response was a long open letter to him, written in imitatively patronizing terms and spelling out each and every error he had made in his supposed rebuttals. She sent this essay to several hundred members of the Académie, and de Mairan was forced to retreat in disarray.

We don't know who first had the idea of translating the *Principia*, Voltaire or du Châtelet, but it must have been obvious to both of them that she was the only one up to the job. She spent some years on the task, and in the later stages was working at breakneck speed, often seventeen hours a day. What made matters even more difficult for her was that by

---

1. A hypothetical invisible and undetectable substance that filled all of space and was the medium through which light moved.

now she was pregnant with her fourth child. The reason she was working in such a frenzy was that she was uneasy about this pregnancy and fretted she might not survive it.

The translation itself was an impressive feat, but even more staggering was that she'd added nearly three hundred pages of her own commentary, explaining Newton's ideas in more digestible form, plus an appendix reworking the main proofs using Gottfried LEIBNIZ's more efficient notation for the calculus. In her commentary she proposed the idea of the conservation of energy, exploring the notion that moving objects had energy (kinetic energy). She also garnered complementary essays from some of the best scientists of her time, including the Swiss physicist Daniel Bernoulli.

Thereafter came tragedy. Du Châtelet managed to beat her deadline, and gave birth to a daughter, Stanislas-Adélaïde, on September 3, 1749. Within a week du Châtelet was dead, and within less than two years so too was the child.

Oddly enough, despite having been so influential in getting du Châtelet started on this immense achievement, Voltaire didn't see that it was brought into print. In the end, a decade after her death, Alexis Clairaut, who had helped du Châtelet with some of the work in the supplement, organized its publication. The year in which it appeared, 1759, also saw the reappearance of Halley's Comet, fulfilling a prediction that lay at the heart of Newton's gravitational model of the solar system.

Du Châtelet possessed a towering intellect that ranged far and wide in its interests—she even wrote a commentary on the Bible—and her early death robbed Europe, and particularly France, of more than it knew. ■

BUT THERE'S MORE . . .

■ A popular and very approachable (but obviously dated) account of the love affair between Voltaire and Émilie du Châtelet is Nancy Mitford's *Voltaire in Love* (1957). David Bodanis's *Passionate Minds* (2006) and Judith P. Zinsser's *La Dame d'Esprit* (2006) are two more recent but equally spirited biographies. Laurel Corona's novel *Finding Émilie* (2011) imagines that Stanislas-Adélaïde ("Lili"), Émilie's daughter, survived to seek the truth about her mother; it's a great read. A French TV movie about du Châtelet is *Divine Émilie* (2007), in which she's played by Léa Drucker.

■ The asteroid 12059 du Châtelet is named in her honor, as is a crater on Venus.

CAROLUS LINNAEUS
(1707–1778)

The Swedish botanist who brought order to the natural world.

Imagine a library where all the books were stuck on the shelves any which way, with no attention paid to subject or to alphabetical order. Now imagine if the titles on the books' spines didn't always stay the same—one day a book could be called *Fungal Fresh!*, the next day it could be called *Cooking with Mushrooms*, and the day after that something else entirely.

Imagine trying to find the book you were looking for in a library like that. Imagine trying to recommend a book to your friends. This was roughly the problem facing naturalists in the eighteenth century and before. There was no agreed scheme for the naming of plants and animals, and certainly there was no logical arrangement so that lifeforms that seemed similar were grouped together. Then along came the Swedish naturalist and physician Linnaeus.

Carl, or Carolus, Linnaeus—in later life known under the aristocratic name Carl von Linné—was born in Råshult, in southern Sweden. An inspirational schoolteacher kindled his interest in botany. In 1727 he went to study medicine at the University of Lund but spent most of his time pursuing his botanical interests, and a year later he moved on to the more prestigious University of Uppsala, again supposedly to read medicine but again to spend much of his time immersed in botany. By 1830 he had become a lecturer in botany there.

While at school, Linnaeus had encountered the system of classification of plants devised by the French botanist Joseph Pitton de Tournefort, one of several attempts that had been made by earlier scientists. Like the others, de Tournefort's was fairly haphazard, although he did develop the concept of the genus.[1] Working at Uppsala, Linnaeus realized in about 1730 that a better way of organizing plant classification was by comparing the sexual organs—the stamens and the pistils—of the different species. At the time, the idea of plant sexuality was still somewhat controversial among botanists, but Linnaeus correctly backed the progressive

---

1. The genus is the next taxonomic level up the scale from the species. You're a specimen of *Homo sapiens*—you belong to the species *sapiens* of the genus *Homo*.

school of thought on this issue. He also became the first person to use the symbols ♂ and ♀ for male and female, respectively. A couple of field trips, including one to Lapland, enabled him to expand his catalogue of plants and refine the classification system he was developing.

In 1735 Linnaeus went to the Netherlands, where he gained a medical degree from the University of Harderwijk. By now he had become a famous botanist, and wealthy patrons flocked to finance his researches. Most important of these was the Dutch banker George Clifford III, who hired Linnaeus to oversee the botanical garden he'd established near Haarlem. One result of this liaison was the book *Hortus Cliffortianus* (1737), an exhaustive catalogue of Clifford's botanical collection, with exquisite illustrations by Georg Dionysius Ehret.

But a far more important book that Linnaeus published while in the Netherlands, even though its first edition was just twelve (large) pages long, was his *Systema Naturae* (System of Nature; 1735), in which he set out in full the taxonomic system he'd devised. He produced expanded versions of this book over the years, the most important being the two-volume tenth edition (1758).

In Linnaeus's system, the natural world could be divided up, first, into three *kingdoms*: animal, vegetable (plant), and mineral. (The parlor game Twenty Questions still echoes this distinction, with its opening question of "Animal, vegetable, or mineral?") Each kingdom was divided into *classes*, the classes were divided into *orders*, and so on down the scale through *families*, then *genera*, and finally *species*. Later scientists would introduce the further subdivision of *subspecies*.

Clearly the kingdom in which Linnaeus himself was primarily interested was the plant one, and in his catalogue in *Systema Naturae* plant species outnumbered animal ones by a ratio of about three to two. *Systema Naturae* was soon followed by *Genera Plantarum* (Plant Genera; 1737), which followed the same taxonomic system in its descriptions of the plant genera known to European botanists at the time—935, in all.

When he returned to Sweden in 1738 he discovered that, although his international fame had reached his homeland, no one actually had a job for him. He thus had to fall back on his medical qualifications, working as a doctor and soon becoming Physician to the Swedish Navy. He also helped found the Swedish Academy of Science, in 1739; now known as the Royal Swedish Academy of Sciences, this is one of the world's most revered scientific organizations and is responsible for administrating the Nobel prizes in Physics and Chemistry.

In 1741 Linnaeus was appointed as a professor of medicine at the

University of Uppsala, a position that he was able to adjust so it covered aspects of botany as well. He held this post for most of the rest of his life, while continuing to do fundamental research in botany. As well as producing sequences of revised editions of his earlier important works, such as *Systema Naturae*, he wrote a flora (1745) and fauna (1746) of Sweden, the major work *Philosophia Botanica* (Botanical Philosophy; 1751)—a radical expansion of his earlier *Fundamenta Botanica* (Foundations of Botany; 1736)—and the book he regarded as his most important of all, *Species Plantarum* (The Species of Plants; 1753), a mammoth catalogue of some 8,000 plant species that aimed for comprehensiveness and, within the terms of European botany at the time, more or less succeeded.

The significance of Linnaeus's classification system, as laid out in the various editions of *Systema Naturae* and applied in others of his works, wasn't its accuracy. In fact, he made lots of mistakes (such as that whales were fishes, a statement he didn't discover was erroneous for over two decades). The importance lay in the fact that, through rigorous application of the principles of science, he was able to create a taxonomy that could be developed and added to by others with a minimum of misunderstanding. It's a system that we still use (in developed form) today. ∎

BUT THERE'S MORE . . .

- You can find *Species Plantarum* on Project Gutenberg for free download; obviously this isn't something you'd actually want to read, but it's well worth a quick look just to get an idea of how Linnaeus's mind worked.
- Tore Frängsmyr's *Linnaeus: The Man and His Work* (1983) contains four essays on various aspects of Linnaeus's science. Designed for younger readers, Margaret Jean Anderson's *Carl Linnaeus: Father of Classification* (1997) offers a useful introduction.
- There's a crater on the Moon named for Linnaeus. In 1866 astronomers noticed unusual changes going on in the crater, and for a time there was speculation that—oh, so fittingly!—they'd discovered evidence of lunar vegetation. No such luck.
- Founded in London in 1788, the Linnean Society is one of the world's premier scholarly societies; it was here that DARWIN chose for the first presentation of the theory of evolution by natural selection. There are/were other Linnean/Linnaean societies around the world.
- In 1965 Sweden honored Linnaeus by putting his image on the 50-kronor banknote; it's been out of circulation since 1990. Later, from 1986, he appeared on the country's 100-kronor banknote.

MIKHAIL LOMONOSOV
(1711–1765)

Russia's best-kept secret—the polymath who repeatedly made scientific discoveries decades before his Western counterparts.

You've likely never heard of the Russian scientist Mikhail Lomonosov—most people haven't. Yet Lomonosov was a genius who made scientific contributions in several fields that were far ahead of their time. He was also an accomplished poet and dramatist, helped found the University of Moscow, wrote what was possibly the first history of Russia, and created the country's first geographically accurate map. The reason he was ignored for so long was that he was a Russian. During the eighteenth and nineteenth centuries it was widely assumed in Europe that Russians weren't good at science, and so it was the habit simply to ignore any science that might be coming out of that country.

Mikhail Vasilievich Lomonosov was born in Denisovka, a village near Archangel that was later renamed Lomonosova. His father was a successful shipper. In his late teens Mikhail left for Moscow, where he briefly trained for the priesthood. He was sent to St. Petersburg and, while there, attended lectures at the Academy of Sciences. Those lectures changed the direction of his life.

He decided to specialize in chemistry. The state of chemistry education in Russia was pretty poor at the time—in fact, the country didn't yet have a university—so the Academy of Sciences sent him to the University of Marburg, in Germany, in 1736. There he studied under, among others, the philosopher Christian Wolff, one of whose books he much later translated into Russian.

After finishing at Marburg, Lomonosov immersed himself in German culture. He also, in 1740, married Elizabeth Zilch, his landlady's daughter. In 1741 he returned with her to St. Petersburg, where he was given a lowly job at the Academy of Sciences. He would remain there, rapidly climbing the academic ladder, for many years.

In 1745 Lomonosov read a paper to the Academy that effectively demolished the phlogiston theory (see page 92); it was some three decades later that science in Western Europe caught up with him, thanks to the work of Antoine LAVOISIER. Lomonosov quite correctly interpreted heat as representing the motion of particles, with greater heat implying faster motion. It would be the end of the century before anyone outside Russia caught up with *this* notion, thanks to the work of Benjamin Thompson, Count Rumford, in 1798. Lomonosov speculated about Absolute Zero, the temperature at which all such motion would stop; here he wasn't the first, but he was certainly in the vanguard. Again anticipating Lavoisier, he suggested (although he didn't rigorously investigate) the idea that there's a conservation of mass in chemical reactions.

He was an ardent supporter of the wave theory of light—almost everyone at the time thought light must be made up of little particles—long before the work of Thomas Young established that light was indeed made of waves.

He was also interested in astronomy. During the 1761 transit of Venus across the face of the Sun, Lomonosov was able to observe that the planet had an atmosphere; again, decades would pass before this discovery was repeated in Western Europe. In 1762 he designed an improved version of the reflecting telescope; when his design finally reached Western Europe, people discovered that he'd invented the Herschelian telescope about a quarter century before William Herschel did.

Lomonosov showed that coal, peat, and oil are organic, and that amber is too. On an especially cold Russian winter's night he became the first scientist to observe the freezing of mercury. And a cold night it must have been, because mercury freezes at about −38°F (−39°C)!

Reading about Benjamin Franklin's famous experiment with the kite and the lightning, Lomonosov decided to repeat it—with disastrous consequences, because the friend who was helping him was electrocuted.

Lomonosov was largely responsible for persuading Ivan Shuvalov, the courtier and lover of Empress Elizabeth and de facto Russian minister of education, that a university should be established in Moscow, and in 1755 Elizabeth issued a decree to this effect. In 1940 Moscow State University was renamed Lomonosov Moscow State University at the insistence of Joseph Stalin. Today the university holds the annual Lomonosov Conference on Elementary Particle Physics.

Lomonosov was apparently an argumentative type. He spent much of 1743 under house arrest for his loudly insulting behavior. It's clear he wasn't afraid to speak his mind on matters of science—a characteristic he shared with many of the scientists discussed in this book. When his dander wasn't up, however, he was reportedly the kindest and friendliest of men. ■

BUT THERE'S MORE . . .

■ Lomonosov has craters on both Mars and the far side of the Moon named for him—and there's also asteroid 1379 Lomonosowa, discovered in 1936.

■ The Russian Academy of Sciences awards the Lomonosov Medal each year for outstanding achievements in the sciences and/or humanities.

■ The Lomonosov Ridge runs under the Arctic Ocean. Lomonosov porcelain comes from what was renamed in 2005 the Imperial Porcelain Factory, earlier called the Lomonosov Porcelain Factory.

■ Steven A. Usitalo's *The Invention of Mikhail Lomonosov* (2013) is an attempt to debunk what the author regards as Russia's and then the USSR's gross exaggeration of Lomonosov's achievements. An elderly but worthwhile account of Lomonosov's life and work is B. N. Menshutkin's *Russia's Lomonosov* (1952).

JAMES HUTTON
(1726–1797)

The Scottish "Father of Geology," who showed how landscapes form and how our world is truly ancient.

Hutton, often called the "Father of Geology," was born in Edinburgh, Scotland, the son of a prominent merchant who died when James was three years old. Hutton initially planned to go into the legal profession, but then his interests shifted and he studied medicine instead. By the time he'd gained his medical degree, in 1749, his interests had moved on again, and he spent the next couple of decades first in agriculture and then as owner of a factory specializing in the production of sal ammoniac (ammonium chloride). All through this period he was becoming more and more fascinated by what we'd now call geology.

Before Hutton's time, even scientists generally assumed Archbishop James Ussher's calculation that the Earth had been created in 4004 BCE was correct. But it was obvious the surface of the planet had undergone some pretty radical changes during the supposed few thousand years of its existence. This gave rise to the theory later known as *catastrophism*: the idea that the world had been shaped by various stupendous catastrophes, most obvious of which was Noah's Flood. The Flood offered a plausible explanation as to why, for example, the fossils of sea creatures could be found scattered on high mountain slopes.

This focus on the Flood spawned a variety of catastrophism that was particularly influential in Hutton's era. *Neptunism* was largely the brainchild of the German scientist Abraham Gottlob Werner. The world had originally been covered by ocean, and out of that ocean had precipitated the varieties of rocks observable today. The theory had a little trouble explaining volcanic rocks, but he solved this problem in time-honored fashion—by largely ignoring it, saying that volcanic processes weren't of much importance.

Having sold his factory in 1768, Hutton had time to indulge his passion for rocks and landscapes. He soon realized Werner's theories of rock formation were completely off base. Actual study of rocks indicated that volcanic processes were of paramount importance, because they brought up molten material from the Earth's interior that then cooled and solidified to form rock. Sedimentary rocks were produced when sediment—sometimes made up of animal shells, as in limestone—was compressed over long periods by various natural processes.

The expression "over long periods" was important here. As Hutton continued his fieldwork it became thunderingly obvious to him that it was quite impossible for the Earth to be just a few thousand years old. The landscapes he was looking at were clearly the product of gradual change over *millions* of years—in fact, Hutton at one point wondered if the planet might be *infinitely* old! His great breakthrough was the realization that landscapes and their components could have been created by the very same processes we see at work today, and operating at the same rate as they are today. There was no need to invoke colossal upheavals in the past—catastrophes for which the evidence was flimsy at best.

This principle of uniform change over geological time was the core of the new breed of geology that Hutton's work initiated, *uniformitarianism*. Most geologists bought into it fairly quickly, especially after the idea was championed by Charles Lyell in his *The Principles of Geology* (1830–33), arguably the most influential book in the history of the earth sciences and a major influence on the ideas of Charles DARWIN. Catastrophism did live on a while longer, because it seemed to some people that uniformitarianism had problems of its own.

Which, in a sense, it does. On the local scale, a Himalayan landslide or an earthquake or a volcanic eruption can have a bigger effect on the local landscape in a few minutes than many thousands of years of slow erosion. However, if you look at things on a longer scale, it's obvious that landslides, earthquakes, and eruptions are likewise agents of fairly regular change.

On the other hand, the incident that almost certainly hastened the downfall of the dinosaurs, the impact on Earth about 66 million years ago of an asteroid or cometary nucleus, was inarguably a large-scale catastrophe that profoundly influenced the current state of the planet. Similarly, the global catastrophe that we're living through the start of, climate change, will result in considerable changes to the face of the world. So we now understand that, while uniformitarianism is indeed the key to the geological past and future, catastrophes can contribute.

The final death knell for catastrophism came in the middle of the nineteenth century, thanks largely to the work of the Swiss scientist Louis Agassiz. The remaining catastrophists offered the eroded valleys often found in highlands as clear evidence that those highlands must once have been underwater. Agassiz correctly deduced that the eroding agent was not water but ice. In past eras the surface of the Earth had been far more widely ice-covered than today, and it was the slow advances and retreats of mighty glaciers that carved the valleys out of the landscape. This was a natural process that, yet again, required long ages in which to do its work.

Hutton realized that if landscapes could evolve over time, so too could species of living creatures; he even hinted at a process something like natural selection, although he didn't take the idea very far. It's just feasible that his idle speculation along these lines might have had some sort of subliminal influence on the thinking decades later of Charles Darwin, but Darwin had far stronger and more tangible evidence for his theory than Hutton's musings.

Another of Hutton's speculations was that the Earth should be treated as a living entity, an idea that would resurface independently a couple of centuries later in the Gaia hypothesis promoted by the UK scientist James LOVELOCK.

Hutton's own writings were virtually incomprehensible to lay readers, and indeed to many of his fellow scientists. Luckily, his friend John Playfair, an Edinburgh University professor, produced an interpretation, *Illustrations of the Huttonian Theory of the Earth* (1802).

In a curious way, the most important impact of Hutton's work was not so much his theory of uniformitarianism but its corollary, that the Earth was hugely old. Once this was accepted, sciences like geology, biology, and astronomy could be released from the cage of irrational preconceptions. ■

BUT THERE'S MORE . . .

■ The science-fiction author Stephen Baxter sometimes writes nonfiction, and one of his books, *Revolutions in the Earth* (2003)—retitled *Ages in Chaos* in the US—is about Hutton and the impact of his work. Another very readable account is Jack Repcheck's *The Man Who Found Time* (2003).

■ Craters on both the Moon and Mars are named for Hutton, as is the asteroid 6130 Hutton.

JAMES WATT
(1736–1819)

The self-trained engineer who gave us the first modern steam engine and ushered in the Industrial Revolution.

It's often claimed that the Scottish engineer James Watt invented the steam engine. He didn't do that, but he improved it so hugely that, from being a useful aid in pumping water, it became a device that would spark and sustain the Industrial Revolution.

Watt was born in Greenock, a shipbuilding town near Glasgow, Scotland. His mother died when he was in his teens. He left home to spend some time in London learning how to repair machines and instruments. On returning to Glasgow, still aged only seventeen, he set up a repair shop near the city's university.

This brought him into contact with a number of notable scientists, some of whom recognized the young man's intellectual spark and provided him with an informal education. One was the physical chemist Joseph Black, famous for his investigations of carbon dioxide and heat. Black had been the first to recognize that temperature measures just how hot an object is; equally important is the amount of heat an object contains. Black also discovered *latent heat*: the heat you need to supply to make water go from solid (ice) to liquid and from liquid to gas (steam). The information about latent heat was to be invaluable to Watt as he set about building a better steam engine.

In the mid-1760s the university gave him a working model of a steam engine to repair. The engine was of the type invented by the English engineer Thomas Newcomen, based on earlier versions done by another Englishman, Thomas Savery. Newcomen engines were in widespread use for water pumping, but to Watt the design seemed hopelessly inefficient.

The problem was that the Newcomen engine used just a single cylinder. Steam was introduced into the cylinder and cooled so that it became water; since water fills a lot less space than the same amount of steam, a vacuum formed that moved a piston. For the next cycle, more steam had to be introduced into the cylinder, but much of the heat it brought was wasted in reheating the cylinder. Because of all the heating and cooling required, the Newcomen engine was a real fuel-guzzler, and its operation was slow and clunky.

Watt's first big breakthrough was to introduce a second chamber, or condenser, in parallel with the first. The cylinder remained hot at all times; steam from it was directed into the cold second chamber, where the chill condensed it. Not only did the new design use a lot less fuel, it worked much faster. Black was one of those who invested in Watt's endeavors to devise further improvements and to turn his small-scale designs into a commercial prospect.

In 1768 Watt entered financial partnership with a mine owner called John Roebuck, but in 1772 Roebuck went bankrupt and sold his share of the enterprise to the English industrialist Matthew Boulton. It was during the partnership with Boulton that Watt finally perfected his engine, which Boulton marketed. Soon Watt engines were being put to use in all sorts of areas, from textile manufacture to train engines, and, for better or for worse, the Industrial Revolution had gotten under way.

Watt, who also invented the governor—a device to regulate the power output of steam engines—retired in 1800 as a very wealthy man. As is so often not the case with "mere" inventors and engineers, especially those without paper qualifications, he was highly regarded by the scientific establishment, being elected to the Royal Society. ∎

BUT THERE'S MORE . . .

- The images of Watt and Boulton, as architects of the Industrial Revolution, have appeared on the reverse of the UK's £50 banknote since 2011.
- Watt introduced the (now-obsolete) unit of power called the horse-power (HP) after observing how fast a straining horse could, using a simple pulley, lift a weight through a particular distance; he defined the HP as 550 foot-pounds per second.[1] Today power is usually measured by a different unit, the Watt, introduced in the UK in 1882 and adopted in 1960 by the Système Internationale d'Unités (SI). There are about 746 Watts to one HP.
- The name of Edinburgh's Heriot–Watt University commemorates the engineer. The Watt Memorial Library, in his native Greenock, had its origins in the collection of science books he left on his death. A

---

1. Other definitions have been used, but all have about the same value.

permanent exhibition at the Science Museum in London is called *James Watt and Our World*. There's a crater on the Moon named for him, plus the asteroid 11332 Jameswatt.

- Although he was buried in Birmingham, an enormous statue of him was erected in 1825 in London's Westminster Abbey; it was replaced in 1960 by a more modestly sized bronze bust and is now on display at the Scottish National Portrait Gallery.
- A good short biography is Ivor B. Hart's *James Watt: Pioneer of Mechanical Power* (1962).

ANTOINE LAVOISIER
(1743–1794)

The French chemist who demolished the phlogiston theory and revealed the composition of the air we breathe.

Antoine-Laurent de Lavoisier is often called the "Father of Chemistry" or the "Galileo of Chemistry," because he took a topic that was still mired in tradition and mysticism and turned it into a science. The French revolutionaries, however, chose to ignore the contributions he made not just to science but to the welfare of the common people, and he met his death on the guillotine.

He was born in Paris, son of a wealthy lawyer who wanted young Antoine to follow in his footsteps. A sickly child who had to stay at home a lot, the boy became fascinated by science and, although in due course he went along with Daddy's wishes so far as to get a law degree, it was in the sciences that he made his career.

Lavoisier realized that accurate measurements were crucial to an understanding of chemistry; unless you could precisely describe what was going on, you didn't have a hope of understanding it. This scientific approach led him to what is often regarded as his greatest achievement, the demolition of the phlogiston theory.

When you burn something, it's obvious that it changes; paper becomes ash, for example. What isn't at all obvious is what has actually happened. In 1700 the German chemist Georg Ernst Stahl and others declared there must be some as-yet-undetected substance that contributed to the process of combustion; Stahl called this substance phlogiston. Substances that were rich in phlogiston burned readily and hotly, and what was left behind after the conflagration was accordingly far lighter than the stuff you'd started with. This seemed to make a good deal of sense to the scientists of the day, and the phlogiston theory was generally accepted.

There were recognized problems, though. For example, sometimes what was left behind after combustion was actually *heavier*; this was the case in the process of rusting, which Stahl recognized was essentially a form of combustion. The idea that phlogiston could have negative mass might have been just about acceptable, but that its mass could be sometimes positive, sometimes negative, was much harder to swallow—impossible, even. Another conundrum was that the air around something that had been burned was now presumably phlogiston-rich; why didn't that air *itself* readily catch fire?

Lavoisier, with his passion for measurement, brought science to the phlogiston table. He burned things inside closed containers so he could establish exactly what was going on in terms of the mass changes. (One of the things he burned in this way was a diamond, which he did by using a lens to focus the sun's rays on it through the glass walls of the container.) He found that, no matter the weight of the ash left behind, the *total* weight of everything in the container, including the air, was unchanged. Lavoisier generalized this observation to state that, in any chemical reaction, the mass of all of the products, added together, is exactly equal to the mass of what you started with. This law of conservation of mass has remained an important principle to this day.

Another thing he found: If you sucked all the air out of the container before you started, the substance wouldn't burn.

It was while UK chemist Joseph Priestley was visiting Paris in 1774 that Lavoisier finally figured out what was happening. Priestley had been researching what was then called "dephlogisticated air," and was only too ready to tell Lavoisier what he'd discovered. He had heated mercury in air to create a red substance (we now know it was mercuric oxide). When he focused concentrated heat on this substance, it decomposed back to mercury, while at the same time giving off a gas in which things burned far more fiercely than in ordinary air. Clearly, Priestley reasoned, this was air that lacked phlogiston.

Lavoisier made a radical conceptual leap. What if it wasn't that the gas was phlogiston-deficient air but that ordinary air consisted of more than one gas? One of these gases was far more reactive than the other, so combustible materials burned readily in it, rusting happened faster, and so on. Lavoisier called the reactive gas *oxygen* and the nonreactive one *azote*.[1]

Although a few scientists dug their heels in and refused to relinquish the phlogiston theory, most readily accepted Lavoisier's reasoning.

---

1.   Greek words meaning roughly "acidifier"—because he thought, wrongly, that all acids contain oxygen—and "lifeless," because animals confined to it soon suffocated. *Azote* was renamed *nitrogen* in 1790 by Jean-Antoine Chaptal.

Lavoisier went further. Others had already realized that respiration was in effect another special case of combustion, even if, like rusting, it didn't look much like it. Animals took in air by breathing. The inert nitrogen constituent of the air was unaffected, but *something* must be happening inside the body, because we exhale carbon dioxide and water.

In 1783 the UK chemist Henry Cavendish had discovered that, when acids attacked metals, a gas was given off that, if burned, produced water. Cavendish had attempted to explain this in terms of the phlogiston theory and gotten nowhere. Lavoisier realized this gas must be another element, which he called *hydrogen*. Water must be the product of the reaction between hydrogen and oxygen; in other words, water—which many chemists still assumed to be an element—must be a compound of these two. So, Lavoisier reasoned, what must be happening in the body was that, somehow, the oxygen that was inhaled must be combining with carbon and hydrogen from foodstuffs in order to produce the carbon dioxide and water of the exhalation.

Lavoisier had a bad habit of annoying people. When he published his discoveries about oxygen and respiration he didn't bother to give credit to the foundational work of Priestley and Cavendish. While scientists might be able at most to grumble and fume about this, some of the other people he annoyed were more powerful. In fact, his biggest mistake was to piss off the French people as a whole.

The French should have had every reason to be grateful to this pioneering scientist. He contributed to better street lighting; he introduced improvements in agriculture that benefited everyone; he discovered a way of manufacturing saltpeter, a crucial component of gunpowder, so the French would have an advantage in war. But he also invested heavily in one of the most reviled companies in France, the Ferme Générale (General Farm).

The French government—this was still the era of the monarchy—had discovered it could save money by privatizing the collection of taxes. Each year the Ferme Générale paid the government an agreed-upon sum of money that notionally represented the year's revenue from taxation, then set about collecting taxes from the citizens. The company's profits came from the difference between what it paid to the government and what it actually collected, so clearly the incentive was for the Ferme Générale to extract as much as it could from everyone—often more than was actually owed. No wonder people hated the "tax farmers."

To make matters look worse, Lavoisier married the daughter of one of the bosses of the Ferme Générale, so now he wasn't just an investor in the company but was married into it.[1]

As if being loathed by the French citizenry weren't enough, Lavoisier earned the undying enmity of the journalist Jean-Paul Marat. Marat dabbled in the sciences, and had set his heart on being accepted into the Académie des Sciences. Lavoisier, who'd been accepted by the Académie when he was just twenty-five, was one of those who spoke out stridently against Marat's candidacy. Little did Lavoisier know that Marat would become a powerful figure after the Revolution and, his resentment having festered over the years, would be the person whose enthusiastic prosecution would bring Lavoisier to the guillotine.

Lavoisier's services to chemistry were many. One was his role in the invention of the system of nomenclature used to specify chemicals. Before his time, every chemist used his own terminology, so it was difficult for one scientist to build upon the work of another—or even to understand what the results of the other's work *were*. Lavoisier's system dictated that a chemical's name should indicate the elements of which it consists: copper sulfate, for example, or sodium chloride. (The biggest exception is of course water, which is almost always just called water.) Lavoisier and his colleagues Guyton de Morveau, Claude-Louis Berthollet and Antoine de Fourcroy published this system in book form as *Méthode de Nomenclature Chimique* (Method of Chemical Nomenclature; 1787).

Even more important was Lavoisier's solo effort *Traité Élémentaire de Chimie* (Elementary Treatise on Chemistry; 1789), which laid out all of his discoveries in the science that he'd almost single-handedly created. Effectively the world's first chemistry textbook, this was read all over

---

1. The fact that Marie-Anne Pierrette Paulze was just thirteen when they wed might seem shocking to us now, but it wasn't so outrageous in those days, and in fact Lavoisier was doing her and her father Jacques a favor. A very pretty girl, she'd attracted a proposal of marriage from a powerful nobleman four times her age. Desperate to avoid this, Jacques begged Lavoisier, then in his late twenties, to marry the girl instead. In fact, it proved to be a love match; furthermore, Marie-Anne was very intelligent, and became a more than competent assistant in her husband's researches.

Europe and in the New World, and was immensely influential; large parts of it are still applicable today. Unfortunately, there were errors, too. Although Lavoisier had played his part in banishing forever the ancient Greeks' notion of the four elements—earth, air, fire, and water—in the *Traité* he gave heat and light the status of elements. Even worse, in order to explain heat, he introduced the idea of caloric, an invisible, weightless constituent of substances that could be released as heat.

The irony of Lavoisier debunking one imaginary substance, phlogiston, yet inventing another, caloric, is obvious; adding to the irony is that the scientist who debunked caloric was Benjamin Thompson, Count Rumford . . . the widowed Marie-Anne's second husband. ■

BUT THERE'S MORE . . .

■ There's a crater on the Moon named for Lavoisier. The asteroid 6826 Lavoisier was discovered in 1989. In 1960 the Antarctic island called Ile Nansen, after the polar explorer Fridtjof Nansen, was renamed Lavoisier Island to avoid confusion with the *other* Nansen Island in the Antarctic.

■ A good although slightly out-of-date biography is *Antoine-Laurent Lavoisier* (1975) by Henry Guerlac. Also to be recommended is Madison Smartt Bell's *Lavoisier in the Year One* (2005). Among several recent short biographies aimed at younger readers is Lisa Yount's *Antoine Lavoisier* (2008).

■ Lavoisier and his wife Marie-Anne are pictured in a famed double portrait by the French artist Jacques-Louis David. It now hangs in New York's Metropolitan Museum of Art.

■ Sadly for Lavoisier's memory, an Australian science-denialist organization takes its name from him: the Lavoisier Group, founded in 1999 to advocate climate-change denial.

EDWARD JENNER
(1749–1823)

The English country doctor who began the conquest of smallpox.

W e tend to underestimate what a killer smallpox was. The disease was successfully eradicated by the late 1970s thanks to stringent vaccination programs. But that was the end of a war that had been waged for well over two hundred years. Before the start of that war, smallpox devastated human populations. In the seventeenth and early eighteenth centuries in London, smallpox was likely responsible for about 10 percent of all deaths, and some estimates put the toll as high as twice that.

A technique was developed by the early eighteenth century that could sometimes give people protection against the deadly disease. This practice, called variolation (from the Latin name for the disease, *variola*) or inoculation, involved opening a vein and pushing into it a small quantity of pus from one of the sores of a smallpox sufferer. If the patient survived the process, the method was very effective; the patient would have a mild attack of smallpox that would soon clear. The trouble was that, often enough, patients contracted a fatal case, which had the additional disadvantage that, before dying, they could infect friends and family.

Edward Anthony Jenner was a doctor in the English county of Gloucestershire. He had a passion for natural history, and was the first person to discover that it was the cuckoo chick that heaved the other eggs out of the nest and not, as had earlier been thought, the adult host birds. For this work he was in 1788 elected to the Royal Society.

There was a disease that infected many people in the English countryside. Called cowpox, because initially it took hold of cows' teats and from there spread by contact with the hands of milkers, it was rather like a very mild form of smallpox; it had some of the same symptoms, but people rarely died from it and often suffered no more than a mild fever. Jenner, as a country doctor, noticed that patients of his who'd had cowpox seemed completely immune to the effects of smallpox, even when he'd inoculated them. He even saw instances where smallpox had wiped out entire families except for those family members who'd earlier suffered cowpox.

In 1796 Jenner did something for which we must all be thankful, even though his act was totally unethical. Aged just eight, James Phipps was one of Jenner's patients. Although there was nothing wrong with the boy, Jenner deliberately infected him with cowpox. A few weeks later, after James's attack of the disease had come and gone, Jenner deliberately inoculated him with live smallpox pus . . . and James showed complete immunity. Just to check, Jenner repeated the smallpox inoculation a few months later, with the same result. Of course, had Jenner been wrong about cowpox conferring immunity to smallpox, the child could very well have died. Luckily he wasn't wrong, and so was born the era of vaccination (from the Latin *vaccinus*, "of a cow").

Curiously, the Royal Society declined to publish his results, since the notion that one disease could confer immunity to another seemed beyond the bounds of science. He thus published them himself in a book called *An Inquiry into the Causes and Effects of the Variolae Vaccinae* (1798), and within a very few years he became in consequence a very rich man. In 1853 the British Parliament mandated the vaccination of all infants and, as a result, by the end of the century smallpox fatalities in the UK had declined by about 98 percent.

What's not generally known is that Jenner wasn't the first to discover the principle of vaccination. A couple of decades earlier, in 1774, the English county of Dorset was devastated by a major smallpox epidemic. A farmer there, Benjamin Jesty, noticed the immunity to the killer that prior infection with cowpox seemed to confer, and in desperation infected himself and his family with the lesser disease. Jesty went public with the success of his "experiment" but, presumably because he was a farmer rather than a physician, nobody took too much notice. Even earlier, in 1765, the physician John Fewster, a friend of Jenner's, wrote a paper noting the immunization cowpox offered against smallpox—although, since Fewster never published it and Jenner was a teenager at the time, it's quite possible the younger man knew nothing of the paper's existence. ∎

BUT THERE'S MORE . . .

- There are surprisingly few biographies of Jenner, aside from some for young children. F. Dawtry Drewitt's *The Life of Edward Jenner* (1931) is a little old-fashioned in style, but is quite readable and reasonably short.
- There's a lunar crater named for Jenner. The asteroid 5168 Jenner was discovered in 1986.

JOHN DALTON
(1766–1844)

A Quaker chemist who revealed that matter is made of atoms.

Greek philosophers of the fifth century BCE like Democritus and Leucippus, as well as the later Epicurus, speculated that all matter was made up of invisibly tiny indestructible particles: atoms. The Roman poet Lucretius was another to develop the idea. Various Indian groups of roughly the same vintage had a comparable concept. In the eleventh century CE, some of the Islamic scientists had atomistic ideas. The seventeenth-century French scientist Pierre Gassendi picked up the idea from Lucretius and developed it.

So the English chemist John Dalton was far from the first to come up with an atomic theory. What he did was turn the idea of the atom from a piece of speculative whimsy into a sober, experiment-based scientific hypothesis about the nature of matter.

Dalton was born in Cumberland (now Cumbria), in the north of England; his exact birth date isn't known, because his parents were Quakers, and so as a matter of principle didn't register the birth. (He himself became a lifelong Quaker.) His schooling lasted just until he was eleven years old; by the time he was twelve he was employed as one of the school's teachers. Although self-taught, he might well have qualified for a place at Oxford or Cambridge, but those two universities were barred to Quakers, being open only to congregants of the Church of England.

In due course he got a teaching job in Manchester, a major city, and joined the Manchester Literary and Philosophical Society, one of the intellectual groups that had sprung up in the UK following the formation in 1660 of the Royal Society. Among the subjects he investigated under the society's aegis were color-blindness (he suffered himself, and to this day it's sometimes called *daltonism*) and the density of water; his counterintuitive discovery was that pure water is at its densest at a temperature of 42.5°F (6.1°C).

But his great love was meteorology, and from about 1787 until the end of his life he kept a detailed diary of local weather conditions. His first book was a treatise called *Meteorological Observations and Essays* (1793).

His interest in meteorology naturally led him to think about the atmosphere, and from there it was a short step to studying air, and gases in general. From experimentation he derived an important principle about the behavior of gases, now known as Dalton's law of partial pressures. If you put a gas in a container, it exerts an outward pressure on the container's walls. Dalton's law says that, if you have a *mixture* of gases in a container, each of those gases exerts the same outward pressure that it would if that were all the gas there was in the container.

But what could gases be made of? Scientists like Robert Boyle and Isaac NEWTON had explained the pressure exerted by contained gases in terms of tiny particles bouncing against the container walls, and this explanation made sense to Dalton. But he went one step further: What if it wasn't just gases that were made up of these tiny particles, but *all* forms of matter?

He put this speculation together with an observation made by the French chemist Joseph Louis Proust. Proust had discovered that, when you separated the chemical copper carbonate into its constituents and weighed those constituents, you always got the same ratio between them, no matter where the copper carbonate had come from or how it had been produced. Proust repeated his experiments with other chemicals and got similar results. Moreover, the ratios could always be expressed in terms of simple whole numbers. He thus put forward his law of definite proportions: When elements combine to form a compound, they always do so in the same proportions. But Proust didn't get very far in trying to explain the *why* of this.

Dalton did. It seemed obvious to him that it was the *atoms* of different elements that were combining to make compounds. All atoms, he thought, were made of the same basic "stuff"; they were indistinguishable from each other except in terms of their masses.

The mass of an atom determined the element to which it belonged. If you split up a simple compound like carbonic acid (which we now call carbon monoxide, CO), you found that, by weight, the ratio between the two constituents was always three parts carbon to four parts oxygen. This indicated, Dalton concluded, that a carbon atom had a mass 75 percent that of an oxygen atom. When carbon and oxygen combined instead to make carbon dioxide, CO_2, the ratio between the weights of the two constituents was measured as three parts carbon to eight parts oxygen. This confirmed Dalton's (correct) view that in carbonic acid two atoms of oxygen combined with one of carbon.

He wasn't so successful in his other assumptions, though. He thought water was a simple one-to-one combination of hydrogen and oxygen, HO, rather than the H_2O we now know it to be, and he thought sulfuric acid was SO_3 rather than H_2SO_4.

Dalton presented all his conclusions about atomic weights, wrong and right, in *A New System of Chemical Philosophy* (1808). Although a few chemists fought tooth and nail against his ideas, most accepted them fairly readily since they seemed to explain so much that had been mysterious about chemical reactions. Moreover, the idea of arranging elements according to their atomic weights gave some kind of order to things. Later scientists, like the Swedish chemist Jöns Berzelius, corrected Dalton's errors and improved upon his scheme of symbols for the elements while retaining his general principles.

A big breakthrough came in the 1860s when the Russian chemist Dmitri Mendeléev developed the Periodic Table, demonstrating that the seemingly disparate properties of the sixty-four then-known elements in fact had an order to them, and that those properties could be predicted through knowledge of the particular element's atomic weight. In fact, in an 1871 paper he predicted the existence of three undiscovered elements that would fill gaps in his table, and described the properties those elements must have. Many chemists thought the claim risible, but over the next few years the elements gallium, scandium, and germanium were discovered, and they fitted Mendeléev's predictions to a T.

There are now (as of April 2016) 118 recognized elements, the last four having been isolated in late 2015. When element no. 101 was discovered in the mid-1950s it was named *mendelevium* in the great Russian chemist's honor.

Of course, Dalton knew none of this. Toward the end of his life he became increasingly reclusive, although he did play a part in the 1831 founding of the British Association for the Advancement of Science (now called the British Science Association), a major organization dedicated to spreading scientific knowledge among the public and, through its annual conferences, aiding interdisciplinary communication among scientists.

The Manchester Literary and Philosophical Society bought Dalton a house, in which he lived for many years, and after his death it was preserved, complete with many of his papers, as a memorial. Unfortunately, in 1940 a Nazi bombing raid destroyed the house and many of the papers. ■

BUT THERE'S MORE . . .

■ Dalton has been honored with the naming of a lunar crater. The unit designating one atomic mass is occasionally called the *dalton* (Da). The University of Manchester presents various awards bearing Dalton's name. The Royal Society of Chemistry publishes the peer-reviewed journal *Dalton Transactions*.

■ Frank Greenaway's *John Dalton and the Atom* (1966) and Roberta Baxter's *John Dalton and the Development of Atomic Theory* (2012), for younger readers, are both recommended. An old but still readable biography is J. P. Millington's *John Dalton* (1906); you can find it for free on Google Books.

WILLIAM SMITH
(1769–1839)

The humble artisan who methodically unpicked the secrets of the strata.

The notion of the stratigraphic column might not sound like one that would have you or me leaping from our seats in excitement, but it's among the most important ideas in the development of modern science.

James HUTTON had argued that when rock faces were exposed—perhaps as a cliff—it was a pretty safe bet that the layers (strata) at the bottom were the oldest and the ones at the top were the youngest. On occasion this pattern would be broken if, for example, there'd been some upheaval that upset things, but even then it was usually pretty clear what had gone on. William Smith took this line of reasoning a whole lot further, which is why he's often known as the "Father of Stratigraphy" and nicknamed "Strata" Smith.

He was born in Oxfordshire, England, the son of a blacksmith who died when William was just eight. A decade or so later, in 1787, a surveyor visiting the town where William lived hired him as a temporary assistant. The surveyor was so impressed by William's intelligence that he took him on as an apprentice. William seems to have taken to the trade like a duck to water, because within a few years he was single-handedly working on some fairly major surveying jobs, his specialty being canals and proposed canal routes. He became so interested in the strata of the rocks through which the canals were dug that he traveled to look at canals all over the country.

What Smith saw was that the collection of fossils in one stratum was quite distinct from the collection in another. In other words, you could use the fossils present in any stratum as a means of identifying it. Even if a layer had been disrupted by more recent events—erosion, earthquakes, subsidence, or whatever—you could still identify it through its fossils. In fact, you could use this method to tell if a layer at one place had been laid down at the same time as one hundreds of miles away.

Smith realized the importance of this discovery but, being a man of modest birth, he didn't rush to publish it—he didn't have access to the swanky scholarly societies in London. Instead, he spent the next couple of decades producing an elaborate stratigraphic map of the whole of England and Wales. In this enterprise he was helped financially by the great botanist and scientific philanthropist Sir Joseph Banks; when the map was finally published, in August 1815, Smith dedicated it to Banks.

The effort of researching and publishing the Map that Changed the World, as it's now often called, practically bankrupted Smith, and he was desperate that it sell as many copies as possible so he might recoup his losses. Unfortunately, a few years later one George Bellas Greenough published a rival map that was quite obviously based on copies of Smith's drafts, supplied to Greenough by one John Farey, an ex-apprentice of Smith's. It was difficult for Smith to do anything about this rank act of plagiarism, because he was but a humble artisan while Greenough was a cofounder and past president of the Geological Society of London.

Greenough's version was published in 1820 but, long beforehand, the publication was trumpeted far and wide, and many potential subscribers assumed that a map backed by the society would surely be better than Smith's; just to twist the knife, the plagiarized version was quite a lot cheaper. Smith's sales plummeted and in 1819 he went bankrupt, spending a few months in debtors' prison. The irony was that Greenough's map, when it eventually appeared, was widely condemned as lousy and sold very poorly.

For a decade or so Smith scraped a living as a freelance surveyor, but then one of his employers took up the cudgel to make sure he got the recognition he deserved. In 1831 the Geological Society of London, the same organization that had defrauded him, honored him with its first Wollaston Medal, which came with a handy cash award. Today the society presents an annual William Smith Lecture in his honor. Not until 1865, though, long after Smith's death, did the society start putting a full acknowledgment of his work on its stratigraphic maps.

Smith's recognition that different strata contained different collections of fossils had another important impact. It was quite obvious that the fossils in the oldest strata were of organisms far less like modern ones than the fossils in the more recent strata. The *stratigraphic column*, as it's called, doesn't just tell us about rocks; it offers us a history of life. And that history shows us, quite clearly, that there's been an evolutionary process at work. A couple of decades after Smith's death, DARWIN published his *Origin of Species* (1859), spelling out just what this process was. ∎

BUT THERE'S MORE . . .

- A tremendous book about Smith is *The Map that Changed the World* (2001) by Simon Winchester.
- Smith's nephew, John Phillips, published *Memoirs of William Smith* (1844); you may be able to find a copy in a specialist library.
- There's a crater on Mars called Smith in honor of the "Father of Stratigraphy."

MICHAEL FARADAY

(1791–1867)

A brilliant experimenter who revealed the mysteries of electromagnetism and the fraudulence of spirit mediums.

Arguably the greatest experimental scientist of the nineteenth century, if not of all time, Michael Faraday discovered electromagnetic induction, benzene, and the laws of electrolysis; invented the transformer, the electric motor, and the electric generator; investigated polarized light; and even took time out to debunk Spiritualism. He coined the words *electrode*, *anode*, and *cathode*. Throughout his life he was a devout Christian, a member of the Sandemanian sect, which held that the accumulation of wealth is sinful. He also took great delight in communicating science to the public, and in 1825 created the annual Christmas series of scientific lectures for children given at the Royal Institution in London, a tradition that continues to this day; he himself gave nineteen series of these lectures.

Michael Faraday was born the son of a blacksmith in Newington Butts, a hamlet that's since been absorbed by London. After a basic education, he was apprenticed to a London bookbindery, where he had the opportunity to read widely. He soon developed a passion for science. To learn more, he attended public science lectures wherever he could find them, a favorite haunt being the City Philosophical Society. When his apprenticeship was up, in 1812, a friendly customer gave him a set of tickets for lectures given at the Royal Institution by the great chemist Sir Humphry Davy.

Faraday decided to switch careers, from bookbinding to science. He first approached Joseph Banks, president of the Royal Society, who rebuffed him. He then tried Davy, who essentially told him to stick to the day job. However, Davy remembered the eager young man when, the following year, the Royal Institution had a vacancy for a laboratory assistant. After Davy damaged his eyesight in a laboratory accident, Faraday served also as his notekeeper. Additionally, Davy took him on an extended tour of Europe in 1813–15, giving him the chance to meet such distinguished figures as the physicists André-Marie Ampère and Alessandro Volta.

Back in London, Faraday rejoined the Royal Institution, where his star began to rise; he also helped Davy in the invention of the miners' safety lamp.[1]

In 1821 he made his first major scientific discovery. The Danish physicist Hans Christian Oersted had found in 1820 that a wire carrying an electric current deflected the needle of his compass, thereby showing that magnetism and electricity are two faces of the same phenomenon, electromagnetism. This seems very obvious to us now, but at the time it was a paradigm shift. Every scientist in sight started experimenting on electromagnetism, and Faraday was no exception. He theorized that the electricity-bearing wire must produce lines of magnetic force—a magnetic field, in other words—and to demonstrate this he set up a complicated piece of apparatus that was, in effect, the first electric motor. Although practical electric motors use a very different design, they rely on the principle Faraday worked out.

The irony is that Faraday succeeded in this and other electrical experiments despite having entirely erroneous ideas of what electricity actually *was*. He thought electricity was a type of vibration that put the molecules of an object under stress; that stress could be conveyed to the molecules of the air and thus to those of another object nearby. He also did his investigations without any reliance on mathematics, which he despised. He was the last scientist of any note not to use math in his work.

Faraday reasoned that, if an electric current could create a magnetic field, then surely a magnetic field should be capable of generating an electric current. It took him some years, starting in 1824, to get this notion to work, but in 1831 he did so, producing the first transformer and thereby discovering the principle of electromagnetic induction—that electricity can be created in a circuit by altering a magnetic field around it. Soon after, following the same line of investigation, he produced the world's first electric generator.

What Faraday didn't know was that another UK physicist, Joseph Henry, had discovered the principle the year before but hadn't yet been able to publish his results; the two are generally listed as co-discoverers. Moreover, Faraday couldn't know the importance of his creation of the

---

1. A problem for miners was the constant risk of encountering pockets of inflammable gas. This was particularly dangerous when carrying a naked flame. Davy devised a lamp that, while still horrifyingly dangerous by today's standards, saved countless miners' lives.

transformer, because in order for the device to be of any practical use you need to have mastered alternating current, something that would have to wait until the work of Nikola Tesla in the 1880s.

All this while, Faraday had also been pursuing his researches in chemistry. In 1823 he managed to produce liquid chlorine, and soon followed this by liquefying a scad of other gases. In 1835 he managed to isolate benzene and, around this same time, discovered how platinum, despite its reluctance to engage in chemical reactions, could catalyze (facilitate) reactions between other substances. Most importantly, he discovered that much of the chemical behavior of substances is electrical in nature—yet another astonishing conceptual leap.

A further electromagnetic discovery came about through a suggestion in 1845 from the influential physicist Lord Kelvin, then still a young man. Faraday was able to show that a magnetic field could rotate the polarization of a beam of light (the so-called Faraday effect). This established a connection between light and electromagnetism, and by 1846 Faraday was groping toward the idea that light might be some kind of electromagnetic radiation—an idea brought to fruition later by James Clerk MAXWELL. Faraday even thought it possible that light was a vibration that could be transmitted through empty space without the need for the luminiferous aether (see page 139). Not until EINSTEIN came along would Faraday's intuition on this be confirmed.

Faraday's interests were wide-ranging. In 1848 people on both sides of the Atlantic were fascinated by the case of the Hydesville Rappings, in which a trio of New York State sisters had seemingly established communication with the dead. The craze of Spiritualism spread like wildfire, and many acquaintances of Faraday's got caught up in it, attending—for a fee!—séances run by spirit mediums or simply conducting amateur séances themselves. These ghostly cavortings offended Faraday as both a scientist and a Christian. He thus devised various experiments to determine what was actually going on.

For example, one of the most popular tricks the "spirits" performed was table-turning, or table-tilting. The participants in a séance would sit around a table, their fingers resting lightly on it, and all of a sudden the table would tip up. Faraday created a special compound table surface that was sensitive to the least pressure upon it and, sure enough, demonstrated that table-tilting could be quite adequately explained through unconscious (or fraudulent) movements by the sitters.

Throughout his life, Faraday was a very modest man, as prescribed by his Sandemanian tenets, the same tenets that made him a lifelong pacifist. He accepted the various honors showered upon him reluctantly, if at all; he refused both the presidency of the Royal Society and a knighthood. ∎

BUT THERE'S MORE . . .

- You can find quite a few of the more recent Royal Institution Christmas lectures, given by scientists like Carl Sagan and Richard Dawkins, on the institution's YouTube channel.
- Various of Faraday's works are available at Project Gutenberg; among them is the book version of his 1848–49 series of Christmas lectures (repeated in 1860–61), *The Chemical History of a Candle*. Also at Gutenberg are some elderly biographies of Faraday, including *Michael Faraday* (1872) by J. H. Gladstone and *Faraday as a Discoverer* (1868) by John Tyndall. A very good modern biography is James Hamilton's *Faraday* (2002).
- The SI unit for capacitance, the *farad* (F), is named for Faraday, as was the *faraday* (F), a unit for electrical charge that has now been superseded by a different (far smaller) unit, the Coulomb.
- The Royal Society gives its annual Michael Faraday Prize to people who've excelled in the communication of science to the UK public. Every three years the Royal Society of Chemistry awards its Faraday Lectureship Prize to someone who's made a great contribution to physical and/or theoretical chemistry; the society's Electrochemistry Group has its own Faraday Medal. The Institution of Engineering and Technology gives its Faraday Medal annually (most years) for advances in science/engineering. The Institute of Physics's Faraday Medal and Prize (a single award, despite the name) annually recognizes advances in experimental physics.
- Between 1991 and 2001 Faraday appeared on the UK's £20 banknote, and he was also the subject of a 22p postage stamp there in 1991.
- There's a crater on the Moon named for him, and an asteroid, 37582 Faraday.
- The counterterrorism expert played by Jeff Bridges in the movie *Arlington Road* (1999) is called Michael Faraday, but there the resemblance ends.

CHARLES DARWIN
(1809–1882)

The naturalist who, through elucidating the mechanism of evolution, made possible the modern biological sciences.

Today Charles Darwin is one of the most revered but also one of the most loathed of all scientists. He offered the first rigorous explanation of what drives evolution.

He was born the same day, February 12, 1809, as Abraham Lincoln. His father, Robert Darwin, a wealthy physician, didn't think young Charles was ever going to amount to anything: "You care for nothing except shooting, dogs and rat-catching. You will be a disgrace to yourself and all your family." At school Charles was happiest studying nature specimens and doing science experiments; his nickname was "Gas."

Despairing, Robert Darwin pulled his son out of school and employed him as an assistant. Charles proved to have some talent at this, and so he was dispatched to Edinburgh University to study medicine. Unfortunately, Charles spent much of his time goofing off. The clincher came when, as part of his studies, he witnessed a couple of surgical operations. There were no anesthetics in those days, so the hapless patients suffered agonies during surgery. The experience turned Charles off medicine entirely.

Attending a lecture by John James Audubon stirred a new interest in him: taxidermy. He took lessons in bird taxidermy from a former slave called John Edmonstone; the two became fast friends and, as they worked together, Edmonstone taught him a great deal about natural history.

Robert Darwin concluded the Edinburgh experiment was another failure. He next sent Charles to Christ's College, Cambridge, to study theology with the aim of becoming a vicar. Yet again Charles was bored by his studies. One of the things he did was join the Glutton Club, which met weekly to eat odd foods. Apparently the club disbanded in dismay after trying to eat a tawny owl, which was by all accounts disgusting. However, all through his life Darwin showed a willingness to try anything once, foodwise.

Also while at Cambridge, Darwin started attending the lectures given by botany professor John Henslow as well as the informal gatherings Henslow held. There was an important consequence of the friendship with Henslow. In 1831 Robert FitzRoy, skipper of an exploratory ship called the *Beagle*, offered Henslow the position of ship's naturalist on its upcoming two-year voyage around the world. Henslow didn't want the job, and proposed Darwin in his stead. After some negotiation, Darwin was signed on for the expedition.

THE VOYAGE OF THE *BEAGLE*

HMS *Beagle* was quite a small ship and of a class nicknamed "Coffin" because of a propensity for sinking. Darwin must have felt the name particularly apt because, within hours of the *Beagle* setting sail from Plymouth, Devon, for South America on December 27, 1831, he was suffering the most horrific seasickness. Frequently during the *Beagle*'s voyage—which eventually lasted nearly five years instead of the planned two—he had to retreat to his cabin for days, capable of not much else but lying on his bunk, moaning.

When he wasn't puking, his job aboard the *Beagle* was twofold. He was expected not just to be the ship's naturalist but to serve as a companion to Captain FitzRoy. FitzRoy was an interesting character in his own right—in the 1850s and 1860s he pioneered modern meteorology, inventing the term *weather forecast*—but he and Darwin were in many ways like chalk and cheese. In particular, the conservative FitzRoy enthusiastically supported slavery, which Darwin vehemently opposed.

The voyage of the *Beagle* took it all the way down the eastern coast of South America and then back up the western coast. From there it sailed to Australia, going along the southern coast of that continent, and then to the Cape of Good Hope, at the southern tip of Africa. So that he could formally claim the ship had gone all the way around the world, FitzRoy then crossed the Atlantic to briefly revisit Brazil before returning to England, landing at Falmouth on October 2, 1836.

All through the voyage Darwin was collecting specimens, notes, and drawings,[1] and shipping them home to Henslow, who arranged for the specimens to be examined by experts. One of those experts was the ornithologist John Gould.

---

1. By the *Beagle*'s artists, Augustus Earle and later Conrad Martens, and sometimes by FitzRoy or Darwin himself.

Famously, one of the *Beagle*'s ports of call was the Galápagos Islands, an archipelago on the equator a few hundred miles west of Ecuador and renowned for its giant tortoises. The vice-governor there told Darwin you could tell which island a tortoise was from simply by examining its shell. Darwin himself noticed the archipelago's mockingbirds varied from island to island, and likewise the islands' finches. Although it's the bit about the finches that's best known today, it wasn't a discovery Darwin himself made. He thought the differences were just variations within a single species, and didn't even make proper notes of them. It was only after he'd returned home that he learned from John Gould that the finches he'd collected were in fact of different species.

Darwin immediately realized the importance of this. The obvious explanation was that, as with the tortoises, the finches had spread from one island to the next along the archipelago—perhaps aboard human vessels. Each island's finch population was then effectively isolated from the next's by the barrier of the sea. Breeding in isolation, the finches in each population became subtly different from those of the others until, over a long period of time, they formed distinct species. Here was an example of evolution in action.

Evolution (although not the word itself) was an idea very much in vogue in the nineteenth century. Before Darwin, the most important hypothesis to explain evolution came from the French biologist Jean-Baptiste, Chevalier de Lamarck, who thought the characteristics animals acquired during their lifetimes could be passed on to their offspring. For example, giraffes had long necks because generations of giraffes had stretched their necks to eat the topmost leaves, and had passed down that "stretchedness" to their offspring. It was Darwin's genius that enabled him to show this idea was wrong, and to unravel what was really going on.

Also during the voyage of the *Beagle*, Darwin saw coral reefs, and he developed a theory to explain how they form. He said that corals initially colonize the shores of volcanic islands. Over time, as the islands gradually subside beneath the waves, the corals grow upward—to keep their heads above water, as it were. Eventually the island is lost to view, leaving only a ring of coral above the surface. Darwin's explanation has since been shown to be perfectly correct.

BARNACLES

By the time he got home, Darwin was famous. The generous-spirited Henslow had made sure that all his adventures and discoveries were kept in the public eye. Among the scientists eager to make his acquaintance were the geologist Sir Charles Lyell and the paleontologist Sir Richard Owen. The latter would eventually turn bitterly against him, jealous of having his limelight stolen by the young upstart, but Lyell remained a lifelong supporter and friend—even though he would disagree with Darwin's evolutionary ideas. Lyell was a great popularizer of the theories of James HUTTON, who'd deduced that the world was not thousands but millions of years old. The notion of deep time would prove immensely important to Darwin's thinking.

Darwin had various obligations to fulfill. One was the writing of volume 3 of FitzRoy's four-volume *Narrative of the Surveying Voyages of His Majesty's Ships "Adventure" and "Beagle"* (1838). Darwin's contribution proved tremendously popular, and so the publisher reissued it as a solo volume. Since its first publication, *The Voyage of the "Beagle"* has never been out of print.

That same year, 1838, Darwin proposed marriage to his cousin Emma Wedgwood. It proved to be a love story for the ages. Emma was deeply devout. Charles slowly lost his religion.[1] The situation could have been ripe for disaster, yet the two loved each other enough that they made it work: Emma helped Charles formulate the ideas with which she so much disagreed, while he went out of his way not to offend her with the implications of those ideas.

The notion of what we'd now call speciation, which had begun glimmering in his mind while he was in the Galápagos and then to gleam more brightly after he'd discovered that those finch specimens represented distinct species, became more and more a preoccupation. In 1837 he began the first of a series of notebooks in which he recorded his ideas about, and the evidence he'd discovered for, what he called the "transmutation of species." In 1842 he expanded these notions into a fairly comprehensive scientific paper, yet he held back from publishing it. A major reason was that while he had credentials as a naturalist and an author on natural history—*The Voyage of the "Beagle"* had been followed by other successful books, like *The Structure and Distribution of Coral Reefs* (1842)

---

1. Not just because of his elucidation of the mechanism of evolution but also in the wake of the death of his adored first daughter, Annie, from tuberculosis in 1851.

and *Geological Observations on the Volcanic Islands* (1844)—he wasn't recognized as a professional biologist.

In 1846 he decided to rectify this situation, and so he started an exhaustive investigation of barnacles that was to take him nearly eight years. It remains today the definitive study on the subject, and has great scientific value. On the other hand, even though throughout his life he was a near-obsessive cataloguer of nature, it bored him silly. Halfway through his work on them, he wrote that "I hate a barnacle as no man ever did before."

THE TRANSMUTATION OF SPECIES

Although Darwin had started compiling his notebooks on the transmutation of species as early as 1837, he still wanted to amass more evidence. In 1844 he wrote a far longer version of his 1842 essay—more like a short book—but the only person he showed it to was his friend Joseph Dalton Hooker, Director of the Royal Botanic Gardens at Kew. More years passed as Darwin dithered.

In 1855 Lyell pointed out to him that he wasn't the only fish in the evolutionary pond. A young naturalist called Alfred Russel Wallace had published a paper advocating ideas on speciation that were quite close to Darwin's. Darwin wasn't much worried but did agree it was about time he got his act together and wrote his ideas up as a book. He envisaged this as a multivolume work called *Natural Selection*.

He was still beavering away on it in June 1858 when Wallace, researching in Malaysia, sent him an essay that sketched out exactly the theory that Darwin had been so painstakingly developing. Wallace had read the book *An Essay on the Principle of Population* (1798) by the English clergyman Robert Malthus. Malthus pointed out that an ever-increasing human population would lead inevitably to poverty and suffering; fortunately, populations were kept (somewhat) in check by factors such as war, disease, and birth control. Like Darwin, who'd read the book a couple of decades earlier and come to a similar conclusion, Wallace realized that herein lay a clue to the rise of new species.

Living organisms produce far more offspring than their environments can support. A pair of frogs, for example, can produce hundreds of eggs in a single breeding cycle. Of those hundreds, however, only a few will survive the tadpole stage. Of course, luck will play a big chance in determining which tadpoles will make it to become frogs, and the same is true concerning which frogs will survive long enough to breed with other frogs. But, Darwin and Wallace reasoned, there's not only luck at play.

Except in very rare cases (identical twins), the offspring of living creatures show a natural variation from one another. Some of the chance variations may be advantageous to an individual's survival. Let's think back to those giraffes. Because of natural variation, some giraffes will grow to have longer necks and legs than others. Such giraffes will be able to feed on leaves that are out of reach of their less fortunate siblings, and so they'll be more likely to survive and reproduce.

Darwin and Wallace were well aware of the process of artificial selection, whereby breeders of plants and animals encourage desirable characteristics and discourage others. But, the two men reasoned, nature likewise exerts a selection pressure on living creatures—the pressure of survival.

Because of all the random variations within a species, that species will become gradually better adapted to its environment. If you introduce the species to a different environment, then you can expect a different set of adaptations to appear over the generations—either that or the species may die out. Through the course of generations, the creatures in the new environment may become sufficiently unlike the ones left behind in the old (which are also changing) that the two strains can no longer interbreed. They've become two separate species, each adapted to its own environment.

There's a lot more to the theory of evolution by natural selection than this—such as the importance of extinctions to the whole process, whereby old species die out as environments change and new, better adapted species appear—but this was the gist of the notion at which Darwin and Wallace independently arrived.

Wallace sent Darwin his paper with a request for advice as to whether it was worth publishing. Obviously Darwin thought it was—very much so! At the same time, he wasn't too keen to see his own decades of work on the theory overshadowed. Just to make matters worse, the youngest of his and Emma's ten children, still an infant, was dying, and another was gravely ill. He sought the advice of his friends Lyell and Hooker. They persuaded him to conquer his grief and produce a paper in a hurry that summarized his own conclusions. The two papers, Darwin's and Wallace's, could then be presented alongside each other at a meeting of the scholarly Linnean Society.

The joint presentation was made to the society on July 1, 1858. The society's president, Thomas Bell, was unimpressed. Summing up 1858 in his annual presidential report, he remarked: "The year which has passed

DARWIN MYTHS

Plenty of myths have grown up around the memory of Charles Darwin:

- One that may have arisen because of the use of the word *races* in its antiquated sense in the subtitle of *Origin of Species* is that Darwin was an ardent racist. He lived in a racist society but he himself, with his vigorous opposition to the slave trade, was far broader-minded than was the norm.
- Another is that Darwinism inspired the Nazis to perpetrate the Holocaust and Stalin to carry out his own mass murders; in fact, both the Nazis and Stalin's regime specifically *rejected* natural selection—with Stalin supporting instead the crackpot notions of Trofim D. Lysenko, which had more to do with Lamarck's hypothesis than with anything Darwin produced.
- Yet another myth is that Darwin invented both eugenics and Social Darwinism. In fact, the pseudoscience of eugenics was the brainchild of Darwin's cousin Francis Galton (Darwin rejected it), while "Social Darwinism" refers to the sociological ideas of the philosopher Herbert Spencer, who coined the term "survival of the fittest." Darwin quite liked the term, and used it in later editions of *Origin of Species*, but he disliked the philosophy.
- You'll often hear it said that, just before he died, Darwin announced to family and friends that he no longer believed in his own theory of natural selection. This refers to a lie told in 1915 by the evangelist Elizabeth Cotton, Lady Hope, who claimed to have visited the bed-ridden Darwin at home a few months before his death to find him reading the Bible and espousing creationism. According to Darwin's children, their father never recanted his theory, and, so far as they could establish, Lady Hope never visited him.

has not, indeed, been marked by any of those striking discoveries which at once revolutionize, so to speak, the department of science on which they bear." He never spoke a wronger word.

Rather than spend the next few years finishing the planned multivolume *Natural Selection*, Darwin decided to rush out a pared-down version. That book, *On the Origin of Species by Means of Natural Selection, or The Preservation of Favoured Races in the Struggle for Life*—usually called just *Origin of Species*—came out in November 1859 and sold out on publication day. Several further editions followed.

We tend to think that *Origin of Species* set the world in uproar—a war between science and religion—but that isn't really what happened. Many theologians and ordinary Christians found they could quite easily incorporate evolutionary notions into their worldview. To be sure, some found the new ideas abhorrent, among them Darwin's old shipmate Robert FitzRoy. FitzRoy attended—and loudly heckled—a famous debate in Oxford between the Bishop of Oxford, Samuel Wilberforce, and Darwin's good friend, the biologist T. H. Huxley. Wilberforce was widely known as "Soapy Sam" because of his unctuous skills as an orator. After the debate, in which Huxley wiped the floor with his opponent, Huxley became known as "Darwin's Bulldog," and he played a major part in pugnaciously championing the theory of natural selection, something Darwin himself was too ill and reticent to do.

Where there was more controversy about the theory was within the scientific community. Darwin and Wallace couldn't explain why those chance variations between individuals—the mutations—actually came about; that mechanism wouldn't be known until the rediscovery in 1900 of MENDEL's work on heredity. Even after the new science of genetics had emerged, there was still some dispute—not over the fact of evolution, which had long been near-universally accepted by biologists, but over natural selection as its driving force. For much of the first half of the twentieth century geneticists like J. B. S. Haldane strove, in the end successfully, to marry genetics and natural selection.

In *Origin of Species* Darwin deliberately avoided discussing the evolution of human beings (the word *races* in the book's full title refers to animal and plant subspecies). He took the plunge over a decade later when he published *The Descent of Man, and Selection in Relation to Sex* (1871). This was another best seller, as was *The Expression of the Emotions in Man and Animals* (1872). The book that apparently did best of all for him, however, had little to do with evolution. It was *The Formation of Vegetable Mould through the Action of Worms, with Observations on Their Habits* (1881), and was an invaluable text for, among others, gardeners.

Within a few months of that book's publication, Darwin died. Despite the fact that Emma wanted him to have a quiet family burial, he was given a state funeral, being laid to rest in Westminster Abbey. ■

BUT THERE'S MORE . . .

■ There have been dozens of TV documentaries about Darwin and his ideas. A couple of fictionalized screen versions of his life are recommended: *Darwin's Brave New World* (2009), an Australian TV mini-series starring Socratis Otto as Charles, Katie Fitchett as Emma, and Rick Jon Egan as Huxley; and especially the magnificent movie *Creation* (2009), starring Paul Bettany as Charles, Jennifer Connelly as Emma, Benedict Cumberbatch as Hooker, and Toby Jones as a very funky but oddly credible Huxley.

- Darwin's *Autobiography* is a tremendous read; it's available at Project Gutenberg (as are other books by him). If you want a definitive biography, Janet Browne's two-volume epic *Charles Darwin* (1995/2002) may be for you, but there are some good short biographies around. I enjoyed Tim M. Berra's *Charles Darwin* (2009), Bruno Leone's *Origin* (2009), and Jonathan Clements's *Darwin's Notebook* (2009). A different take is offered by Janet Browne's *Darwin's "Origin of Species": A Biography* (2006)—a "biography" of the book. Of related interest is John Gribbin's *FitzRoy* (2003).

- A tongue-in-cheek novel about Darwin, supposedly subverting the "official" version, is *The Darwin Conspiracy* (2005) by John Darnton.

- Darwin's birthday is celebrated worldwide every February 12—including by many Christians—as Darwin Day.

- Darwin has featured on the UK's £10 banknote since 2000.

- Locations named for him are found all over the world: Mount Darwin, Darwin Falls, and the town of Darwin, all in California, plus several other places, in the US; Darwin Sound, Darwin Channel, Darwin Island, and the Andean peak Mount Darwin, plus others, in South America; Zimbabwe has another Mount Darwin; Antarctica has Darwin Glacier and the Darwin Mountains, plus others; while in Australia there are Darwins galore: Darwin International Airport, the Charles Darwin National Park, Charles Darwin University, the Charles Darwin Reserve, Northern Territory's Darwin River and town of Darwin, plus Tasmania's town of Darwin, Darwin Dam, and yet another Mount Darwin.

- A vast collection of Darwin's writings can be found at Darwin Online: darwin-online.org.uk. Thousands of his letters are collected at the Darwin Correspondence site: www.darwinproject.ac.uk. For more on the myths about Darwin and evolution in general, the Talk Origins site is useful: www.talkorigins.org.

- Charles Darwin's son George produced a theory to explain the origin of the Moon that was for decades rejected but is now (in modified form) widely accepted.

ADA LOVELACE

(1815–1852)

The poet's daughter who became a mathematician and devised what's arguably the first computer program.

Although for some while she was kept in the dark about it, Ada Lovelace was the daughter of the poet Byron. Byron was married to Ada's mother, Anne Isabella Milbanke, for only about a year before the couple separated; Ada was born a few weeks prior to that separation, and never knew her father, who died in Greece when she was just eight. Her mother, determined Ada should be anything but a poet, schooled her rigorously in math, a subject in which Ada wasn't then much interested. (She enjoyed geography, though.)

However, when she was eighteen she met the mathematician Charles Babbage, who was trying to build what we now recognize as the first computer. She realized the potential of the idea, and suddenly the math that had seemed so tedious became far more interesting. The following year Ada married William King, who in 1838 became the First Earl of Lovelace and was himself enough of a scientist to be elected to the Royal Society in 1841.

Everyone agreed Ada had a brilliant mind. She was mentored by Mary Somerville, the extraordinary polymath who, in an age when women were generally barred by social pressures from the sciences, showed what nonsense that was by educating herself to rival the menfolk. In 1835

Somerville became one of the first two women, along with Caroline Herschel, to be admitted as members of the Royal Astronomical Society. Among Ada Lovelace's other acquaintances were Charles Dickens and scientists of the caliber of Charles Wheatstone, Michael FARADAY and Augustus De Morgan; De Morgan thought Lovelace was a diamond in the rough—that she could have been a significant scientist had she only had a formal training. Unfortunately, such training wasn't available to women in Victorian England.

On the other hand, no one had ever tried to build a computer before, so perhaps her very lack of formal training was helpful when it came to assisting Babbage. Babbage had done a great deal to help British mathematics catch up with that of the European continent, behind which it had lagged for many decades through adopting the calculus of NEWTON rather than that of Gottfried LEIBNIZ. He pioneered the idea of assembly-line production in factories, an idea Henry Ford would bring to fruition. He was the first to demonstrate that it actually saved the postal services money if the price of the stamp for a domestic letter was the same no matter how far away the letter's destination (the system was adopted in the UK in 1840 and spread all around the world), invented skeleton keys and the first ophthalmoscope, developed the first practicable speedometer and the actuarial table, and did much else.

From about 1822 he began to envisage the possibilities of machines that could compute. People like Leibniz and Blaise Pascal had already developed calculating engines (and of course devices like the abacus had been around for centuries), but Babbage dreamed of something far more ambitious. In 1823 he began building—and got government backing for—the device eventually called Difference Engine No. 1. Calculations were done by giving numerical values to rotating wheels. Difference Engine No. 1 was extremely slow and bulky.

In 1834, soon after Lovelace had become absorbed by and involved in the project, Babbage realized he'd spent a decade heading down a blind alley and drew up plans for Difference Engine No. 2. By now, though, the government had lost interest. During Babbage's lifetime the idea never got off the drawing board, but between 1985 and 1991 a team of scientists at the Science Museum in London built Difference Engine No. 2, and, within its limitations, the device actually worked.

Babbage's next idea was far more advanced. His Analytical Engine was to be operated through the use of punched cards, much like those in modern voting machines. With the help of the enthusiastic Lovelace, he worked out many of the principles that a century later would be incorporated into the first working programmable computers.[1] The trouble was that Babbage didn't have electronics. The Analytical Engine never came to anything because he was stuck with using strictly mechanical devices.

It might seem as if Babbage was the senior partner in the work that he and Lovelace did together. What we can see in hindsight, however, is that in the long term Lovelace's contribution was far more significant. Whereas Babbage produced lots of good ideas for devices that he couldn't get to work, Lovelace devised something that would come to have universal application in the field of computing. Although some scholars have disputed the claim, it seems a near-certainty that Lovelace wrote an algorithm that was in effect the very first computer program.

Lovelace was only thirty-six when she died. Her later years became a quicksand of alcoholism, unsuccessful gambling (she'd devised this mathematical system, you see), depression and adultery. Bearing in mind Victorian England's ruthless suppression of female scientific ambitions, it may seem unsurprising to us that the extremely gifted Ada Lovelace reacted in this way. ■

BUT THERE'S MORE . . .

■ A good novel that portrays Lovelace is the early steampunk classic *The Difference Engine* (1990) by William Gibson and Bruce Sterling. The movie *Conceiving Ada* (1997) is about a modern-day computer scientist who, obsessed with Lovelace, believes she can somehow genetically engineer a living version of the pioneer. The title of Sydney Padua's graphic novel *The Thrilling Adventures of Lovelace and Babbage: The (Mostly) True Story of the First Computer* (2015) speaks for itself.

■ Ada Lovelace Day, celebrated annually in mid-October (the precise date varies), encourages the advancement of female scientists. The British Computer Society awards the annual Lovelace Medal for achievement in information systems. The computer language Ada, in use from the 1970s onward, was named in her honor, as was the lunar crater Lovelace.

---

1.   The first electronic computer I ever worked on involved the use of hundreds and thousands of punched cards, and was regarded as modern in that it didn't use punched tape. I was the kid paid to punch the data onto the cards!

IGNAZ SEMMELWEIS
(1818–1865)

The Hungarian physician whose discovery of the importance of hospital hygiene has saved countless millions of lives.

In the mid-1840s a doctor working in one of the two maternity wards at the Vienna General Hospital, Ignaz Philipp Semmelweis, was disturbed that the mortality rate among the mothers there was, at 11 percent, about six times higher than that suffered in the other maternity ward. The killer was puerperal fever, often called childbed fever. The really puzzling factor was that the ward where so many mothers were dying of the fever was the posher of the two, where there were highly trained doctors and surgeons to hand and serious medical research was done. In the other ward, the births were handled by mere midwives.

In those days nobody really understood fevers. It wouldn't be until a couple of decades later that PASTEUR would come out with his germ theory of disease, the understanding that infectious illnesses are caused and spread by microbes. In Semmelweis's time, HIPPOCRATES's notion of the four humors still had an important hold on the minds of physicians; unfortunately, the principle of "First do no harm" was less revered. Medicine wasn't really a science, just a matter of following established procedures even if there was no real evidence they worked.

So Semmelweis's first breakthrough was the idea that the Scientific Method could be applied to the problem. He compared the practices in the two wards and put forward several hypotheses as to what might account for the difference in mortality rates. He then tested each in turn by making adjustments to the way his own ward was run.

None of the adjustments made any difference.

One difference was that his own ward was a training establishment. The young doctors working there performed dissections as part of their training in between tending the mothers. At first this didn't seem important to Semmelweis, but then a friend of his, Jakob Kolletschka, was accidentally cut while performing an autopsy and soon afterward died of what looked for all the world like puerperal fever.

Was it possible, Semmelweis thought, that there was some kind of "cadaveric material" that could fatally infect hitherto healthy people? Were the trainee doctors unwittingly carrying it on their hands from the dissecting theater to the patients?

To test this new hypothesis, he insisted that, before working with the mothers, the medical and nursing staff washed their hands in a solution of chlorinated lime. He instituted this practice in May 1847, and by 1848 the death rate from puerperal fever in his ward had dropped by a factor of nearly ten, to a mere 1.27 percent. That's still high by modern standards, but it was an incredible achievement.

However, the doctors at the Vienna General Hospital were a stupid bunch. They bitterly resented being forced to wash their hands the whole time—both because it was a nuisance and, in some cases, because they felt the smell of cadaver on their hands was a mark of distinction!—and they refused to believe the new measure had anything to do with the decrease in fatalities. And, as a clincher, Semmelweis was a Hungarian—he was born in what's now a suburb of Budapest—and therefore to be looked down upon by proud Austrian doctors.

Semmelweis's superiors found an excuse to fire him. By the fall of 1860 the mortality rate of puerperal fever in the ward, which Semmelweis's regime had reduced to just over 1 percent, was at an appalling 35 per-cent—in other words, over one-third of the mothers who gave birth there died soon after.

Semmelweis, meantime, had returned to Budapest and continued to work in obstetrics, now at the St. Rocaus Hospital. Naturally hygiene was an important part of his regime and so, almost alone in the whole of Europe, the St. Rocaus Hospital saw few deaths in its maternity ward.

In 1861 Semmelweis gathered the evidence he'd accumulated and wrote a book, *The Etiology, Concept and Prophylaxis of Childbed Fever*, which he sent to every significant medical society in Europe. In most countries the medical profession largely ignored him. The exception was the UK, where at least some of the medical establishment had taken note of a much earlier paper by the US physician Oliver Wendell Holmes, "The Contagiousness of Puerperal Fever" (1843).

In 1865 the UK surgeon Joseph Lister, working in the medical school of Glasgow University, made the connection between Semmelweis's re-searches on the importance of hygiene in hospitals and Pasteur's germ theory and started insisting on sterilization of instruments, treatment of surgical wounds using a powerful antiseptic, initially carbolic acid (phenol) —which must have hurt the patients like crazy, but did the trick—and other measures. Post-operation death rates plummeted in Glasgow, and Lister forced the rest of the medical establishment to take heed.

There wasn't to be a happy ending for Semmelweis. Perhaps because of his horror at the death toll wreaked by the European medical profession's refusal to acknowledge what he'd discovered, or perhaps just out of simple frustration, in 1865—the same year Lister made his breakthrough—he fell into a chronic depression and was committed by his friends to a mental institution. Within a few weeks of the committal he was dead . . . seemingly of puerperal fever. ■

BUT THERE'S MORE . . .

■ In Hungary you can find the Semmelweis University in Budapest and the Semmelweis Hospital in Miskolc, while Vienna has the Semmelweis Clinic.
■ Various movies have been made about Semmelweis and his adversities, of which one, *That Mothers Might Live* (1938), was awarded an Oscar for Best Short Film.
■ The asteroid 4170 Semmelweis was discovered in 1980.

GREGOR MENDEL
(1822–1884)

The quiet monk whose deciphering of the laws of heredity would lead eventually to the modern science of genetics.

It's generally agreed there are three scientific papers that stand head and shoulders above all others in biology, and Gregor Mendel's "Versuche über Pflanzenhybriden" ("Experiments on Plant Hybridization"; 1865), in which he outlined his ideas on heredity, is one of them.[1]

It was published in the *Proceedings* of the Natural History Society of Brno, but that was just a local group of amateurs, and it seems the members were merely bewildered by the work. Copies of the *Proceedings* went to scholarly organizations around Europe but seemingly went unread. Mendel bought forty offprints and mailed them to some of the titans of contemporary biology; again, it seems they went unread.

One recipient who probably did not read the essay was Charles DARWIN. Furthermore, Darwin owned a copy of a book called *Die Pflanzen-Mischlinge, Ein Beitrag zur Biologie der Gewächse* (Plant Hybrids: An Offering in the Biology of Plants; 1881) by the German botanist Wilhelm Olbers Focke, in which there was a brief discussion of Mendel's ideas on heredity. That copy still survives. The pages of the relevant section remain uncut—Darwin never got round to reading or even opening that bit. He was *within the thickness of a few sheets of paper* of discovering the mechanism whereby natural selection functioned, a problem whose solution eluded him until the end of his life.

Johann Mendel—he took the name Gregor years later, on becoming a monk—was born in what is now Hynčice, Czech Republic, to a poor family. By freelancing as a tutor, he paid his way through a couple of years of college before, in 1843, entering holy orders at the Abbey of St. Thomas in Brünn (now Brno); he was ordained a priest in 1847.

---

1. The other two are the presentation by DARWIN and Wallace to the Linnean Society of their ideas on natural selection in 1858 and the proposition in *Nature* in 1953 by Crick and Watson, based to a great extent on work done by Rosalind FRANKLIN, that DNA had a double-helix structure.

The priests were expected to teach in the local schools, and for training purposes he was sent in 1851 to the University of Vienna to study math and a range of sciences, including botany. But he kept failing the teaching exams!

In 1856 or 1857 he began growing peas in the monastery's garden and investigating how they reproduced. He maintained this hobby for the next eight years, and by the end of 1864 was ready to present his results to the local natural history society, of which he was a member. His presentation was greeted with, by all accounts, a stony silence; as soon as Mendel started getting into the math of what he'd been doing, it seems everyone's eyes glazed over. Even so, as a courtesy the society published his lecture in its *Proceedings*, with the dismal results we've seen.

His most important experiments were with pea plants, of which the monastery had two types: tall ones and dwarf ones. Mendel took great precautions when breeding these to make sure there was no cross-pollination from one plant to another.

He discovered that seeds from the dwarf plants always produced more dwarf plants. When he grew the seeds of the second generation and self-pollinated them as before, once again the offspring were all dwarf plants. No matter how many generations he bred, the results were always dwarfs.

The situation with the tall plants was a bit different. About one-third of his tall plants bred true, like the dwarf ones, but the seeds from the others produced a mixture of tall and dwarf offspring. It seemed to him there must be two types of tall plant: the ones that bred true and the ones that didn't.

He next determined to find out what happened when he crossbred dwarf and tall plants. The plants produced from this mix were all tall, but, when he self-pollinated these offspring as before, he found about one-quarter of the new generation were true-breeding dwarfs and about one-quarter were true-breeding talls, while the rest—half the total— were non-true-breeding tall plants.

Mendel concluded that all of the non-true-breeding tall plants contained the potential for dwarfness, but that this was suppressed when the potential for tallness was present. In plants that lacked the potential for tallness, the dwarfness always could and did express itself. The tallness was a *dominant* trait in that, when present, it dominated the dwarfness; conversely, the dwarfness was a *recessive* trait.

He repeated his experiments, now focusing not on height but on other characteristics, such as blossom color, and got similar results.

What Mendel had managed to demonstrate was that heredity isn't a matter of the parents' characteristics averaging out, as people had assumed. The offspring contains characteristics from both parents, but not all of these characteristics show.

This would have been tremendous news for Darwin had he been a bit more diligent about his reading. Darwin and Wallace were convinced evolution operated via natural selection based on random mutations that occurred during reproduction. But, if everything evened out, favorable mutations would in a few generations disappear. The laws of heredity demonstrated by Mendel's experiments showed there was no such averaging-out. At last there was a way for natural selection to act as a powerful driver of evolution.

In 1868 Mendel was promoted to be Abbot of St. Thomas's, and thereafter he had far less time for science. (He did, though, find the time to keep an accurate weather diary.) Moreover, the distinguished local botanist Carl Wilhelm von Nägeli, to whom Mendel sent a copy of his paper with a specific request for comments, essentially dismissed it as worthless; he may well have been, like the stalwart members of the Natural History Society, baffled by the math.

Mendel died assuming all of his endeavors with the abbey's pea plants had been just so much wasted effort. But in 1900 the Dutch botanist Hugo de Vries, the German botanist Carl Erich Correns, and the Austrian agronomist Erich Tschermak von Seysenegg independently discovered Mendel's epochal paper and recognized its importance. De Vries had performed his own experiments in plant breeding and come to conclusions about heredity similar to Mendel's.

Ironically, de Vries used his own and Mendel's discoveries about heredity to produce a theory of evolution that differed quite radically from Darwin's: mutationism. Where Darwin's theory of natural selection envisaged minor mutations accumulating to produce major changes over many generations, de Vries's mutationism assumed evolution progressed in fits and starts, that every now and then there'd be a major mutation so advantageous the individual concerned became parent to a whole new line.

Through much of the first half of the twentieth century, biologists wrestled with the problem of marrying the laws of heredity, as established by Mendel and refined by others, with the theory of evolution by natural selection. The term *genetics* was coined by the UK biologist William Bateson around 1905 to describe this new branch of science. The UK biologist J. B. S. Haldane was at the forefront of those who succeeded in elucidating the role of Mendel's heredity in the process of evolution. Today, although we haven't yet pinned down every last detail of the process of evolution, we can recognize Darwin and Mendel as the two major contributors to our knowledge of where we came from. ∎

BUT THERE'S MORE . . .

- Simon Mawer's novel *Mendel's Dwarf* (1998) depicts a geneticist, the great-great-great nephew of Mendel, who has difficulty being taken seriously both socially and professionally because he's a dwarf. Large parts of the book are concerned with Mendel's own life and the discoveries he made. Mawer, a biology teacher, has also written a good short nonfiction account of Mendel and early genetics, *Gregor Mendel: Planting the Seeds of Genetics* (2006); this was originally published as a complement to an exhibition at Chicago's Field Museum (and later on tour). Another good short biography is *Gregor Mendel and the Roots of Genetics* (1999) by Edward Edelson. Longer, but not hugely so, is Robin Marantz Henig's highly readable *The Monk in the Garden* (2000). A great scientific biography of him is Vítezslav Orel's *Gregor Mendel: The First Geneticist* (1996).
- The Mendel Museum of Genetics, now part of Masaryk University, was founded in 2002 in Brno within the grounds of St. Thomas's Abbey. Also in Brno is Mendel University, formerly the Mendel University of Agriculture and Forestry. The Gregor Mendel Institute of Molecular Plant Biology was founded in Vienna in 2000. The Mendel Polar Station was established on James Ross Island, Antarctica, in 2006.
- Craters on both the Moon and Mars are named in the scientist's honor, as is the asteroid 3313 Mendel.

LOUIS PASTEUR
(1822–1895)

*Despite arrogance and possible dishonesty, Pasteur gave us
pasteurization and the germ theory of disease.*

The man who produced the germ theory of disease and pioneered vaccination, Louis Pasteur was born in Dole, in eastern France, although his family moved twice when he was a small child, and so he grew up in the town of Arbois. He was only an average student until he attended some lectures by the celebrated chemist Jean Baptiste André Dumas, who infected him with a zeal for chemistry. He got a BA in 1840 from Besançon's Royal College, which two years later awarded him a BS. He then entered the Ecole Normale Supérieure in Paris, where he gained his doctorate in chemistry in 1847.

His first major piece of work was in the field of crystallography—at least, that's where it began. Scientists had noticed that the polarization of polarized light could be rotated when the light passed through, for example, quartz crystals; solutions of certain organic chemicals had a similar effect. But what was puzzling was that different batches of the same substance in solution could have different effects: some batches rotated the light clockwise, some rotated it counterclockwise, and some didn't rotate it at all. One such substance was tartaric acid, which existed in two forms: ordinary tartaric acid and the so-called racemic version, which appeared identical in all respects except that, in solution, it didn't rotate polarized light.

Earlier scientists had examined crystals of racemic tartaric acid in search of clues, but without any luck. Pasteur repeated this and discovered that, while at first sight all the crystals of the racemic form looked identical, in fact they were of two kinds, one being the mirror image of the other. It occurred to him that perhaps the two kinds rotated polarized light in opposite directions but that, when mixed in solution, each neutralized the rotating effect of the other.

With incredible patience he sorted the tiny crystals of his sample into two piles, one of each kind, and from each pile he made a new solution. As he had anticipated, one of his solutions rotated polarized light clockwise, the other counterclockwise.

We now say that the two forms of tartaric acid are optical isomers.

However, in solution the tartaric acid was clearly no longer in crystalline form. Pasteur speculated (correctly) that it wasn't only crystals of tartaric acid that came in two mirror-image forms but the actual *molecules* of the stuff. This was the first time anyone had realized such a thing was possible, and it led to the birth of a new discipline, stereochemistry, the study of the spatial arrangement of the atoms in molecules. Pasteur also noted, some years later, that living creatures are able to use only one or the other of any pair of optical isomers.

A BOOZE PROBLEM

In 1854 Pasteur was appointed dean of the newly created Faculty of Sciences at Lille University. In 1856 he was approached by a local businessman about a major problem in the French wine industry. Ideally, wine should mature in the bottle. But quite often vintners were getting a nasty surprise on opening their treasured bottle of plonk, discovering it had soured to the point of undrinkability. The problem was costing the industry a fortune.

Pasteur put samples of wine under the microscope and found there were two types of yeast involved. In correctly maturing wine, the yeast cells clumped together to form spherical globules. In souring wine, there were also elongated yeast globules; rather than producing alcohol they were producing lactic acid.

He was able to offer a solution to the problem because of his realization that fermentation was a biological process—that it involved living organisms—rather than a chemical reaction, as was widely believed at the time. What the winemakers should do, Pasteur advised, was make sure they used the right variety of yeast—and likewise brewers, who were having similar problems with beer.

In practice, it was often difficult to keep lactic-acid-producing yeasts out of the fermentation mix—they're floating around in the air, after all—and so a few years later Pasteur was able to produce a better "fix." The winemakers should gently heat their wine before bottling, to a temperature of about 50°C (120°F), and keep it there for a while. This wouldn't damage the wine but would kill all the yeast cells in it. After it was put into bottles, the airborne lactic-acid-producing yeasts wouldn't be able to get at it, and so there'd be no souring.

Initially skeptical, the winemakers tried it and it worked. Today all sorts of foods, notably milk, are routinely pasteurized to stop the growth of undesirable microorganisms in them. Countless human lives have been saved by this precaution.

Pasteur's next project concerned spontaneous generation (often called *abiogenesis*). For centuries people had believed living creatures could emerge spontaneously from inanimate material, and this seemed to be backed up by observation: leave food lying around, for example, and sooner or later you'll find it crawling with maggots. Even scientists as distinguished as Francis BACON and William HARVEY subscribed to the belief; Robert Hooke, NEWTON's bitter enemy, thought mushrooms and molds must be abiogenetic.

Sometime before 1668 the Italian naturalist Francesco Redi demonstrated that maggots formed only in meat with which flies had been in contact—no flies, no maggots—but even he thought abiogenesis was possible in other instances. And when, in 1674, the Dutch microscopist Antonie van Leeuwenhoek discovered microbes—"animalcules"—it seemed obvious *they* must appear abiogenetically.

In the middle of the eighteenth century the English biologist John Needham and the French naturalist Georges-Louis Leclerc, Comte de Buffon, produced the hypothesis that living creatures were made up of a mixture of ordinary material and "vital atoms"; it was these latter that made the difference between living and dead. Needham did a series of experiments that seemed to demonstrate microbes could generate from gravies he'd earlier sterilized. The Italian biologist Lazzaro Spallanzani repeated these experiments but took proper precautions to ensure air didn't come into contact with the gravies. Sure enough: no microbes. And there the matter seemed to rest.

By the middle of the nineteenth century, however, the theory of spontaneous generation was becoming popular again. The German biologist Ernst Haeckel, who spread DARWIN's ideas around continental Europe but otherwise had some odd notions, claimed that Spallanzani, through heating the air above his gravies, had destroyed some sort of life-giving principle in it. Pasteur decided to test whether or not there was any basis for this claim.

He was certain materials became contaminated through coming into contact with airborne dust particles that bore microbes. He demonstrated first that, if a sterilized gravy was allowed to come in contact with dust, microbes appeared. For the second part of his demonstration he placed sterilized samples in containers whose long necks, bent like a flush toilet's U-bend, allowed air to reach the gravies but trapped dust at the bottom of the U. As expected, the samples didn't become contaminated.

The final blow for spontaneous generation came in about 1880 when the Irish physicist John Tyndall showed that organic matter didn't putrefy in air that had been scrubbed clean of contaminants.

GERMS

The wine industry wasn't the only one to call for Pasteur's aid. In the early 1860s a new disease hit the silkworm farms of southern France, and no one could explain it. There was a good chance the French silk industry could be destroyed altogether. Pasteur discovered there was a microscopically small parasite preying upon the worms. He told the farmers they should destroy all the infected worms and the mulberry leaves they ate, and start over again with healthy worms. As with the winemakers, the initial reaction of the silk farmers was horror, but eventually they complied with Pasteur's advice and the problem was solved.

If tiny organisms were capable of spreading disease among silkworms, was it possible that even tinier ones were responsible for the spread of disease among animals, including humans? He wasn't the first to come up with this idea; a full century earlier, in 1762, the Viennese physician Marcus Plenciz had suggested that invisibly small "animalcules" in the air around us were responsible for the spread of disease. Plenciz spoiled his case somewhat by claiming that the "animalcules" could also produce gnats, leeches, and beetles. Another precursor was Ignaz SEMMELWEIS, who'd realized the spread of disease could be stanched in hospitals through proper hygiene. Semmelweis had no clear idea *why* this method worked, and unfortunately he died at about the same time Pasteur produced the explanation. The agents responsible for infectious diseases are creatures so small (germs) that they're invisible except through the microscope (and some of them too small even for that, in Pasteur's day).

Pasteur's germ theory of disease was arguably the single most important breakthrough in the history of medicine. Once you've discovered the reason why something happens, you're halfway or more toward being able to control it. Much later discoveries like antibiotics could never have happened without the realization that bacteria are responsible for many of our most debilitating diseases.

By now Pasteur had become a superstar, much like EINSTEIN in the twentieth century. Unfortunately, the celebrity seems to have gone to his head.

In the 1870s he started to examine yet another problem that plagued (pun intended) French industry: anthrax. Anthrax could devastate herds of sheep and other agricultural animals. Although some biologists claimed anthrax wasn't a germ disease, Pasteur maintained (as usual, correctly) that it was. He also discovered that the bacteria responsible can survive long periods of adversity in spore form; a pasture once inhabited by infected animals can remain infected for years afterward. In 1876 Pasteur recommended that the best way to stop the anthrax infestation was—much as with the silkworm problem—to kill and burn all the infected animals and start over with new ones.

But was there a *cure* for anthrax? Decades earlier, Edward JENNER had discovered that people could be protected from smallpox by vaccination with cowpox pus. That option wasn't open for anthrax, of which there isn't a less devastating sister disease. But could Pasteur apply the same principle by creating a less devastating version of the *germ*?

It seemed so. In 1881 he gave a graphic demonstration of the efficacy of an anthrax vaccine he claimed to have created. He injected half of a flock of sheep with his vaccine and then later injected the whole flock with lethal anthrax. The vaccinated sheep survived; the others didn't. But here the plot thickens.

One of Pasteur's dying wishes was that his notebooks should never be published. In 1964, however, his family donated the notebooks to the Bibliothèque Nationale (National Library) in Paris. Their contents were still kept secret for years, but finally, in the 1990s, a few scientific historians were allowed a peek.

What they found was pretty devastating to Pasteur's reputation. When performing that dramatic demonstration of the effect of his anthrax vaccine on the flock of sheep, he'd discovered at the last moment that the method he'd used to create a weakened version of the anthrax germ didn't actually work. So, in a panic, he created some vaccine using a method devised by the veterinarian Jean Joseph Henri Toussaint—a method he'd publicly scorned. Pasteur never credited Toussaint's role, pretending that the preparation technique was all his own.

Pasteur did valuable work devising further vaccines, for chicken cholera and for rabies. Yet there's some murkiness, too, surrounding his rabies vaccine. The famous tale goes that a nine-year-old boy, Joseph Meister, was brought to Pasteur in 1885 having been badly mauled by a rabid dog. Luckily Pasteur had devised a vaccine, which he'd extensively tested using animal "volunteers." Accordingly, he vaccinated Meister, who made a full recovery.

According to Gerald L. Geison, one of the historians who examined Pasteur's notebooks, the reality was rather different. Trivially, there were two mauled boys, not one. More importantly, neither had yet displayed any symptoms of rabies. Only about one in six humans bitten by a rabid animal actually comes down with rabies, so quite likely neither boy was suffering from the disease. Most significant of all, though, is the fact that *Pasteur hadn't done the animal testing he claimed to have done.* He was therefore, in effect, using the two boys as his experimental subjects for a vaccine that, had he been wrong in his guess about its safety, could very likely have killed them.

Lapses like these seem to have come in the latter part of Pasteur's career, and it's easy to see him as a man whose head had been turned by fame; increasingly intolerant of criticism, he was determined to project to the world the image of infallible master-scientist. Perhaps he even believed in his infallibility himself.

He founded the Institut Pasteur (Pasteur Institute) in Paris in 1887; it still thrives today, with branches all over the world.

Pasteur was a devout Christian. He therefore went against the tide of opinion—and of history—by refusing to accept DARWIN's theory of evolution by natural selection.

BUT THERE'S MORE . . .

■ William Dieterle directed *The Story of Louis Pasteur* (1936), a Hollywoodized version of Pasteur's story, with Paul Muni in the title role. If you can find a copy (I couldn't), there's also a Czech TV miniseries about the scientist's life, *Louis Pasteur* (1977). A more recent TV treatment is the French *Pasteur* (2011), with André Marcon in the title role; it's quite an absorbing drama.

■ Among accessible books on Pasteur and his revolutionary impact are Jane Ackerman's *Louis Pasteur and the Founding of Microbiology* (2003) and John Mann's *Louis Pasteur Bacteriology* (1964). Somewhat meatier fare is on offer in Gerald L. Geison's excellent *The Private Science of Louis Pasteur* (1995), the book that exposed Pasteur's serious ethical lapses.

■ Pasteur was honored in 1966 by an appearance on the French 5-franc banknote. He has craters named for him on both the Moon and Mars, plus the asteroid 4804 Pasteur. The bacterial family Pasteurellaceae contains the genus *Pasteurella*, which, unsurprisingly, is the cause of the disease pasteurellosis. Pasteur himself identified the first species in the genus, now called *Pasteurella multocida*, as the cause of chicken cholera. The little pipettes generally known as eye-droppers are more correctly termed Pasteur pipettes.

■ The racehorse Pasteurized won the 1938 Belmont Stakes.

BERNHARD RIEMANN
(1826–1866)

The mathematician whose explorations of what we now call non-Euclidean geometries laid the foundations upon which Einstein could build his general theory of relativity.

Georg Friedrich Bernhard Riemann was born in Breselenz, Germany, the second of six children of a Protestant preacher. Bernhard very early showed an exceptional aptitude for math. The plan was that he would be a preacher like Dad, and so in 1846 he entered the University of Göttingen to study theology and philology. It soon became obvious, though, that math was his passion, and his father allowed him to switch allegiances. After a two-year sojourn to the University of Berlin, which at the time had a far better math department, he returned to Göttingen, where things had improved.

With the great mathematician Carl Friedrich Gauss as his supervisor, Riemann attained his PhD with a dissertation called "Foundations of a General Theory of Functions of a Complex Variable." Gauss had a couple of cavils but, overall, recognized this as the work of a mathematical genius.

The system in Germany in those days was that, after you'd gained your PhD, if you wanted to stay in academia you had to produce another dissertation and a lecture; in effect, a second, posher PhD. For the paper "The Representability of a Function by Means of a Trigonometric Series" (1854), Riemann picked up some ideas of Gauss's and explored their consequences. Although unpublished until after Riemann's death, this is now regarded as a classic of math.

But it was the lecture that was so revolutionary. Gauss had asked Riemann to produce three possible topics, of which Gauss would pick one. Riemann assumed this was a formality, so he offered the topic of his paper plus a couple of other ideas "for Gauss to reject." But Gauss startled him by picking one of the "to reject" topics, "On the Hypotheses that Underlie Geometry." This was, in effect, a reexamination of the postulates put forward as axiomatic by EUCLID and accepted without question for centuries.

The fifth of Euclid's five postulates can be boiled down to this statement: Two parallel lines, even if extended infinitely, will never either meet or grow further apart.

The Hungarian mathematician Bolyai Farkas spent much of his working life trying to prove the postulate, but more significant was the endeavor of his son, Bolyai János, who investigated what geometry might emerge if the postulate was actually *wrong*—if parallel lines in fact diverged from each other. The Russian mathematician Nikolai Lobachevsky had the same idea, and developed the notion of hyperbolic geometry[1] even further. One consequence was that, because he seemed to be scandalously dissenting from Euclid, he got fired from his position at the University of Kazan. Gauss, too, had investigated hyperbolic geometry.

Riemann took a different approach. Another way of looking at the postulate is to say that two straight lines drawn through the same point can't be parallel—they'd be the same line, drawn on top of itself! But what if an infinite number of parallel straight lines could be drawn through any particular point?

This brought some interesting corollaries. The sum of a triangle's angles would no longer be 180° but a total always greater than 180°. There was no such thing as an infinitely long straight line. The shortest distance between two points wasn't a uniquely defined straight line; lots of equally short straight lines could be drawn between those two points.

All of this sounds like some sort of bizarre fantasy, but in fact we're quite accustomed to a form of geometry in which such things are true: the geometry of the surface of a sphere. If you draw a triangle on the surface of a sphere, its angles always add up to more than 180°. And two lines that start off as parallel will eventually meet.

---

1. So called because the surface defined by such a geometry is a hyperboloid—roughly saddle-shaped. Lobachevsky is direly slandered in the uproariously funny Tom Lehrer song "Lobachevsky."

Riemann took this a lot further. As physicist Sean Carroll vividly put it in a 2015 blog post, "Thanksgiving," celebrating the centenary of the publication of Einstein's general theory of relativity, Riemann

> provided everything you need to understand the geometry of a space of arbitrary numbers of dimensions, with an arbitrary amount of curvature at any point in the space. It was as if Bolyai and Lobachevsky had invented the abacus, Gauss came up with the pocket calculator, and Riemann had turned around and built a powerful supercomputer.

It's unclear as to whether Riemann thought this work had any real-world applications or if he just intended to put forward a demonstration of clever mathematics. After all, the universe didn't *look* as if it were ellipsoidal, which is the surface that Riemann's geometry would imply. But over half a century later, as Einstein began grappling with the problem of the geometry of spacetime, he discovered that Riemann had in effect done all the math for him.

Tragically, Riemann died of tuberculosis aged just thirty-nine. He made several other significant contributions to math, notably in the field of prime numbers, but nothing else on the scale of "On the Hypotheses that Underlie Geometry." It's almost alarming to speculate what he might have achieved had he lived a reasonable lifespan. ∎

BUT THERE'S MORE . . .

- I haven't found any popular biography of Riemann, and there may in fact not be one. John Derbyshire's *Prime Obsession* (2003) is an investigation of the Riemann hypothesis concerning prime numbers. Dan Rockmore's *Stalking the Riemann Hypothesis* (2005) covers similar territory; you may find it more approachable.
- Numerous concepts within mathematics are named in honor of Riemann's work, as are a crater on the Moon and the asteroid 4167 Riemann.

JAMES CLERK MAXWELL
(1831–1879)

The "Scottish Einstein."

lthough he was only forty-eight when cancer took his life, this Scottish physicist made enormous contributions to our understanding. Not for nothing has he been called "the Scottish EINSTEIN."

He was born in Edinburgh to a prosperous branch of minor nobility; his father was born John Clerk but took the additional surname "Maxwell" for legal reasons connected with the family estates. James was schooled at Edinburgh Academy and then Edinburgh University before going to Cambridge. In 1856 he was appointed Professor of Natural Philosophy (as science was often then called) at Marischal College in Aberdeen, Scotland; in 1860 he moved to King's College, London, where he remained as Professor of Natural Philosophy and Astronomy until 1865, when, his father having died, he retired from academia to manage the family estate and focus on his own research. In 1871, however, he was tempted into becoming Cambridge University's first Professor of Experimental Physics. In 1874 he set up the famed Cavendish Laboratory there.

He was still an undergraduate at Edinburgh when he made his first important contribution. Many years earlier Thomas Young had theorized that white light was made up of the three colors red, green and blue, and that we can see all the colors that we do because the retina has receptors sensitive to these three shades, with color blindness being due to an absence of functional receptors of the relevant type. Over the next dozen years or more, Maxwell was able to demonstrate the truth of this experimentally; for good measure, in 1861 he produced as an offshoot of his research the world's first ever color photograph.

During the 1850s he tackled the problem of the rings of Saturn. GALILEO was the first to notice that Saturn seemed to be an odd shape, but with his primitive telescope he couldn't tell more. In 1665 Christiaan Huygens was able to discern that the planet had rings, but until the time of Maxwell no one had any idea what they were made of. He analyzed the problem and demonstrated conclusively that, if the rings were solid structures, they'd soon enough collapse under Saturn's gravity, while, if they were made of some sort of liquid or gas, they'd disintegrate. The rings, then, must comprise innumerable tiny solid moons of the giant planet. It wasn't until 1895, over a decade after Maxwell's death, that spectroscopic analysis of the rings proved he was correct, and it wasn't until 1979 that visual confirmation was attained, with the arrival in Saturn's system of the *Pioneer 11* spacecraft.

Maxwell tended to work on several topics at once. While tackling the problem of Saturn's rings, he was also carrying out his most important investigation, exploring electromagnetism. Here he built on the work of Michael FARADAY; however, where Faraday had been an experimental scientist with little knowledge of math, for Maxwell, the theoretical genius, math was a way of thinking—*and* he was no mean experimenter! He was helped in many of his experiments by his wife Katherine.

As far back as NEWTON, people trying to explain the nature of light had assumed there must be some sort of invisible substance—the luminiferous aether—that permeated all of space. This was particularly important to those theories about light that claimed it was a wave motion; after all, how could you have a wave if there wasn't anything for it to be a wave *in*? Maxwell, as a person of his time, accepted the existence of the aether, and was interested in the properties it must have to explain why electricity and magnetism—which it seemed obvious to him were likewise propagated via the aether—behaved the way they did. He showed that, according to his theoretical model, a moving electrical/magnetic charge would set up a series of transverse waves in the aether—rather as a pebble dropped in a pond will set up transverse waves (ripples) in the water. He discovered, too, that these waves in the aether would travel at the same velocity as light.

From here it seemed not too great a leap to the conclusion that light, electricity, and magnetism must all, in some sense, be the same thing. In order to prove this he had to establish the precise nature of the electromagnetic field, and this he did in a series of equations he derived during the 1860s. He published these as "A Dynamical Theory of the Electromagnetic Field" (1864–65) and in more fully rationalized form in his ambitious book *A Treatise on Electricity and Magnetism* (1873).

Not only was it plain that light was electromagnetic, it seemed likely there were other forms of electromagnetic radiation, corresponding to different wavelengths, of which we knew nothing. Confirmation came after Maxwell's death with the discovery by Heinrich Hertz in 1888 of radio waves. We now, of course, know there's an entire electromagnetic spectrum, running from very long wavelengths right up to gamma rays,

MAXWELL'S DEMON

Maxwell's work on the kinetic theory of gases led him to think more deeply about the Second Law of Thermodynamics. This is the one that creationists get excited about, because it says in essence that, in any closed system, things get progressively less organized (entropy increases)—they tend to even out. How could something as organized as life emerge in such a context?[1] More particularly, if you put something hotter next to something colder, heat flows from the hotter to the colder object until both objects are at the same temperature.

However, this is a statistical effect. This means you can't in theory absolutely guarantee it'll happen every time. Maxwell, who had a tremendous sense of fun, devised a thought experiment to show how the "law" could be violated. He envisaged two bodies of gas separated by a wall with a door in it. A creature (the term *demon* came along later) stands by the door. Whenever a fast-moving molecule approaches from one side, but not the other, the creature opens the door to let it through. The net result is that one of the two bodies of gas gets a lot hotter while the other cools down.

Maxwell's purpose in devising the thought experiment was to show that the Second Law isn't inviolable. Later researchers showed that, while entropy is decreasing if you think only about the gas, the demon is part of the system too. Once you count in the energy the demon has to expend on, for example, identifying the fast-moving molecules, the Second Law is upheld.

---

1. The flaw in the argument is that our world isn't a closed system. It's the recipient of a constant supply of energy from the Sun. That energy fuels the organization that underpins life.

which have extraordinarily short wavelengths and thus high frequencies and energies. Astronomy, which in Maxwell's time was restricted to observing light, is now carried out in all ranges of the electromagnetic spectrum.

Maxwell also considered the possibility that the waves of electromagnetic radiation didn't need the aether in order to propagate—that the aether might be just a figment of the imagination. The final death blow for the aether came in 1905, delivered by EINSTEIN.

Also during the 1860s and into the 1870s, Maxwell was working on the kinetic theory of gases. The kinetic theory, first presaged in any coherent form in the 1730s by the Swiss scientist Daniel Bernoulli—a friend of Émilie DU CHÂTELET—was developed in the 1850s by the German scientist Rudolf Clausius. It sought to explain why you have to do work in order to compress gases—or, to turn that around, why a gas in a container exerts pressure on that container's inner walls. Like Bernoulli, Clausius envisaged gases as being made up of countless individual molecules moving around in random directions at high velocity, constantly bumping into and bouncing off one another. The pressure a gas exerts against its container walls is thus a consequence of lots of molecules bouncing off those walls. The pressure is steady because there are so many molecules, and thus so many impacts happening in every instant, that everything evens out.

One unexpected experimental discovery Maxwell made was that the viscosity of a gas doesn't depend on pressure; instead, it's dependent upon temperature. This caused Maxwell to revise his thinking about what the molecules in the gas were doing. Rather than bouncing off one another, he concluded, they must be responding to some sort of mutually repellent force.

Maxwell applied statistics to the problem of the range of velocities the molecules in a gas must have, and in this way was able to explain most of the properties of gases. A big exception was the conduction of heat. This piece of the jigsaw puzzle was supplied by the Austrian scientist Ludwig Boltzmann, who revised Maxwell's statistical equations to produce what's now called the Maxwell–Boltzmann distribution law. Both men made later modifications to the kinetic theory as it approached the form in which we know it today.

Maxwell died of abdominal cancer, the same disease that had killed his mother. It's impossible, really, to enumerate all the implications that Maxwell's work—especially on electromagnetism and the kinetic theory—has had for modern scientific knowledge. Newton famously once remarked that all the scientific progress he'd made had been possible because he was standing on the shoulders of giants. When Einstein made a similar acknowledgment of his predecessors it wasn't only Newton whom he mentioned. He also singled out James Clerk Maxwell. ∎

BUT THERE'S MORE . . .

■ Construction on the James Clerk Maxwell Telescope at Hawaii's Mauna Kea Observatories was completed in 1987. With a main mirror about 49 feet (15 m) across, it's the world's largest telescope for observing the universe in far-infrared to microwave frequencies. The annual James Clerk Maxwell Prize in Plasma Physics is awarded by the American Physical Society.

- Also named for him are a mountain range on Venus, a crater on the moon, the asteroid 12760 Maxwell, and, more pertinent to his work, the Maxwell gap and the Maxwell ringlet, two related structures within the C-ring of Saturn. In the CGS system, the maxwell (Mx) is a unit of magnetic flux.

- The James Clerk Maxwell Foundation exists to promote knowledge of the man and his work. Its website, at www.clerkmaxwellfoundation. org, has a tremendous amount of information about the man, even including some of his fairly dire poetry! At the time of writing, its patron is Nobel laureate Peter Higgs, of Higgs Boson fame.

- The standard early biography is *The Life of James Clerk Maxwell* (1882) by Lewis Campbell and William Garnett; you can find it online for free at www.sonnetsoftware.com/bio/maxbio.pdf. A couple of more recent books are Basil Mahon's *The Man Who Changed Everything* (2003) and P. M. Harman's *The Natural Philosophy of James Clerk Maxwell* (1998); the latter's for the more serious student.

MARIE CURIE
(1867–1934)

The only person ever to win two Nobel science prizes, Curie explored the newly discovered phenomenon of radioactivity . . . and died for her science.

The matriarch of a truly extraordinary scientific family, the recipient of both the Nobel Chemistry Prize (1903) and the Nobel Physics Prize (1911), Marie Curie is a blazing star in the firmament of science. Yet, despite her fame, she lived in great poverty throughout much of her life, believing the discoveries she made should be used to benefit humanity rather than exploited for personal enrichment.

Maria "Manya" Salomee Skłodowska was born in Warsaw. Her family was extremely short of money. She was able to get herself a basic school education, and proved an outstanding student; but in those days in Poland—and through much of the world—it was widely assumed there was no real point in educating women further than that.

Marie begged to differ. She took whatever jobs she could get in order to save money toward being able to go live in Paris with her elder sister Bronia and attend the Sorbonne.

She managed it in 1891, specializing in physics and mathematics. Once again, she was an exemplary student, graduating at the top of her year despite having been so poor that at least once she fainted from hunger during a lecture. In 1894 love entered her life when she met a physicist some years older than herself, Pierre Curie. They married in 1895.

Marie is such a dazzling light that it can be easy to forget Pierre was likewise a scientist of great distinction. His greatest contribution—aside from serving as Marie's colleague and assistant from not long after their marriage until his death—was his discovery in 1880 with his brother Paul-Jacques of the phenomenon of piezoelectricity. When certain crystals are squeezed, they produce an electric potential of size proportional to the amount of pressure you're applying. Or you can turn things around by putting the crystal into a changing electric field so that its faces vibrate at high frequencies; it's this phenomenon that's exploited in all sorts of sound devices today. In the 1890s he studied how heat affects magnetism. The Curie temperature (Tc), or Curie point, the temperature at which a particular substance loses its magnetic properties, was named for him.

The discovery of X-rays by Wilhelm Röntgen in 1895 and, soon after, the observation by Henri Becquerel that atoms of uranium emit penetrative radiation sparked interest throughout the scientific world in *radioactivity*—a term that Marie coined. She discovered there are three types of radiation involved—alpha, beta, and gamma—a conclusion that others came to as well, notably Becquerel and Ernest Rutherford.

Using a clever adaptation of Pierre's piezoelectric research, Marie discovered a way to measure the intensity of radioactive radiation. She showed that the radioactivity of various uranium compounds is directly attributable to the uranium they contain—that there are no contributions from the other elements in the compound. Similar investigations led in 1898 to the discovery that the element thorium was likewise radioactive.

Investigating the uranium ore pitchblende (uraninite), Marie discovered it emitted more radioactivity than could be accounted for by its uranium content alone. She knew none of the other recognized elements in the ore were radioactive, and concluded (rightly) that there must be some other element present in such tiny quantities that no one had detected it before; further, if such minute amounts could produce so much radioactivity, this element must be very radioactive indeed. In 1898 the Curies were able to isolate it; they called it polonium, for Marie's homeland.

A few months later they found a yet more radioactive element, which they called radium. However, it was present in pitchblende in even tinier quantities, so all they could detect of it beyond its radioactivity was a trace when the ore was analyzed spectroscopically. In order to find out more, they needed somehow to obtain a sample that was at least visible to the naked eye.

So began one of the loopier examples of scientific determination. The silver mines of Bohemia had been worked for centuries, and huge quantities of leftover pitchblende had accumulated. Nobody knew what to do with it, and nobody wanted it . . . at least until the Curies came along. For the cost of shipping the stuff to Paris, they could have it. That cost wasn't minimal—it more or less bankrupted the couple—but it gave them enough to work with for the next four years. At the end of that time they had reduced 10 metric tons of pitchblende to obtain a single gram of radium.

QUELLE FAMILLE

Marie and Pierre Curie founded a lineage of such scientific distinction that it's hard to credit. Their elder daughter, Irène Joliot-Curie, and her husband, Frédéric Joliot-Curie (they met when both working as Marie's assistants and he took her surname as a mark of respect), shared the 1935 Nobel Chemistry Prize for their discovery of artificial radioactivity. They were also active in the Resistance during the German occupation of France; when she applied for membership of the American Chemical Society in 1954 Irène was rejected because of her association with left-leaning organizations during this period and after. (It seems a Curie family habit to be demonized by second-raters.) Irène's younger sister, Ève Curie, was a journalist and concert pianist; she wrote a biography of her mother. Ève's husband, Henry Richardson Labouisse Jr., received the 1965 Nobel Peace Prize on behalf of UNICEF.

Irène and Frédéric Joliot-Curie had two children. Hélène Langevin-Joliot became a nuclear physicist; her husband, Michel Langevin, was grandson of the very same Paul Langevin whose affair with Marie had scandalized a nation; Hélène and Michel met while working together at the Institut Curie. Irène and Frédéric's son Pierre Joliot became a biochemist of note. Hélène's and Michel's son Yves is an astrophysicist.

Their researches into radioactivity brought the Curies the 1903 Nobel Physics Prize, which they shared with Becquerel. (It was thanks to Pierre's complaints that Marie was mentioned in the citation; originally the all-male committee had intended to leave her off because she was a mere woman.) The discovery of polonium and radium, and the years-long effort to isolate radium, brought Marie the 1911 Nobel Chemistry Prize; even though the work had been done jointly with Pierre, she had to accept it solo, because he had been killed in 1906 in a traffic accident while crossing the road in Paris.

A couple of years earlier, Pierre had been appointed professor of physics at the Sorbonne. Marie was now appointed in his place, becoming the first woman ever to teach there. This generated much hostility toward her in the right-wing newspapers, which vilified her as a Jew (which she wasn't) and a foreigner (which she obviously was). When the Académie des Sciences voted on whether to admit her, in 1911, her election was narrowly defeated. Her detractors in the gutter press were given additional fuel for their hate campaign when it emerged, not long before she was awarded her second Nobel, that the widow Curie had been carrying on an affair with physicist Paul Langevin, who was both younger than her and married.

By now Poland was beginning to realize quite what it had discarded when the young Marie left for Paris, and offers of distinguished academic appointments came in from there. Since she was being so viciously and routinely abused in France, it's hard to understand why she didn't give Paris a traditional hand gesture and go live in Warsaw. The reason is probably the inducement that the French government had earlier been able to offer her: the establishment in 1909, specifically for her, of the Institut du Radium[1] (Radium Institute).

In 1914 war broke out, and Marie served as an ambulance driver and also supervised, for the International Red Cross, the installation and use of X-ray equipment in ambulances. Naturally this act of bravery and French patriotism was widely ignored in the newspapers that had so eagerly hounded her for being a foreigner. After the war, she continued researching at the institute, her focus becoming the use of radioactive materials as a means of fighting cancer. Ironically, it was cancer that killed her—leukemia, to be specific, developed as a consequence of the long periods she'd spent in close proximity to highly radioactive materials. ■

BUT THERE'S MORE . . .

■ The French 500-franc bill issued in 1995 and extant until 2002 showed the image of Marie Curie, with Pierre looking over her shoulder. In Poland, the 1989 20,000-złoty bill showed Marie on her own, as does the 2011 Polish 20-złoty bill.

■ Ève Curie's *Madame Curie* (1937) is for obvious reasons a standard source. Barbara Goldsmith's *Obsessive Genius* (2005) offers a very clear and readable overview of Curie's life; the book's usefulness is considerably reduced, though, by its lack of an index. Shelley Emling's *Marie Curie and Her Daughters* (2012) somewhat breathlessly recounts Curie's personal life and her relationships with Irène, Ève, and Langevin. Lauren Redniss's *Radioactive* (2010) focuses on Marie and Pierre's work together. Useful short biographies are Marilyn Bailey Ogilvie's *Marie Curie* (2004) and, for younger readers, Rachel A. Koestler-Grack's *Marie Curie* (2009).

---

1. Now called the Institut Curie.

- The lunar and Martian craters called Curie were both named for Pierre—surely an example of sexism extending far beyond Marie's grave (the Martian crater was named as late as 1973). On the Moon, a smaller crater near Curie is named Skłodowska, so Marie is not entirely overlooked.
- Technically speaking, the unit of radioactivity called the curie (Ci) is likewise named for Pierre, although here Marie was a member of the committee that decided on the name. The radioactive element curium (Cm), atomic number 96, is named for both of them.

LISE MEITNER
(1878–1968)

The German physicist who, because of the Nazis' anti-Semitic bigotry, was robbed of a Nobel Prize for her co-discovery of nuclear fission.

Several of the scientists discussed in this book were ignored for a Nobel Prize that should surely have been theirs, but in no instance was the oversight more glaring than in that of the Austrian physicist Lise Meitner. One of the most important scientists of the twentieth century, she had to battle against the repressive forces of establishment sexism and Nazi anti-Semitism.

Elise "Lise" Meitner was born in Vienna; although her parents were Jewish, she and her seven siblings were raised Christian. By the time she was in her teens she had decided to be a physicist. Not only was this an almost unheard-of profession for women at the time, there was a strong sentiment within the scientific establishment that science had by now discovered almost everything there was to know. The discovery of X-rays by Wilhelm Röntgen in 1895 and of radioactivity by Henri Becquerel in 1896 rather put a sock over that notion, but as late as 1899 US commissioner of patents Charles H. Duell was telling President William McKinley that "everything that can be invented has been invented."

Despite her physics aspirations, her parents directed Lise to study French at school on the grounds that language-teaching was a good career for a woman who troublesomely wished to be independent. But she taught herself science well enough in her spare time that in 1901 she was awarded a place at the University of Vienna. There, as a rare female student, she encountered quite a lot of sexism but also the encouragement of the significant physicist Ludwig Boltzmann.

In 1907, having graduated, she attended Max Planck's lectures in theoretical physics at his German Physical Society, in Berlin. However, she searched in vain for an academic position that would allow her to do experimental work. Relief came at last in the form of the chemist Otto Hahn, who was investigating the chemistry of radioactivity and wanted a physicist to help him. There was one problem. Hahn was working at Berlin's Chemical Institute, run by Emil Fischer, and Fischer did not permit women scientists there. Ludicrous though it sounds, he did permit the pair to convert an old carpentry workshop in the building, accessible from a side entrance, to use as a laboratory; so long as Meitner didn't sully the main building with her loathsomely female presence, Fischer was satisfied. A disadvantage for her was that, whenever she needed a pee, she had to rely on a friendly nearby hotel. Luckily, the rule barring women was relaxed a couple of years later.

In 1912 she moved to the Kaiser Wilhelm Institute for Chemistry in Berlin–Dahlem. When World War I came along, Meitner volunteered as an army nurse. (Hahn worked on developing poison gas for military use.) After the war, Meitner became, as head of the institute's physics department, Germany's first female physics professor. She engaged in weekly meetings where she exchanged ideas and research results with other physicists including Planck, EINSTEIN, SCHRÖDINGER, Gustav Hertz, and Walther Nernst; Einstein called her "our own Marie CURIE." Around this time, she and Hahn identified a relatively stable form of protactinium, of which element they're generally credited as discoverers.[1]

For the next decade or more Meitner studied radioactivity and radioactive decay. With hindsight we can see that much of her work during these years was misguided, because nobody knew anything about the structure of the atom. But then, in the first half of the 1930s, a series of breakthroughs changed all that, including the discovery of the neutron in 1932 by James Chadwick (its existence had been predicted by Ernest Rutherford as early as 1920) and the positron (the positively charged electron, or antielectron) in the same year by Carl Anderson, following a prediction by Paul Dirac in 1931.

In 1934 Meitner and Hahn started working together once more. In Italy, Enrico Fermi had discovered that uranium atoms bombarded with neutrons gave rise to other radioactive atoms that he assumed must be those of heavier uranium isotopes. Meitner and Hahn repeated Fermi's work, but weren't satisfied with Fermi's explanation; they thought the products of the collisions might be new elements (transuranium elements) of higher atomic weight than uranium, and Hahn convinced himself he'd discovered several of these. Meanwhile, Marie Curie, doing similar research, had noted that some of the products showed behavior

---

1.   An extremely short-lived isotope of protactinium had been discovered a few years earlier by a different team.

reminiscent of elements of *lower* atomic weight. This went against all received wisdom, and Curie seems to have pursued the idea little further.

All this while, Hitler was in the ascendant in Germany. Although Jewish by birth, Meitner was initially left alone by the Nazis because she was Austrian; when the Nazis annexed Austria in 1938, however, the situation changed. Friends smuggled her into the Netherlands, and from there she traveled to Copenhagen in Denmark, where Niels Bohr welcomed her to his home. She then moved on to Sweden, where she'd been offered a post at the recently opened Nobel Institute.

She was still in contact by phone and letter with Hahn, and the two continued to collaborate as best they could. Hahn was working in the lab with his student Fritz Strassmann, and reported to her that they'd identified some of the products of uranium bombardment as isotopes of radium.

Meitner was unconvinced, and asked the two men to redo their work. This time they told her it seemed the products were barium isotopes rather than radium ones. This seemed impossible, because the general assumption was that neutron-bombardment must create products *heavier* than uranium—either heavier isotopes or transuranium elements. Barium is not much more than half as heavy as uranium (atomic weight ~137, as opposed to uranium's ~238).

Supposedly while the pair of them were out on a country walk, Meitner talked over this issue with her physicist nephew Otto Frisch, visiting from Copenhagen, and she realized that what must be happening was that the nucleus of the uranium atom was being split into two; they called the process "fission." Hahn had come to a similar conclusion but, when he published his relevant paper in 1939, avoided the idea of nuclear fission because he didn't have the nerve to suggest such a radical notion. Meitner and Frisch, less reticent, announced their discovery soon afterward, and noted that the process released copious energy.

Very luckily for the Allies during World War II, their scientists realized the potential of the discovery while those in Germany generally didn't; besides, many of Germany's smartest scientists, whether Jewish or otherwise, had been driven out by the Nazi menace—in fact, many of the scientists who'd work on the Manhattan Project to develop the atomic bomb, which exploited those enormous energies released by the process of nuclear fission, were German refugees. Meitner was invited to the US to join that project, but she firmly rejected the offer.

Otto Hahn was awarded the 1944 Nobel Chemistry Prize for his discovery of nuclear fission. Meitner, as joint discoverer—and in fact (with Frisch) by far the more important contributor to the discovery—was disregarded. Neither of them made any issue of this—after all, Hahn was still in Berlin and it could have been risky for him to speak out on behalf of a Jew—and Meitner appears to have been delighted by his Nobel recognition. In succeeding years she was showered with other international awards and honors; when you look at the list, the lack of a Nobel sticks out like a sore thumb.

After the war's end, Meitner was invited to return to the Max Planck Institute, but this was another offer she rejected; seemingly the thought of working alongside scientists who'd compromised with the Nazi regime was repugnant. She spent a few months in 1947 working in the US, but otherwise she remained in Sweden until her retirement in 1960, when she moved to Cambridge, UK. There she died just before what would have been her ninetieth birthday. ■

BUT THERE'S MORE . . .

■ A full-scale biography is Ruth Lewin Sime's *Lise Meitner* (1996). Shorter biographies include Deborah Crawford's *Lise Meitner* (1969), which is for young adults, and, primarily for younger readers, Janet Hamilton's *Lise Meitner* (2002). Craters on both the Moon and Venus are named for Meitner, as is the asteroid 6999 Meitner.

■ Discovered in 1982, element no. 109 is named meitnerium (symbol Mt) in her honor.

ALBERT EINSTEIN

(1879–1955)

The twentieth century's indomitable superstar scientist.

In his *A Brief History of Time* (1998), Stephen HAWKING tells how astrophysicist Arthur Eddington was once asked by a journalist about the claim that just three people in the world really understood Albert Einstein's general theory of relativity. Eddington was slow to respond, but then said: "I'm trying to think who the third person is."

Albert Einstein was born in Ulm, Germany, the first child of an unsuccessful electrician and his musician wife. He was apparently a very ugly baby, prone throughout childhood to unreasoning tantrums, and so slow to start speaking that his family grew worried he might be developmentally disabled. When he was still an infant the family moved to Munich, where his father went into business with a brother and, reversing the earlier pattern, became successful. Albert was already highly interested in puzzles and other mental games; his fascination with science is generally dated to his father's lending him a compass when he was about five. What could be the mysterious force that kept the needle always pointing in the same direction?

Albert didn't do well at school, partly because—as would be the case throughout his life—he had difficulty focusing on subjects that didn't interest him, partly because the highly structured German educational system inhibited anything other than rote learning, partly because he instinctively rebelled against senseless discipline, and partly because, as a Jew, he was in a small minority among predominantly Catholic students.

At home it was a different matter. His uncle taught him a love of algebra and set him problems that Albert regarded as games rather than work. Even more important, an ophthalmology student whom the family had befriended, Max Talmey, saw the boy's nascent passion for science and nurtured it by lending him science books and talking ideas through with him. In due course Einstein fell in love with mathematics, and by the time he was in his early teens his skills had developed beyond anything Talmey could follow. He also fell in love with music, and for the rest of his life he'd play the violin enthusiastically, albeit—by all accounts—not very well.

Eventually he dropped out of school, one of his teachers having told his father he'd never amount to much. He did, however, manage in 1896 to get himself—at the second attempt—a college place at the Federal Institute of Technology in Zurich, Switzerland. This meant he dodged Germany's compulsory military service; he'd been a pacifist since childhood, and would remain one all his life. Very much later in life he'd come to believe that the danger posed by Hitler—in particular by the possibility that the Nazis might develop the atom bomb—was so serious that the use of armed force to counter it was justified. Not only did he urge President Franklin D. Roosevelt to create what would become the Manhattan Project but also, in 1944, he put up for auction a handwritten copy of his paper launching special relativity, the proceeds to be donated toward the war effort. It's a measure of Einstein's fame that the winning bid was for no less than $6 million.

LOVE, THE PATENT OFFICE, AND THE ANNUS MIRABILIS

At the Federal Institute of Technology, Einstein wasn't the most popular of students, primarily because of his arrogant impatience with anyone he regarded as his intellectual inferior—which was just about everyone. This included his professors, which, bearing in mind that they included distinguished figures like Hermann Minkowski and Heinrich Weber, was foolish of him.

He did, however, make some strong friendships. The math student Marcel Grossmann not only let Einstein borrow the notes he took for the many lectures Einstein skipped but, much later, helped him with the math for the general theory of relativity. And then there was Mileva Marić, a young Serbian student who soon became Einstein's girlfriend. Even though his mother loathed Mileva on sight, the pair planned to get married once they'd graduated and Einstein was settled into a reasonably paying job.

Nothing went smoothly for them. Although Einstein graduated, Mileva failed. In order to get a job, Einstein had to become a Swiss citizen. Once he'd cleared that hurdle, he discovered that jobs in academia were hard to find, and in 1902 had to settle for a junior post at the Bern patent office. By then, Mileva, temporarily in Hungary with her parents, had given birth to their first child, Lieserl, who seems to have been given up for adoption; the whole matter was kept very hush-hush. In January 1903 they were finally able to marry, and in May 1904 they had their first "official" child, Hans Albert.

By now Einstein was flourishing at the patent office. Somehow he managed to juggle a full-time job, a busy social life, and the responsibilities of fatherhood while working on his PhD dissertation and continuing his own theoretical research. The neighbors became accustomed to the sight of Einstein pushing a baby carriage into which he'd occasionally dip for his notebook.

The year 1905 is usually referred to as Einstein's annus mirabilis (miracle year). During it he published no fewer than five papers in the prestigious scientific journal *Annalen der Physik* (Annals of Physics). Those five papers would establish him as the world's leading theoretical physicist.

The first concerned the photoelectric effect, a phenomenon that had puzzled physicists for some decades. If you shine a light on certain metals, the surface gives off electrons. A major part of the puzzle was that the energy of those electrons had no relationship to the intensity of the light; a brighter light caused more electrons to be emitted, but the energy of each electron was the same as for a dimmer light. On the other hand, changing the color of the light could affect the energy of the emitted electrons, with a blue light producing more energetic electrons than a red light did. This was all inexplicable in terms of the universally accepted wave theory of light.

Einstein's breakthrough idea was to apply the new quantum physics to the problem. Quantum theory had been worked out a few years earlier by Max Planck, but no one had been much interested: it seemed to be a solution without a problem. Einstein realized the photoelectric effect could be explained if light was not simply a wave motion but a stream of discrete packets—or quanta. When a quantum of light (a photon) muscled its way into one of the metal atoms, it pushed out an electron with an energy appropriate to the energy of the photon. Supply higher-energy photons (i.e., bluer light) and you force the atoms to give out higher-energy electrons.

The importance of the paper was not just that it offered a theoretical explanation (experimentally confirmed a few years later) for the photoelectric phenomenon but that it revolutionized our perceptions of what light *is*. Quantum physics was placed firmly on the scientific map as a result. Years later, in 1921, Einstein received the Nobel Physics Prize for this achievement.

Yet that was just the start of what he did in 1905.

Another paper concerned the phenomenon of Brownian motion. As early as 1827 the Scottish botanist Robert Brown noticed that microscopically small pollen grains in water moved in a sort of erratic, jiggling dance. His first explanation was that the living pollen grains were, in effect, swimming. But, like a good scientist, he repeated the experiment using nonliving dye particles, and discovered they moved in the same way.

Before Einstein, various scientists suggested the pollen grains were being jostled by the molecules of the water, which were dashing around in all directions at high speed. Individual molecules don't have much mass and there are a lot of them, so, if you put a normal-size object—such as your finger—into still water, you don't notice any buffeting effect, because all parts of your finger are being hit at the same time by almost exactly the same large number of molecules. But a microscopically small object like a pollen grain is being hit by far fewer molecules at any one moment. If by chance a few more molecules hit one of its sides than the other, the pollen grain is punched out of position. These chance variations are happening all the time to the pollen grain, which is why it jiggles around in the water.

Einstein not only put forward this theory, he went into it with full mathematical rigor. This latter aspect was important, because it meant that if you knew the mass of the pollen grains, you could start to calculate the masses of the individual water molecules and thus of the individual atoms. To realize quite how revolutionary this all was you have to recognize that at the time there were still a few physicists around who didn't buy John DALTON's atomic theory—in other words, who weren't convinced that atoms and molecules actually existed. Einstein's explanation of Brownian motion effectively silenced those doubts.

Even if he'd done nothing else, these two achievements would have earned Einstein a place in science's hall of fame. But, still in 1905, he produced another paper that eclipsed them. That paper was his formulation of the special theory of relativity: "Zur Elektrodynamik Bewegter Körper" ("The Electrodynamics of Moving Bodies"). In effect, he rewrote our understanding of the universe—an understanding that had remained largely unchanged since NEWTON had put forward his theory of universal gravitation.

All through the nineteenth century it was assumed light was a wave motion. It was therefore reasoned, since waves—like ripples in water—require something to be waves *in*, that space must be full of some as-yet-undetected light-bearing medium, the luminiferous aether. Toward the end of the nineteenth century the US physicists Albert Michelson and Edward Morley conducted experiments to try to measure the speed with which the Earth was moving through the aether, and to their surprise could detect no trace of the aether. This didn't prove the aether didn't exist, but it was worrisome.

Einstein, who may or may not have been aware of the Michelson-Morley experiment, concluded there was no such thing as the aether; after all, he'd already shown light wasn't a simple wave motion but instead was made up of a stream of "particles," and so it didn't need a medium to move through.

He also assumed that the observed velocity of light in a vacuum is always the same, no matter how fast the source of the light is moving or how fast the observer is moving. This was really a consequence of his discounting the existence of the aether. Without a stationary aether to measure against, you can't meaningfully think of anything being at absolute rest, and nor can you measure any motion in absolute terms. All motion is relative to something else—to whatever handy frame of reference you choose to use. Usually we pick our frames of reference without thinking (if you're waiting to cross a road, you say the cars are passing you, not that you're passing the cars), but this doesn't have to be the case. If we assume the laws of physics hold good in whatever frame of reference we choose, then the constancy of the velocity of light in all frames of reference seems an inevitable conclusion.

This has some odd consequences. If there's no absolute motion, there's nothing absolute about the passage of time, either. Indeed, Einstein was able to show that the rate at which time passes depends upon the speed at which you're moving—hence all those old science-fiction stories about astronauts coming home to find the Earth has aged by centuries. Without an absolute time, simultaneity becomes a problem: You can't be sure if two events are simultaneous, or if one happened before the other . . . or was it the other that happened first? In fact, it doesn't make too much sense to talk about time and space as separate entities; really, they're both part of a single entity, spacetime.

Mass and energy are likewise two sides of the same coin, and Einstein was able to deduce the relationship between them in the form of a very simple equation, the most famous equation in human history:

$$E = mc^2$$

where E stands for energy, m for mass, and c for the velocity of light. Since the velocity of light is extremely high, it's clear that even a tiny amount of mass can produce a very great deal of energy, as would be demonstrated a few decades later by the development of nuclear weapons and nuclear power stations.

GENERAL RELATIVITY

The odd thing was that, despite his having revolutionized physics, universities weren't clamoring to offer Einstein a job. He got a part-time lectureship at the University of Bern, but the money was peanuts and he still wasn't able to give up his full-time post at the patent office. Finally, in 1909, he was given an associate professorship at the University of Zurich, to which city he and his family moved. The pay wasn't any better than he'd been getting at the patent office, and some of his new colleagues were dubious as to whether he was the right stuff—this in the year he was first being recommended for a Nobel Prize![1]

In 1911 the Einsteins moved to Prague, where he'd been offered a much better job at the German University. They didn't stay there long, but long enough to make the acquaintance of the writer Franz Kafka. Then Grossmann, by now dean of the Physics Department at the Federal Institute of Technology in Zurich—the very place where Einstein had toiled as a student—offered him a full professorship there. In 1913 he was offered a professorship at the Humboldt University of Berlin with minimal teaching responsibilities and all the research facilities he could wish for.

The Einsteins arrived in Berlin in 1914. Mileva hated it, not least because it meant they were living close to her dreaded mother-in-law,

1. For the special theory of relativity.

who still loathed her. Later that year, World War I broke out. Mileva and the children—Hans Albert by now had a little brother, Eduard—moved back to Zurich, on the understanding that Einstein would visit them whenever he could. Unfortunately, with war raging throughout Europe, that wasn't often. Relations between Einstein and Mileva were already strained; the prolonged separation spelled the end of the marriage, as did the blossoming friendship in Berlin between Einstein and his divorced cousin Elsa. (After the war, Mileva and Einstein divorced, leaving him free to marry Elsa, which he did in 1919.)

Einstein had been thinking about gravity since 1907, when it had struck him that someone in free fall wouldn't feel their own weight. If you jumped off the Empire State Building you'd feel yourself weightless as you accelerated groundward; *finally*, you'd get a nasty reminder that you do indeed have mass, but not before impact. In that year he published a paper proposing that gravitational attraction is equivalent to acceleration. He also suggested that gravitational fields distort time locally and both bend light passing by them and increase its wavelength (i.e., redshift it). In a 1911 paper he put a mathematical value to the bending of light by a gravitational field.

All of these ideas and more came together in a 1916 paper in the *Annalen der Physik*, "Grundlage der Allgemeinen Relativitätstheorie" ("The Foundation of the General Theory of Relativity"); you may recall the centennial of this paper being celebrated in early 2016.

Spacetime, Einstein said, was not flat and uniform as Newton had assumed and, centuries earlier, EUCLID had decreed. Instead it was curved in a manner strongly reminiscent of the geometries Bernhard RIEMANN had explored in the mid-nineteenth century. In the region of a massive object, spacetime was distorted; the distortion produced the force we call gravity.

This is difficult to imagine, since spacetime is four-dimensional and it's hard to visualize four-dimensional curvature. In three dimensions, imagine a rubber sheet stretched out tautly with something heavy put in the middle of it. The heavy object obviously indents the sheet quite steeply. Now imagine you flick a marble across the sheet. As the marble gets close to the indent, its path is deflected; if you've got your flick just right, the marble will briefly "go into orbit" around the heavy object.

Now all you have to do is imagine that in four dimensions . . .

In his 1916 paper, Einstein pointed out three areas in which the predictions of general relativity differed from those of Newtonian physics:

- The precession of the orbit of the planet Mercury. The orbits of the planets aren't quite perfect ellipses. In each of its orbits, the position of the planet when it is (say) at its most distant point from the Sun is slightly along from where it was in the previous orbit (orbital precession).

Only in the case of Mercury is orbital precession large enough to be obvious to astronomers, and it had puzzled physicists for some time. General relativity did indeed explain it precisely, but of course this wasn't really a prediction.

- The redshifting of light by a gravitational field.

For this to be noticeable, you need to find yourself a very powerful gravitational field, and luckily scientists had one at hand. Well, not precisely at hand, but only a few light-years away. This was the Pup, the small, very dense white-dwarf companion of the bright star Sirius. In 1925 the US astronomer Walter Adams, at the suggestion of Arthur Eddington, searched for a redshift of the light from the Pup, and found it to be exactly as predicted by general relativity.

- Light bends as it passes a massive object.

Although we're now quite familiar with the concept of gravitational lensing on very large scales across the universe, at the time astronomers simply didn't have the tools or the techniques to look for such a phenomenon. However, they could do so closer to home, using the Sun as the massive object.

In March 1919 a total eclipse of the Sun was visible from much of the southern hemisphere. The Royal Astronomical Society sent out two expeditions. One, led by Eddington, went to Principe, off the coast of West Africa; the other was based in northern Brazil. The idea was that at the moment of total eclipse, you could see stars whose light rays had passed close by the Sun on their way to the Earth. Eddington's team had difficulty with clouds, but photographs taken by the Brazil team, when analyzed later, bore out Einstein's predictions very closely.

In a follow-up paper in 1916, Einstein made a further prediction:

- It should be possible to detect gravitational waves.

For almost a century, despite some very determined efforts, no one was able to find gravitational waves. This didn't undermine general relativity at all, because it was accepted that the task was so difficult as to be almost impossible. But in 2015 the picture changed.

About 1.3 billion years ago two black holes closely orbiting each other in a distant galaxy finally collided to become one. For a fraction of a second they emitted more energy than all the stars of the universe put together. The gravitational waves from that gigantic implosion spread out through spacetime at the velocity of light, and finally reached the Earth on September 14, 2015. The first person to notice the signals was a postdoctoral student at the Albert Einstein Institute in Hannover, Marco Drago. Using his computer, he'd been remotely observing the data from the two detectors set up by the National Science Foundation's LIGO[1] project in Livingston, Louisiana, and Richland, Washington. The trace he saw represented an event that lasted a tiny fraction of a second; on reaching LIGO's apparatus, it caused a deviation in a laser beam so small that it was compared to the thickness of a human hair over the distance from here to the nearest star.

This observation, announced in February 2016, was perhaps the final confirmation that Einstein had got things right in the general theory. Just as disciplines like radio astronomy and X-ray astronomy have revealed to us scientific information about the universe that traditional optical astronomy couldn't, so gravitational astronomy is expected to open up a great new territory of human knowledge. These are very exciting times we live in.

THE GRAIL OF THE UNIFIED FIELD THEORY

After Eddington's announcement in 1919 of the bending of starlight by the Sun's gravitational field, Einstein was an international celebrity—a sort of rock star of science. His 1921 Nobel Prize was the icing on his cake of fame. Universities all over the world showered awards on him and naturally were keen to attract him as a visiting lecturer. Meanwhile he was living in Berlin with Elsa and various members of her family.

His marriage to Elsa was unconventional. They didn't share a bedroom, and it was no secret between them that Einstein was cutting something of a swath among the pretty young women of Berlin academia. There's little question but that the two of them loved each other

---

1. Laser Interferometer Gravitational-Wave Observatory.

greatly; like the SCHRÖDINGERS, they just did marriage differently from the way most people do.

Although Einstein continued producing good scientific work, he never again attained the heights of that decade or so between 1905 and 1916 when he completely altered the face of science. In part this was because he had great difficulty accepting many of the conclusions of quantum mechanics, such as HEISENBERG's uncertainty principle. ("God does not throw dice," he famously commented.) It's certainly true that to this day, no one has successfully patched together quantum mechanics and general relativity. The two theories have each been confirmed time and time again, yet they actually disagree with each other in some important ways. Since the two deal with very different aspects of nature—one with the very large and the other with the very small—for the most part this disagreement can be (uncomfortably) ignored. At some point an explanation will be found. A delight of science is that scientists don't know everything; there's always something new to discover.

Another reason Einstein's later years were comparatively unproductive was that he devoted much of his time to what still seems a fool's errand: an attempt to find a unified field theory—a theory that would explain gravitation and electromagnetism (plus, ideally, the weak and strong nuclear forces) as manifestations of a single field. Einstein got more or less nowhere with this.

In 1930 Einstein accepted a visiting professorship at the California Institute of Technology, in Pasadena. A few years later Hitler came to power in Germany, and the Einsteins wisely decided not to go home to a country where anti-Semitic politicians persecuted scientists whom they accused of "Jew science." Einstein himself was pilloried in his absence by the ignorant Nazi thugs as the epitome of this "Jew science"; had he returned home he might have found himself in a concentration camp. Any nation that demonizes science and scientists, pretending to itself that science is some great hoax, deserves what the Nazis eventually got.

Although Einstein helped lay the political groundwork for the Manhattan Project, as a lifelong pacifist he was depressed by the outcome, and by the world's buildup of nuclear weaponry during the Cold War years. He was an outspoken advocate of nuclear disarmament, and equally outspoken about the evils of McCarthyism, the anti-Communist (and anti-gay) witch hunt mounted in the US in the 1950s and spearheaded by the demagogue senator Joe McCarthy. To Einstein, a refugee from Nazi Germany, the scourge of McCarthyism in his new homeland must have seemed like something born of nightmare.

Elsa died in 1936, and Einstein never remarried. In 1951 his younger sister Maria ("Maja"), whom he'd invited to join him in the US in 1939 to escape Mussolini's anti-Semitism in Italy, died after a long illness. In his last years Einstein was alone except for his colleagues and his science. In 1952 he was offered the presidency of Israel but refused it. When, in 1955, he was taken to hospital suffering internal bleeding, he declined surgery on the grounds that the artificial prolongation of life was unsavory.

Einstein once said, "I very rarely think in words at all. A thought comes, and I may try to express it in words afterwards." Perhaps that was the secret of his success. ■

BUT THERE'S MORE . . .

- A good explanation of the basics of relativity for the general reader, despite its age, is Bertrand Russell's *The ABC of Relativity* (1925). Two books giving us unusual perspectives on Einstein are Hans C. Ohanian's *Einstein's Mistakes* (2008) and Dennis Overbye's *Einstein in Love* (2000). Also recommended are *Albert Einstein* (2005) by Alice Calaprice and Trevor Lipscombe and *Annus Mirabilis* (2005) by John and Mary Gribbin. Jerome Pohlen's *Albert Einstein and Relativity for Kids* (2012) is one of those great books that's just as useful—and just as much fun—for adults as it is for the kids of the title.
- So far as I can work out, the first appearance of Einstein as a quasi-fictional character in the movies was in 1944's *Arsenic and Old Lace*, where he was played by Peter Lorre. For some reason, outside docu-dramas and biopics, Einstein is usually played for laughs in the movies (maybe it was the hairstyle); typical is the 1994 movie *I.Q.*, a fact-free romantic comedy in which Walter Matthau stars as Einstein. If you can find it, the 1985 four-part TV miniseries *Einstein*, with Ronald Pickup in the title role, is worth watching.
- Israel honored Einstein in 1968 on its 5-lirot note; the bill went out of circulation in 1984. Element no. 99, discovered in 1952, was named einsteinium in his honor.

ALFRED WEGENER
(1880–1930)

The meteorologist and polar expeditioner who formulated the theory of continental drift.

Although qualified as an astronomer and a meteorologist, the Berlin-born Alfred Lothar Wegener is today remembered for a theory he proposed and promoted that was quite outside his professional sphere: the idea that the continents move—"drift"—around the surface of the planet.

Wegener first presented his theory of continental drift in a book called *Die Enstehung der Kontinente und Ozeane* (The Origin of Continents and Oceans; 1915). He proposed that, millions of years ago, all the Earth's continents were crammed together as a single vast landmass, which he called Pangaea. Eventually, for reasons unknown, Pangaea split up, and the continents we know today are its fragments, still drifting relative to one another.

The evidence he offered for this conjecture fell into four main categories:

- Measurements indicated Greenland was moving away from Europe. Although the rate was very slow, it was reasonable to assume the great distance now between them could have arisen over a period of many millions of years.
- The Earth's crust comes in two major varieties: the lighter continental crust and the much heavier crust under the oceans. (Around the edges of the continents are areas—the continental shelves—where continental crust is beneath the ocean surface.) Was it not possible that the lighter type of crust could slide over the top of the denser material?
- There are various examples of apparent "jigsaw fits" between opposite shores. The most obvious case is that of South America's eastern coast with Africa's western one. In fact, if you compare the continental shelves rather than the actual coastlines, the fit becomes even more striking.
- On opposite sides of these "jigsaw fits" there are often similarities in the fossil record.

As a mechanism for drift, Wegener proposed a hypothetical phenomenon produced as a centrifugal effect by the Earth's rotation: *Polflucht*, or "flight from the poles." Or perhaps the precession of the equinoxes (the slow rocking of the Earth on its axis) could be responsible. But no one has ever observed any evidence for *Polflucht*, and the precession explanation doesn't hold water either. It was easy for the geological establishment, hostile as it was to the idea of moving continents, to dismiss Wegener's conjecture as the witterings of an amateur.

He did have supporters, though. The South African geologist Alexander Logie Du Toit, while on a field trip to South America, discovered that numerous rock formations in western Africa were continued in eastern South America, very clear evidence the two continents had once been joined. In a book called *Our Wandering Continents* (1937), Du Toit proposed that Pangaea had originally split up not into the fragments we see today but into two smaller supercontinents, Laurasia and Gondwanaland. In due course those two landmasses in turn broke up.

Perhaps even more important was the support of the British geologist Arthur Holmes. In 1929 Holmes produced a workable mechanism for continental drift: convection currents in the Earth's mantle (the molten layer underneath the crust) could bring hot rocks to the surface, where they'd cool and spread out, eventually being subsumed back into the mantle and becoming molten again. Holmes's idea was not too far off modern ones.

The clincher for drift came in the 1960s, when the phenomenon of seafloor spreading was investigated. Underneath the oceans there are various ridges—such as the mid-Atlantic ridge—where molten rock is coming up from the mantle to form new crustal material. This pushes the ocean floor away from both sides of the ridge. Elsewhere, like around the famous Pacific Ring of Fire, crustal material is being pushed back down into the mantle. The continents are carried around on top of the ocean crust in a process called plate tectonics. In fact, at one point Wegener briefly toyed with this notion, but seems to have discarded it in favor of his other, implausible mechanisms.

By the time of this dramatic validation of his ideas, Wegener was long dead. As a meteorologist, he had specialized in weather studies done on the Greenland ice sheet, to which he made his first visit in 1906. On his fourth trip there, in 1930, he displayed extraordinary courage in the face of extremely hostile circumstances but in the end lost his life, probably through heart failure brought on by exertion in the cold. The thriller writer John Buchan based part of his novel *A Prince of the Captivity* (1933) on Wegener's last, fatal Greenland adventure. ∎

BUT THERE'S MORE...

■ Clare Dudman's *Wegener's Jigsaw* (2003; retitled *One Day the Ice Will Reveal All Its Dead* in the US) is a tremendous novel about Wegener's life. Although inevitably by now a bit dated, *Continental Drift* (1979) by D. H. and M. P. Tarling is a great introduction to the subject, and conveys the excitement as the theory of plate tectonics revolutionized our understanding of how our world works. Martin Schwarzbach's biography *Alfred Wegener* (1980; translated 1986) looks a bit intimidating when you pick it up but is recommended.

■ Wegener has craters on both Moon and Mars named for him, as well as an asteroid, 29227 Wegener. Antarctica has the Wegener Range of mountains and, offshore, the Wegener Canyon. The Alfred Wegener Institute for Polar and Marine Research is in Bremerhaven, Germany.

ERWIN SCHRÖDINGER
(1887–1961)

The great Austrian physicist who was also the progenitor
of a famous hypothetical cat.

The name of physicist Erwin Schrödinger is one of the best known of any scientist because he invented what's almost certainly the world's most famous thought experiment. That thought experiment came to be called Schrödinger's Cat, and both the name and the idea behind it have permeated all aspects of our culture. It has come to epitomize most people's mental image of the strange, counterintuitional picture of the universe that is painted by quantum mechanics, the highly successful scientific theory of which Schrödinger was one of the main pioneers.

Erwin Schrödinger, an only child, was born in Vienna. His father had inherited an oilcloth factory, so the family wasn't short of money. His mother was the daughter of a chemistry professor. Most of Erwin's early schooling was at home, either with a private tutor or, as he'd later say, more importantly with his father, who'd qualified in chemistry. In 1898 Erwin went to the Vienna Gymnasium,[1] and from there he went to the University of Vienna, where in due course he specialized in theoretical physics, having been bewitched by the lectures there of Friedrich Hasenöhrl. He gained his PhD in 1910, then got an assistant job at the university's Second Physics Institute.

When World War I broke out, Schrödinger signed up with the Austrian army and became an artillery officer. Though it might seem surprising, this gave him plenty of time to continue studying physics from books. It was during this period that he first encountered and then mastered EINSTEIN's theory of general relativity. After the war he went back to the Second Physics Institute for a while before taking up a succession of professorships at various universities. It's obvious the Austrian physics community had spotted him as an up-and-comer. He did some work on quantum theory and some on relativity, but his first significant

---

1. Not a place for PE but a top-notch school.

contributions came in a different area of science altogether: color vision and color blindness.

In 1925, reading a paper by Einstein, Schrödinger came across references to the ideas of the French physicist Louis de Broglie about what are now called matter waves. De Broglie's notion was that every particle should have a wave associated with it. For something as small as an electron, the wave would be relatively large and thus relatively easy to find. (Following de Broglie's lead, in 1927 scientists were indeed able to detect this wave.)

At the time, the accepted model for atomic structure was the so-called Bohr atom, inferred in 1913 by the Danish physicist Niels Bohr. This envisaged the atom as being like a miniature solar system, with electrons ("planets") orbiting the central nucleus ("sun"). The electrons can follow only certain orbits; if an electron transfers from one of these to another, energy (in the form of light) is either released (if the electron goes to a closer orbit) or must be supplied (for an electron to go to a higher orbit). We now know that the model is wrong, but it's still quite a useful way of thinking about the atom—and is certainly a heck of a lot easier to visualize than the reality.

Schrödinger realized that if he applied de Broglie's notion of matter waves to the Bohr atom, he might be able to produce a better model. He deduced that the permitted orbits for an electron were those—and only those—whose circumference corresponded to an exact number of wavelengths of the electron's associated wave. In such a situation, a standing wave is produced and the situation is stable, with no energy being released or absorbed. In effect, the electron *is* the standing wave.

This gave a physical explanation for why electrons could, as Bohr and others had realized, have only certain orbits.

Schrödinger and others researched the math of this and realized they were giving the quantum theory, put forward a couple of decades earlier by Max Planck, a rigorous mathematical underpinning at last. In 1926 Schrödinger published his conclusions, calling his new scheme "wave mechanics." The previous year, HEISENBERG had published a concept called "matrix mechanics" that attempted to explain many of the same phenomena, and it was soon recognized that the two approaches were equivalent. The quantum theory had become quantum mechanics.

In 1933 Schrödinger shared the Nobel Physics Prize for this work with the UK physicist Paul Dirac; Heisenberg, awarded the previous year's prize, received his at the same time. That same year, Hitler's Nazis came to power in Germany. This was bad news for Schrödinger, who

THAT CAT

In the quantum universe, it seems, nothing can be known for sure; everything is just a matter of probabilities. When you observe something actually happening, what you're seeing is the outcome of a contest between different probabilities (the collapse of a wave function, to use the jargon). All of those probabilities *could* in theory have happened. What you're seeing is the one that did.

Schrödinger, worried by this conclusion (even though it had been based in large part on his own work!), put forward a series of thought experiments as to why this could not be so. The most famous was Schrödinger's Cat, which he proposed in 1935.

Everyday events can depend on quantum ones. Schrödinger pictured a cat placed in a steel box with a quantity of radioactive material. Within (say) an hour, there's a 50 percent chance that an atom of that material will decay. If it does, a device will be triggered to smash open a vial of poison, also in the box, and the cat will die. If it doesn't, the cat will survive until eventually an atom decays. The cat's life thus depends on the quantum event.

The only way you can tell if the cat is alive or dead is by opening the box and taking a look. In terms of quantum mechanics, the current status of that atom of radioactive material is that it has neither decayed nor not decayed; not until you open the box will you collapse its wave function, one way or the other, to bring the observed reality into being.

That might seem just about acceptable at the quantum scale. But the decay or nondecay of the atom also affects the welfare of the cat. Until you open the box, is the cat alive or dead? Or is it in the wave-function-not-yet-collapsed state? Schrödinger pointed out that *from the perspective of the cat*, it's pretty obvious whether it's alive or dead.

Schrödinger presented this as a paradox undermining the notion that in the quantum world all sorts of eventualities are equally real until you go check on them. Since then, however, it's become increasingly clear that the universe *does* operate like this, whether we like it or not.

by now was working at the University of Berlin—he'd taken over from Planck as professor of theoretical physics there. While he himself wasn't Jewish, he detested anti-Semitism and watched with fury as the Nazis ousted good scientists for anti-Semitic or other ideological reasons. In 1934 he briefly took up a position at Magdalen College, Oxford, UK, but apparently his lifestyle—he and wife Annemarie had an open marriage, and often enough his mistress du jour would live with them—outraged sensibilities among the dons.

By 1936 he was back in Austria, at the University of Graz. When the Nazis overran Austria in 1938, it was clear to Schrödinger that the writing was once more on the wall. In September of that year he was dismissed from Graz. Luckily in 1940 Éamon de Valera, formerly a math professor at Dublin University and now the Irish taoiseach, set up the School for Theoretical Physics in Dublin especially in order for Schrödinger to be its head. In due course Schrödinger's fellow Nobel laureate Dirac joined him there.

Schrödinger remained in Ireland until 1956, when he returned to Vienna for the last few years of his life. He died of tuberculosis, a disease that had haunted him since his youth. ∎

BUT THERE'S MORE . . .

- Schrödinger's book *What Is Life?* (1944), based on a series of lectures he gave in Dublin, is hardly beach reading, but it's accessible to the persevering lay reader. In the book, Schrödinger didn't exactly predict DNA, but he did predict the properties a replicant molecule (he called it a crystal) should have.
- For a fairly painless introduction to many of the concepts Schrödinger worked with, you could try James Kakalios's *The Amazing Story of Quantum Mechanics* (2010). Paul Halpern's *Einstein's Dice and Schrödinger's Cat* (2015) looks at the debate between the two great scientists as they tried to reconcile the differing views of the universe presented by relativity and quantum mechanics. William T. Scott's *Erwin Schrödinger: An Introduction to His Writings* (1967) is just what it says on the label. In the field of fiction, Robert Anton Wilson's *Schrödinger's Cat* trilogy explores different aspects of existence as implied by quantum mechanics. In Douglas Adams's *Dirk Gently's Holistic Detective Agency* (1987) the eponymous detective is hired to find out what's happened to the cat, discovered through clairvoyance to be missing from the box.
- Release no. 19 of the operating system Fedora was called Schrödinger's Cat. I personally rather like the Czech post-punk outfit Schrödingerova Kočka (Schrödinger's Cat), whose music you can find on Bandcamp.

EDWIN HUBBLE

(1889–1953)

The US astronomer who revealed the vastness of the universe and showed that the distant galaxies are receding from us.

The Hubble Space Telescope (HST), launched in 1990 and still functioning over a quarter century later, is probably the most productive scientific tool ever built. When we think of the HST—often called just the Hubble—it's usually those fabulous photographs of distant galaxies that come to mind. But the Hubble has done much more. It has been used to measure far more accurately than before the rate at which the universe is expanding, from which we've been able to calculate the universe's age and develop a completely new understanding of how our universe operates, complete with concepts like dark energy and dark matter that were totally unknown just a few decades ago.

It's no more than appropriate that the telescope should be named for the US astronomer Edwin Powell Hubble, because his work, too, revolutionized our understanding of the universe.

Hubble was born in Marshfield, Missouri, and initially trained as a lawyer. He was briefly on the Kentucky Bar, but his interest in astronomy and math couldn't long be denied. In 1914 he snagged a research position at the University of Chicago's Yerkes Observatory, then the world's leading observatory. He stayed there until, in 1917, he joined the army. After a short spell in Europe he returned to the US and took up a new research post at the recently opened Mount Wilson Observatory in California. The Hooker telescope there was, with a mirror 100 inches (254 cm) in diameter, the largest in the world, and would remain so until the 200-inch (508 cm) Hale telescope at Mount Palomar was built in 1948.

Hubble's primary interest was nebulae—fuzzy patches in the sky. During his early years as a professional astronomer it was believed the universe consisted only of our own galaxy, plus a few astronomical structures, such as the two Magellanic clouds (today recognized as small satellite galaxies), just outside our galaxy's main body. One puzzle about nebulae was that some were irregular in shape while others were clearly structured. While at Yerkes, Hubble attempted to find a way to tell which nebulae lay within our galaxy and which were outside it, but he could go only so far with the observatory's telescopes. The move to Mount Wilson gave him access to the Hooker telescope.

Other astronomers—such as Henrietta Leavitt, Harlow Shapley, Ejnar Hertzsprung, and Henry Norris Russell—had discovered that variable stars of a particular type, the so-called Cepheid variables, pulsated at a rate that was proportional to the star's average luminosity. In other words, by measuring the rate at which one of these stars pulsates, you can tell how bright it actually is. If you compare this with how bright the star looks in your telescope, you can calculate how far away the star is. Cepheid variables could thus be used as distance markers. It was because of the Cepheid variables in the Magellanic clouds that astronomers knew those clouds were outside our galaxy.

Once at Mount Wilson, Hubble searched for Cepheid variables in some of the regular-shaped nebulae, notably the Great Andromeda Nebula. He discovered the first Cepheid variable there in 1923, and within a year or so found a dozen or so others. All told the same story. Not only was the Andromeda Nebula outside the galaxy, it was *a long way* outside it. Studies of other nebulae led him to the same conclusion. In 1924 he put forward the theory—obvious to us now in hindsight but revolutionary then—that some nebulae weren't dust clouds but distant galaxies.

The universe suddenly became a much bigger place—at least, so far as we understood it.

Hubble continued studying distant galaxies and discovered that most have either an ellipsoidal (squashed sphere) or flattened shape. The flattened ones can be either lenticular (lens-shaped) or, like our own galaxy, structured like a spiral.

Other astronomers discovered the galaxies are receding from us. Adding their observations to his own, Hubble was able to make his next big breakthrough: the discovery that, the farther a galaxy is, the faster it's receding (Hubble's law). He made this discovery through looking at how much the wavelengths of the light from the galaxies were increased (redshifted) by the velocity of their recession. In fact, he concluded, there's a direct mathematical relationship (the Hubble constant) between the distance of a galaxy and the velocity at which it's traveling away from us.

Here was a *really* useful way to calculate distances on a universal scale. But there were more important consequences even than that.

When Albert EINSTEIN put forward general relativity in 1915, there was one great difficulty with it. The theory indicated quite clearly that the universe should be expanding. However, the best astronomy of the time was based on the notion that the universe was static—that it was getting neither bigger nor smaller. So Einstein introduced a fiddle into his calculation, which he called the cosmological constant. (He later called it the biggest mistake he'd ever made!) Hubble's work removed any need for the cosmological constant, thereby vindicating general relativity. It also very quickly led the Belgian cosmologist Georges Édouard Lemaître to put forward the first version of the Big Bang theory—the idea that, at some point in the past, the universe had been concentrated into a very small volume, the "primal atom" or "cosmic egg," which then for some reason exploded.

We know a lot more about the universe today than Hubble ever could—that it's yet more mysterious and wonderful than perhaps he could even have dreamed. But it was his work that led us, in terms of our understanding of the universe and our place in it, out of the cave of our ignorance and, blinking, into the broad daylight of knowledge. ■

BUT THERE'S MORE . . .

■ In 1976 Hubble's home in San Marino, California, was declared a National Historic Landmark. The Edwin Hubble Highway passes through Marshfield, Missouri, his birthplace. There's a crater on the Moon named for him, as well as an asteroid, 2069 Hubble.

■ You can find one of Hubble's books, *The Realm of the Nebulae* (1936), online at the Internet Archive; the book's science is dated but you get an insight into the man's mind. A good biography is Gale Christianson's *Edwin Hubble: Mariner of the Nebulae* (1995).

HOWARD FLOREY
(1898–1968)

The Australian bacteriologist who brought antibiotics to the world.

If you ask people who was responsible for the discovery of penicillin, 99 out of 100 will promptly respond that it was the Scottish bacteriologist Alexander Fleming, and tell you how one day he noticed a funny growth in his petri dish, the rest being history. That's true, so far as it goes, but it's misleading. Fleming deserves full credit for spotting an interesting phenomenon when others might not have noticed it. But the people who discovered how to make and use penicillin, and who thereby started the antibiotics revolution that has saved untold millions of lives, were Howard Florey and his young colleague Ernst Chain.

It was in 1928, while he was researching the bacterium *Staphylococcus aureus* at St. Mary's Hospital, London, that Alexander Fleming noticed that some of the petri dishes he was using to cultivate the *S. aureus* had been contaminated by little spots of green mold, and that any bacterial colonies near the mold had died out. Realizing that anything that killed disease-causing bacteria might be useful, he experimented with the mold, identifying it as *Penicillium notatum* (it's similar to one of the molds that grows on old bread), naming it penicillin, and finding that it killed some strains of bacteria but not others. He also discovered that, despite its bactericidal properties, it was harmless to experimental animals. Pluckily, one of his assistants ate some to demonstrate that it was harmless to humans, too. And that was more or less where Fleming left it.

This wasn't the first antibacterial agent he'd discovered. In 1922 he found that tears, snot, saliva, and other bodily fluids contain an enzyme called lysozyme that acts as a catalyst in breaking down bacterial walls, so helping the body defend itself against infection.

Fleming passed along his samples of penicillin to researchers at the Sir William Dunn School of Pathology at Oxford University, and seems thereafter to have more or less forgotten the matter. The team who received the samples found little use for penicillin in their current research project, but luckily recorded its properties and kept it on file.

Scroll forward a few years and the Sir William Dunn School of Pathology welcomed as its new head an energetic bacteriologist called Howard Walter Florey. Born in Adelaide, Australia, Florey was particularly interested in bactericides, and did some research on Fleming's lysozyme before focusing on penicillin.

Fleming's problem with penicillin had been that he didn't know how to purify it or produce it in any quantity. Working with Ernst Chain, a German-born biochemist, in 1939 Florey was able to extract penicillin in the form of a yellow powder. He and his team then discovered that even an extraordinarily dilute solution of the powder—one part in a million[1]—was effective in wiping out streptococcal infections in mice, leaving the mice unharmed.

There was still the difficulty of producing the stuff in quantity—it took Florey's team almost eighteen months to produce just four ounces (100 g) of the powder. To make matters worse, World War II was under way, and all the commercial laboratories were focusing on producing vaccines. The team managed to increase the rate of production in the lab, but not by much.

This shortage of penicillin was to have tragic results when it came to testing the drug on humans. Naturally, Florey selected only terminally ill patients as experimental subjects. The first subject was a postmaster dying from an infection of his face and lungs. In just a few days he was very much better and looked to be on the road to a miraculous recovery; alas, a few weeks later he died—Florey didn't have enough penicillin for a full course of treatment. Subsequent patients were luckier, and it was clear Florey and his team had their hands on a medical tool whose potential benefits were almost unimaginable.

Eventually the UK wartime government gave permission for the production of penicillin to be farmed out to US companies. Between

---

1. They later found that one part in just 50 million was enough.

1943 and the end of the war, millions of Allied lives were saved through the use of penicillin. After the war was over, commercial pharmaceutical laboratories could be recruited for production of the drug, and the age of antibiotics got into full swing.

However, the person getting all the credit for this was neither Florey nor Chain but Fleming. One of the governors of St. Mary's Hospital, where Fleming had made his lucky discovery, was the distinguished physician Charles Wilson, Lord Moran. Wilson recognized that the hospital could derive very useful publicity from the fact that Fleming worked there, and fortuitously was a good friend of the media magnate Lord Beaverbrook. All of the high-circulation Beaverbrook newspapers trumpeted Fleming as discoverer of the "miracle drug" and essentially wrote Florey and Chain out of the script. In 1945, when the Nobel Prize for Physiology or Medicine was shared by Fleming, Florey, and Chain, there was a general feeling of "Who are Florey and Chain?" Even today, it's hard to reverse the misperception that their contribution was just ancillary.

Not so in Australia, of course, where the primacy of the ex-local boy's work on penicillin was justly celebrated. And slowly the rest of the world caught up. In 1958 Florey became president of the Royal Society, an office he held until 1965. Also in 1965, he was appointed Baron Florey. ∎

BUT THERE'S MORE . . .

- In 1973 Florey's native Australia put his image on the $50 bill, which remained in circulation until 1995. In 1995 Australia commemorated Florey's work with a $2.50 postage stamp, and he appeared again in 2012, this time on the 60¢ stamp. In Scotland, Fleming's image has since 2009 appeared on £5 banknotes issued by the Clydesdale Bank.
- Three good books about Florey and the emergence of penicillin are Eric Lax's *The Mold in Dr. Florey's Coat* (2004), Robert Bud's *Penicillin* (2007), and, at a more elementary level, Francine Jacobs's *Breakthrough: The True Story of Penicillin* (1985).
- The 2009 TV movie *Breaking the Mould*, directed by Peter Hoar, dramatizes the development of penicillin by Florey and his team at Oxford.

CECILIA PAYNE-GAPOSCHKIN

(1900–1979)

The US astronomer who told us what the universe is made of.

In 1835 the French philosopher Auguste Comte declared we would never know the chemical composition of the stars. He added: "I regard any notion concerning the true mean temperature of the various stars as forever denied to us." It's one of the great failed predictions of science history. Within the next two or three decades the new science of spectroscopy so much improved our understanding of the stars that by 1861 the UK astronomer Warren de la Rue claimed:

> If we were to go to the Sun, and to bring some portions of it and analyze them in our laboratories, we could not examine them more accurately than we can by this new mode of spectrum analysis.

In 1802, long before Comte made his doomed pronouncement, the UK chemist William Wollaston noticed that the spectrum of the Sun's light contained not just the spectral colors but also some narrow dark lines. And in 1814 the German optical scientist Joseph Fraunhofer, working much more precisely, discovered there were hundreds of these.

The big breakthrough came in 1859, when Fraunhofer's compatriots Gustav Kirchhoff and Robert Bunsen[1] showed these lines were caused by absorption of some of the Sun's light by chemical elements present in the cooler regions above the Sun's visible surface. Every element produces and absorbs its own spectrum of light, and study of the lines in the solar spectrum could be used—a little like fingerprints can be used to identify criminals—to determine the elements present there.

It's very fiddly work, even for a star as close as the Sun. Imagine how much trickier it is when you're working with the spectra of distant stars, whose light is many millions of times fainter. Even so, it could be done, and it became apparent that stars had different spectra; some were bluer,

---

1. Yes, the same Bunsen who devised the burner.

some redder, and so on. By 1890 the US astronomer Edward Pickering had concocted a catalogue of over ten thousand stars arranged according to spectral type, and by 1924 another US astronomer, Annie Jump Cannon, had increased this number to over a quarter million.

Cecilia Helena Payne was born in Buckinghamshire, England. She studied botany, physics, and chemistry at Newnham College, Cambridge. While there, she attended a lecture by the astrophysicist Arthur Eddington that sparked her interest in astronomy. Although she did well in all her examinations at Newnham, she wasn't awarded a degree; crazily, in those days, women could study at Cambridge University but could not receive degrees.

She thus decided to move to the US, to the Harvard College Observatory in Cambridge, Massachusetts; this was where Pickering and Cannon did their pioneering work on classifying the spectra of the stars. In her PhD thesis, Payne was able to show *why* the stars were of those different spectral types. Earlier astronomers had thought the strength of an element's "fingerprint" in a star's spectrum indicated how much of that element was present there. She correctly deduced that, instead, the lines indicate the temperature of the star. Different elements ionize to different degrees at different temperatures; the strength of the "fingerprints" depended on how much the various elements had ionized.

That piece of work has been described by various astronomers as perhaps the most brilliant PhD thesis ever written. One of those who agreed was Payne's supervisor, Henry Norris Russell. However, he disagreed with her conclusion that stars were made up almost entirely of hydrogen, plus a small amount of the next lightest element, helium, with the other elements present only as traces. At the time, astronomers assumed the elements were present in the same proportions in stars as here on Earth. So Russell advised her to suppress or downplay her conclusion. Because he was one of the most prominent astronomers in the world and she was a mere postgraduate student, she obediently added a comment stating that her inferences were "almost certainly not real"—in other words, that her results were real enough but her interpretation of them was likely faulty.

A few years later, in 1929, Russell changed his mind and published a paper concluding that the stars were—and thus the universe was—made up almost entirely of hydrogen. In this paper he made just an offhand reference to Payne's work, and for many years Russell was credited with the discovery.

In 1934 Payne married Russian astronomer Sergei I. Gaposchkin, a political refugee from the USSR. Throughout the rest of her life she did important work in astronomy and astrophysics, much of it with her husband, studying variable stars, novae, galactic structure, and so on. In 1956 she became Harvard's chair in astronomy, the first woman to attain such a position there. Although there had been other notable female astronomers before her, Payne-Gaposchkin distinguished herself as a theoretician, thereby storming her way into formerly male-only territory and providing an inspiration to many women astronomers and other physicists after her.

But her greatest contribution was the discovery that almost all of the matter in the universe is hydrogen. ∎

BUT THERE'S MORE . . .

- Payne-Gaposchkin wrote a number of popular/introductory books on astronomy, but these are obviously very dated now. She also wrote an autobiography, *The Dyer's Hand* (1979); this was originally printed privately for friends, but in 1984 was published as part of *Cecilia Payne-Gaposchkin: An Autobiography and Other Recollections* (1984).
- Asteroid 2039 Payne-Gaposchkin is named for her.

WERNER HEISENBERG
(1901–1976)

*The "Father of Quantum Mechanics" and the mastermind
behind the Nazi bomb that wasn't.*

Although Erwin SCHRÖDINGER has at least as great a claim, the German mathematical physicist Werner Karl Heisenberg is generally regarded as the father of quantum mechanics, arguably, along with general relativity, the most fundamental theory of modern physics. Heisenberg's breakthrough was his realization that if you want to tease out the workings of the subatomic world—the quantum realm—the best way of doing so is not by thinking of models or pictures. The quantum realm simply isn't like anything we can see or sense, and so attempts to interpret it in everyday terms are doomed. He opted instead to represent the atom in the form of mathematical matrices, ignoring any questions as to what the atom might "look like."

Heisenberg was also responsible for the famous uncertainty principle, whose implications signaled the end of the old, deterministic physics and the ushering in of the new.

He was born in Würzburg, Germany, and entered the University of Munich in 1920, intending to study pure math. Circumstances conspired against this, and instead he enrolled to read theoretical physics under the distinguished scientist Arnold Sommerfeld. Sommerfeld was relatively rare among older physicists in that his focus was on theoretical work rather than experiment. One of Heisenberg's fellow students under Sommerfeld was Wolfgang Pauli, who'd win the 1945 Nobel Physics Prize for his elucidation of what's now called the exclusion principle.[1]

In the early 1920s it was becoming obvious there were serious problems with the hitherto widely accepted model of the atom deduced by Niels Bohr (see page 167). Experimental results were differing from predicted ones—not by a huge amount, but enough to make it clear there was something wrong with the model. Pauli was among the first to

---

1. Every electron has four quantum numbers. According to the exclusion principle, no two electrons in the same atom can have identical values for these.

raise the alarm, and even Sommerfeld, although generally supportive of Bohr's model, acknowledged there were difficulties.

In 1923, having attained his PhD, Heisenberg went to the University of Göttingen to work under Max Born. He tackled the enigma of the Bohr atom by considering the spectral lines of hydrogen, the simplest atom. Where the Bohr model was intended to explain the spectral lines—and wasn't doing so with full success—Heisenberg turned the situation on its head. Instead of trying to make your model explain the lines, why not start with the lines and, through working out a mathematical relationship for them, see what that relationship could tell you about the atom?

With the help of Born, Heisenberg applied matrix algebra to the situation, and thereby evolved a system that he called matrix mechanics. This was effectively the birth of quantum mechanics. Very soon after, Schrödinger published his own conclusions about the nature of the atom, that electrons aren't orbiting particles but are in effect standing waves around the nucleus. In the mid-1940s the mathematician John von Neumann, working in the US, was able to show that, mathematically, Schrödinger's wave mechanics and Heisenberg's matrix mechanics were really the same thing. The Schrödinger approach became the more popular of the two because, while it was impossible to meaningfully imagine an atom constructed like that, at least you could get some sort of image of it in your head.

Heisenberg did much other work of note. As an offshoot of his use of matrix mechanics to study the atom, he predicted that the hydrogen molecule (H_2) should be able to exist in two forms (allotropes): ortho-hydrogen, in which the nuclei of the two atoms have the same direction of spin, and para-hydrogen, in which they have opposite directions of spin. In 1929 this prediction was confirmed.

Far more important was his announcement in 1927 of the uncertainty principle. Put simply, this says you can't know both the position and momentum (mass times velocity) of a particle at the same time. The more exactly you know one of those properties, the less accurately you can know the other—and you can never know either with certainty. Moreover, if you multiply together the mathematically expressed uncertainties of your two attempted measurements, you get a result very close to the value of Planck's constant,[1] suggesting the principle isn't just a philosophical concept but a fundamental property of the universe.

---

1. The relationship between the energy of a photon ("light particle") and its frequency.

This might sound like a fairly obscure point . . . until you consider the ramifications. The principle implies you can't accurately predict the outcome of any event; all you can do is express that outcome in terms of a range of probabilities. This puts under threat the idea that cause must always precede effect, a cornerstone of human reason since time immemorial. The French astronomer Pierre Simon de Laplace had said over a century earlier that, given the position and motion of every particle in the universe in one particular instance, you could (in theory only, obviously!) calculate exactly the universe's entire history from birth to death. The uncertainty principle suggested such notions were at best naïve.

For his deduction of the uncertainty principle, Heisenberg was awarded the 1932 Nobel Physics Prize. For various reasons, this wasn't announced until November 1933, when the winners of the 1933 award, Erwin Schrödinger and Paul Dirac, were also named. You'll sometimes come across the erroneous statement that all three shared the 1933 award.

That same year, 1933, was the year the Nazis came to power in Germany, and the next few years saw a flight of Germany's scientists to other, friendlier nations. First went the Jews, like EINSTEIN; then went people who valued freedom of thought, leftists, and so on. Even though Heisenberg had embraced democratic socialism in his youth, he was somehow able to compromise his views sufficiently to work within the Nazi regime.

Under the Nazis, a new notion of physics emerged. This was Die Deutsche Physik—"German Physics"—and its main stalwarts were two extraordinarily vile men, Philipp Lenard and Johannes Stark. Both were winners of the Nobel Physics Prize, Lenard in 1905 and Stark in 1919. Both presumably felt threatened by the new physics, based as it was on indeterminacy, and both were incorrigible anti-Semites. The idea of German Physics—promoted as the replacement for "Jew Physics"—was that conclusions should be commonsensical, not abstract or indeterminate like those of relativity and quantum mechanics. If you couldn't actually observe something, then either it didn't exist or it was *intended* we should never learn about it. Obviously relativity must be nonsense because it was the brainchild of a Jew, Einstein. You could hardly say Heisenberg was a Jew, because his genealogy represented a sort of Aryan ideal. What you could do, and what Lenard and Stark did do, was call him a "white Jew"—someone who'd betrayed his Aryan heritage in order to go along with the detested Jew Physics.

All of this was, of course, garbage, but since when have people rejected ideas just because they're garbage? Lenard and Stark were saying what the Nazi overlords wanted to hear, specifically what Heinrich Himmler wanted to hear. Himmler, head of the SS, fancied himself to be something of a scientist and often grasped the reins of scientific power in the Nazi regime. This was a bit of a disaster, because Himmler held all sorts of dotty pseudoscientific ideas, from an opposition to the notion of human evolution to support of the hypothesis that the universe was made entirely of ice.

Lenard and Stark mounted a determined campaign against the "white Jew" Heisenberg, and things looked very dicey for him for a while. He might well have been hauled off to death in the camps had it not been for a lucky coincidence. Heisenberg's mother, Annie, knew Himmler's mother, Anna. The two moms got together, and Anna agreed she'd have a word with her Heinrich.

The failure to topple Heisenberg more or less spelled the end for Die Deutsche Physik. Heisenberg's mom's action may have saved more lives than his. Soon Lenard and Stark fell from official favor and, while the practice of real science remained a nightmare within Nazi Germany, at least this particular blight had been removed.

Heisenberg was drawn into the Nazis' project to build an atomic bomb. On paper, given Heisenberg's abilities and past history, this might have made one expect the Germans would get there before the Allies. In practice, they made very little headway. A popular theory is that Heisenberg deliberately led his team down blind alleys, but there's not much evidence for this.

After the war, Heisenberg naturally faced some hostility over his collaboration with the Nazi regime and his participation in the Nazi A-bomb project. Even so, the scientific community managed to rehabilitate him, and although his glory days were over, he continued to do valuable work. In July 1946 he became director of the Kaiser Wilhelm Institute for Physics (now the Max Planck Institute) in Munich. He finally left the institute in 1970, by which time his health was in decline. A few years later he was dead of cancer.

Heisenberg's brilliance is not in doubt. He was a child prodigy not just in math but also as a classical pianist—he continued to play piano for the rest of his life. In addition, he was captivated by philosophy and by classical literature. ■

BUT THERE'S MORE . . .

- For useful background information on Heisenberg's work, try James Kakalios's *The Amazing Story of Quantum Mechanics* (2010). For an account of the scientific revolution that Heisenberg's work inaugurated there's David Lindley's *Uncertainty* (2007). Thomas Powers's doorstop *Heisenberg's War* (1993) describes the German project to develop the A-bomb, and Heisenberg's role in it. There's a good account of this also in John Cornwell's *Hitler's Scientists* (2003). A good but hefty biography is David C. Cassidy's *Beyond Uncertainty*.
- The asteroid 13149 Heisenberg was discovered in 1995.
- Heisenberg's brother-in-law was the economist E. F. Schumacher, best known for the book *Small Is Beautiful* (1973).

RACHEL CARSON
(1907–1964)

The US writer and marine biologist who warned the world about the perils of environmental devastation.

Rachel Carson almost single-handedly brought the topic of the environment to the forefront of public attention in the US and around the world. The big chemical companies mounted a major smear campaign against her because they saw her as a threat to their profits. But, undaunted, she insisted on sticking to the truth. Even today, decades after her death, the attacks from pro-corporate think tanks continue.

Rachel Louise Carson was born in Springdale, Pennsylvania. Her mother was a schoolteacher who was forced to give up her profession on getting married, because that was state law in those days. This was a stroke of luck for Rachel, who, because of a bout of scarlet fever in infancy, had to take several extended breaks from school; unlike many parents, her mother was perfectly capable of educating her at home.

Intending to become a writer, Rachel took English as her major at the Pennsylvania College for Women. However, she also had to take a science minor, and chose biology. After much soul-searching, she opted for that as her major instead, with chemistry as a minor. By that time, she had just a year before graduation in which to catch up on a huge amount of study; nevertheless, in 1929 she graduated with flying colors.

She was accepted at the Johns Hopkins University graduate school, and also got a job as an intern at the Marine Biological Laboratory (MBL) in Woods Hole, Massachusetts. Ironically for someone who made her first big impact on public attention with books about the sea and its denizens, it was only when Carson took up this internship, at age twenty-two, that she saw the sea for the first time.

She moved from the MBL in 1936 to the US Bureau of Fisheries (now called the Fish and Wildlife Service). While there, she wrote the first of her books, *Under the Sea-Wind* (1941), illustrated by Howard Frech (and reillustrated in the 1990s by Robert W. Hines). Although conveying a tremendous amount about the biology and the ecosystems of the sea, the book was written almost as if for children. It was well received but didn't sell especially well until after its sequel, the National Book Award–winning *The Sea Around Us* (1951), appeared a decade later. That book, adapted for the screen as a documentary in 1953, became a major best seller (enough so that Carson was able to give up the day job and become a full-time writer, as she'd dreamed decades before), and it made *Under the Sea-Wind* a belated best seller too.

The Sea Around Us mixed science, history, and personal recollections in a narrative that was (and is) intensely readable. It also presented a viewpoint that was radical at the time: that our planet is basically an ocean world, its land areas being essentially anomalies. So, when we put the health of the oceans at risk through pollution and otherwise, what we're actually doing is endangering the planet as a whole. Its sequel, the third in her "sea trilogy," *The Edge of the Sea* (1955), continued with the same preoccupations but concentrating this time on shoreline environments.

It was her fourth book, *Silent Spring* (1962), that really rocked the boat; the strap line on a recent reissue describes it as "The Classic That Launched the Environmental Movement," and that's a reasonable characterization. Its focus was on synthetic pesticides, which were then being deployed indiscriminately by the agricultural industry, such controls on their use as existed being—because of politicians' complacency, ignorance, or corruption—only laxly enforced.[1] People were turning a blind eye to the side effects of these pesticides, which Carson preferred to term—more accurately, she claimed—*biocides*.

She pointed out that chemicals like DDT, very widely used as an insecticide, were killing all sorts of organisms other than the ones intended as their targets, which anyway tended to build up an immunity. The chemicals accumulate in the environment, enter the diets of other creatures—notably fish and birds—and eventually cause untold destruction. The "silent spring" of the title referred to a powerful image she evoked—of a spring without birdsong.

The book, and its prepublication serialization in the *New Yorker*, caused a public uproar. The chemicals industry attacked it on the grounds that it was junk science (it wasn't) and that Carson had wildly exaggerated the problem (she hadn't). John F. Kennedy instructed the President's Science Advisory Committee (PSAC) to mount an investigation, and the committee's conclusions vindicated Carson's claims in every impor-

---

1. Sound familiar? We have similar problems today, not just with pesticides but with the overuse of antibiotics in the meat industry to fatten up animals.

tant respect. The use of DDT as an insecticide was banned in the US in 1972, and by 2004 the rest of the world had largely followed suit; the only generally accepted use of DDT today is for curbing the mosquitoes that spread malaria.

Silent Spring, listed in 2006 by *Discover* as no. 16 on that magazine's list of the 25 Greatest Science Books of All Time, brought Carson many awards and honors, notably the National Audubon Society's Audubon Medal (she was the first woman to receive this honor) and election to the American Academy of Arts and Letters.

She didn't have long to enjoy these honors, however, because even at the time of the book's publication she was battling breast cancer. On April 14, 1964, complications ensuing from her therapy caused a fatal heart attack.

Today, the National Audubon Society's Women in Conservation group annually honors women whose "immense talent, expertise, and energy" have "greatly advance[d] conservation and the environmental movement, locally and globally," with the Rachel Carson Award. ∎

BUT THERE'S MORE . . .

- Linda Lear's *Rachel Carson: Witness to Nature* (1997) and Arlene R. Quaratiello's *Rachel Carson* (2004) provide excellent introductions to Carson's life and work. Lear has also edited an extremely rewarding posthumous collection of Carson's work, *Lost Woods* (1998).
- In 2012, University of California Television inaugurated a series of six lectures and discussions about ethics in environmental science, the Silent Spring Series, so named in honor of the fiftieth anniversary of Carson's book. You can find the individual shows on YouTube or at the UCTV website (www.uctv.tv). Of particular relevance to Carson is the lecture "Rachel Carson's Legacy: Finding the Wisdom and Insight for Global Environmental Citizenship" (2013) by Mitchell Thomashow.
- The US composer Steven Stucky's symphonic poem *Silent Spring*, again marking the book's fiftieth anniversary, was commissioned by the Pittsburgh Symphony Orchestra and premiered in February 2012. The Thom Yorke song "Silent Spring" entered Radiohead's repertoire in 2015 and, retitled "The Numbers," was included in the band's May 2016 album *A Moon Shaped Pool*.

SUBRAHMANYAN CHANDRASEKHAR

(1910–1995)

The physicist who predicted neutron stars and black holes—
and almost lost his career for doing so.

Sometimes things do really seem to go in families. When Subrahmanyan Chandrasekhar—widely known as just Chandra—won the Nobel Physics Prize in 1983,[1] he became just the second Indian to do so. The first, in 1930, was his uncle, Sir Chandrasekhara Venkata Raman. Just to confuse matters, by the time Chandra became a Nobel laureate, India had been partitioned and the city of his birth, Lahore, was now in Pakistan, while Chandra himself had been a US citizen since 1953!

Chandra was a child prodigy, his initial passion being mathematics. He went to college at age fifteen; there the physicist Arnold Sommerfeld introduced him to the "new physics" of quantum mechanics. He was particularly taken by a paper called "On Dense Matter" (1926) by the UK physicist Ralph H. Fowler. The dense matter with which Fowler was concerned was the stuff found within the particular type of stars known as white dwarfs. It was known that white dwarfs like the companion to the bright star Sirius (Sirius B) were so dense that a teaspoonful of their material would weigh many tons.

Stars are very massive objects, and they require some sort of internal energy source to push back against the inward force of their own gravity, which is trying to make them collapse. In the case of our own star, the Sun, that energy source is the nuclear fusion of hydrogen to helium.

For an object as dense as a white dwarf, however, nuclear fusion is impossible; in essence, all the atoms are already so jam-packed together (in a state called "degenerate matter") that there isn't room for it to happen. Using quantum mechanics, Fowler showed that the electrons inside

---

1. Shared with US nuclear physicist William Fowler.

degenerate matter must be ricocheting around at very high velocities. It's the sum of all those high-velocity impacts that keeps the white dwarf from collapsing in on itself.

When he was just nineteen, Chandra gained a postgraduate position in the UK at Trinity College, Cambridge. During his voyage from India to the UK he entertained himself by applying EINSTEIN's theory of general relativity to Fowler's work. He calculated that if a white dwarf were to be above a certain mass—about 1.44 times the mass of the Sun—even the pressure of those rapidly moving electrons wouldn't be enough to stop it collapsing further. It was hard for people at the time to comprehend how anything could be denser than white dwarfs, but Chandra believed his calculations didn't lie. Stars above what's now called the Chandrasekhar limit must collapse into something even denser: in modern terms, into either a neutron star (pulsar) or a black hole.

The trouble for Chandra was that these new ideas ran slap-bang into the face of the then current theories of Arthur Eddington, a titan of astronomy . . . who just happened to be Plumian Professor of Astronomy at Cambridge University, the very place where Chandra was heading! Eddington thought the final destination in a star's life was the white-dwarf state, and the idea that there could be further collapses was anathema to him.

At first Eddington seemed supportive of Chandra's work, but, when in 1935 Chandra read a paper on his conclusions to the Royal Astronomical Society, the older scientist went ballistic. He condemned Chandra's work in the most devastating terms and, because of his enormous prestige, other astronomers believed him—especially given that his opponent was a fresh-faced young man who'd turned up out of nowhere.

So great was the opprobrium that Eddington heaped on his head that Chandra couldn't get a job anywhere in UK astronomy. In early 1937, however, the University of Chicago's Yerkes Observatory at Williams Bay, Wisconsin, then among the world's leading observatories, recruited him, and he remained with Chicago University for the rest of his life. In 1938 a team led by J. Robert Oppenheimer, later of Manhattan Project fame, worked out the theoretical underpinning for neutron stars in more detail. Although neutron stars wouldn't be directly detected until 1967, by Jocelyn BELL BURNELL, it was obvious to the astronomical community that Chandra was in the right of the argument, Eddington in the wrong.

However, Chandra had been so demoralized by Eddington that for nearly four decades he largely avoided anything to do with superdense stars, instead doing vital work in other areas of astrophysics; although Eddington is still referred to as the "Father of Astrophysics," it's a bit of a toss-up as to which of the two men was more important to the history of the science.

At last, in the mid-1970s, Chandra took up once more the study of black holes. He spent nearly a decade working on *The Mathematical Theory of Black Holes—A Treatise* (1983), one of the staples of the field.

Chandra was by all accounts the mildest and least vain of men, and much loved by his students. His legacy, in terms of our scientific knowledge of how stars work, is immense. ■

BUT THERE'S MORE . . .

■ The Chandra space telescope, more properly known as the Chandra X-ray Observatory (CXO), was launched in 1999 and is still functioning today. It's our primary source of information for the study of X-ray astronomy. The asteroid 1958 Chandra is named for him.

■ Arthur I. Miller's *Empire of the Stars* (2005) recounts the conflict between Eddington and Chandrasekhar; it's a gripping read. Chandra himself wrote a sort of informal scientific autobiography; he made no effort to publish it but left instructions that, should there be interest, others were free to publish it after his death. In cooperation with Chandra's widow, Lalitha, Kameshwar C. Wali edited this for publication as *A Scientific Autobiography: S. Chandrasekhar* (2010); it's heavy going for the lay reader, but worth the effort if you know the background science.

ALAN TURING

(1912–1954)

The English mathematician who cracked the Enigma machine and laid the groundwork for our understanding of artificial intelligence (AI).

A man who had saved the lives of millions of Allied personnel during World War II, Alan Turing committed suicide when he was just forty-one. The reason? He'd been persecuted by UK law because he was gay.

Alan Mathison Turing, one of the most brilliant mathematicians of the twentieth century, was born in London. A distant cousin of his mother's, the Irish physicist George Johnstone Stoney, introduced the term *electron* in 1891. His father, Julius, was a member of the (UK) Civil Service in India, and the pattern of Alan's childhood was that his parents, particularly his father, spent almost all of their time in India while Alan and his elder brother John remained in England, farmed out to family friends.

At age thirteen Alan was sent to Sherborne School in Dorset. He did poorly at most of the classroom subjects but excelled at math and science. About eighteen months after his arrival he came down with mumps, which meant he was confined to the school sanitarium for a few weeks. That illness shaped his future. Left to his own devices, he devoured science books—not least EINSTEIN's works on relativity for the lay reader.

Also at Sherborne, Alan had his first love affair, with a boy a year older than him, Christopher Morcom. The two planned to share rooms at Cambridge University's Trinity College together, but, while Christopher passed the scholarship exam for Trinity in 1929, Alan failed it. And then in 1930, while Alan was still trying to work out what to do, Christopher died from complications of tuberculosis.

Turing responded to this bereavement by passing the scholarship exam for Cambridge's King's College, where he was tutored (mentored) by the mathematician Max Newman (who would later, like Turing, do groundbreaking work during World War II in cracking German codes). It was during this period that Turing published his first important paper, "On Computable Numbers, with an Application to the *Entscheidungsproblem.*"

In 1900 the great German mathematician David Hilbert had presented the mathematical world with a set of twenty-three fundamental philosophical problems that it had yet to solve. In 1928, with most of these having been tackled, Hilbert restated three of them: to prove that math was (a) complete in itself, (b) consistent, and (c) obedient to the rule that the truth or falsehood of mathematical statements could be decided through math. Kurt Gödel soon showed that (a) and (b) were in fact false—in so doing he produced his famous incompleteness theorem—but (c) remained open.

To tackle (c), Turing envisaged a sort of infinite computer that could be programmed using a set of fairly simple rules to make decisions about (again) simple mathematical operations. Through analysis of how such a computer would behave and the logical problems it would face, he was able to show that (c) too was false. The imaginary computers he dreamed up have ever since been called Turing machines.

At about the same time Turing was working on this problem, so was the prominent US mathematician Alonzo Church, who arrived at the same conclusion through an entirely different line of reasoning. Having read Turing's paper, Church invited the young man to study under him. Turing spent a couple of years at Princeton before returning to the UK, and to Cambridge, in 1938.

His interest had turned to codes and decryption, and when war broke out in September 1939 he moved to the UK government's decryption center at Bletchley Park, where he and his team set about trying to crack the coded messages the Nazis were sending via a device called the Enigma machine. The version of this being used by the German military was regarded as virtually uncrackable, in that its periodicity[1] was about one trillion. Nevertheless, using a device that Turing invented called the Bombe—because it ticked ominously, like a time bomb!—his team was able to crack it, and from early 1943 the Allies were effectively listening in on Axis military communications.

After the war, Turing did pioneering work on electronic computers at the National Physical Laboratory in London and then, from 1948, under

---

1. The interval between a character having a particular meaning and its next appearance with that same meaning.

his old friend and tutor Max Newman, at Manchester University. It was while at Manchester that he produced another groundbreaking paper, "Computing Machinery and Intelligence" (1950). Here he put forward the idea that if you're having a conversation (written or otherwise) and you can't in any way tell if it's a machine or a human being you're dealing with, then, if it's in fact a machine, to all intents and purposes that machine is intelligent. This is one of those conclusions that initially seems an affront to reason but, the more you think about it, reveals itself to be making a very profound statement—not just about machine (artificial) intelligence, AI, but about our *own* intelligence. The idea of the Turing test, as it's now called, has not only been influential in AI studies but has also entered the popular consciousness.

One night in 1952, Turing came home to discover his house had been burgled. The burglar, a friend of a lover of Turing's, assumed the scientist wouldn't go to the cops and risk being exposed as a practicing homosexual, which was illegal at the time. That never crossed Turing's mind. The burglar went to jail, but Turing himself was charged with gross indecency. The upshot was that he was given the choice between prison and estrogen treatment ("chemical castration"). He chose the latter, but within a couple of years the misery of his situation became too much for him. He killed himself by eating an apple that he'd laced with cyanide.

The year 2012, the hundredth anniversary of Turing's birth, was declared Alan Turing Year and marked around the world by celebrations of his work. ■

BUT THERE'S MORE . . .

■ A huge but engrossing book, Andrew Hodges's *Alan Turing: The Enigma* (1983) is recommended. Based on Hodges's book, the 2014 movie *The Imitation Game*, starring Benedict Cumberbatch as Turing, covers Turing's time at Bletchley Park and, more briefly, the years afterward. It was nominated for eight Oscars, including Best Picture, Best Director, Best Actor, and Best Supporting Actress (Keira Knightley as his Bletchley colleague—and briefly fiancée—Joan Clarke). The 2011 TV movie *Codebreaker* (aka *Britain's Greatest Codebreaker*) starred Ed Stoppard as Turing. The splendid science-fiction movie *Ex Machina* (2015) is based firmly on the notion of the Turing test, some implications of which it explores.

■ Other useful books are David Leavitt's *The Man who Knew Too Much* (2006), George Dyson's *Turing's Cathedral* (2012), Harry Henderson's

Alan Turing (2011), Simon Lavington's *Alan Turing and His Contemporaries* (2012), and, perhaps most especially, Jack Copeland's gripping biography *Turing* (2014). Jim Corrigan's *Alan Turing* (2007) is for younger readers.

- On June 23, 2012, the centennial of Turing's birth, the Google Doodle depicted a Turing machine. There has been a special Turing edition of the board game Monopoly. Presented since 1966, the annual Turing Award is regarded as the highest recognition of contributions to computing science—the "Nobel Prize of computing."

- Sadly, Turing Pharmaceuticals, the company that hit the headlines in 2015 when it bought the rights to the toxoplasmosis drug Daraprim and immediately raised its price by 5,000 percent to a prohibitive $750 per pill, is also named for the great mathematician. Perhaps the connection is skill with large numbers.

JONAS SALK
(1914–1995)

The US physician who led the campaign to conquer polio.

In 1954, the year that Jonas Salk's anti-polio vaccine was given its first major field test, there were 37,476 cases of polio in the US. In 1955, the first year of large-scale vaccination, that figure dropped to 28,985, with some two hundred of those cases, including eleven deaths, being due to a faultily prepared consignment of vaccine. In 1956 there were 15,150 US cases; in 1957, 5,467; and by 1961 the figure was down to just 1,312. In 2013, thanks to vaccination, there were just 416 cases detected *worldwide*. Were it not for the activities of antivaxxer fanatics, there's a good chance that polio—like smallpox before it—would by now be completely extinct in the wild.[1] Polio vaccination has been one of the great triumphs of scientific medicine.

More properly called poliomyelitis and formerly often known as infantile paralysis, polio is a viral disease that wreaks havoc by damaging the central nervous system. After a mild fever following infection, the sufferer begins to experience paralysis of various muscles, often those that have been recently most in use. In about half the detected cases, the paralysis is long-term and perhaps permanent, and occasionally the disease kills.

In the majority of cases, the symptoms of polio infection are so slight that people don't even realize they've had the disease. This is one of polio's great dangers: people who think they've got just a mild cold may pass the disease on to others.

In 1935 a team led by Maurice Brodie attempted to vaccinate against polio using viruses that had been killed by exposure to formaldehyde; the idea was that the injected viruses, though dead, would spur the body's immune system into producing the relevant antibodies to fight off the disease. Brodie's vaccine had no effect. A few months later a similar attempt mounted by John Kolmer was yet more unsuccessful, not just

---

1. In April 2016 the World Health Organization predicted that polio might be extinct in the wild within twelve months.

being ineffective but actually causing a number of cases of the disease, some fatal. The idea of producing a vaccine from dead polio viruses was put on the back burner indefinitely.

Another difficulty was getting hold of enough polio virus for vaccine purposes. (While bacteria can be cultivated outside living tissue, viruses require it.) Breakthroughs came in the 1940s when it was discovered that viruses could be grown in chicken embryos and, a few years later, when John Enders and his team found they could grow viruses in tissue from miscarried fetuses. The way was open for the mass production of viruses.

The person who put all this together to produce the first effective polio vaccine was Jonas Edward Salk, born in New York City to Polish-Jewish immigrants; his younger brother Lee became a child psychologist who discovered that the sound of the human heartbeat relaxes babies. Jonas's first degree, in 1934 from the College of the City of New York, was in surgery; his doctorate came in 1939 from the New York University College of Medicine. By 1947 he was at the University of Pittsburgh researching viral diseases. When the new methods of cultivating viruses were developed, Salk focused on the polio virus, and on ways of deactivating it.

The first thing he discovered was that there are in fact three strains of polio virus; any effective vaccine was going to have to be able to nullify all three. He managed this, using dead viruses, by 1952. He tested his vaccine successfully on monkeys and then on children who'd already survived the disease; the children were already immune, but Salk was able to detect that the vaccine had increased the levels of antibodies in the children's blood, a sure indication it was doing its stuff. Finally he tried it on his own family and on a few children who *hadn't* already suffered the disease, and again he could measure increased antibody production.

The next step was a large-scale field trial. This came in 1954 and involved about 1.8 million US children; about 650,000 were given the vaccine and about 750,000 a placebo, with a control group of about 400,000 given nothing at all.

The results were spectacular. The vaccine seemed to be 100 percent safe and an estimated 80–90 percent effective, a figure that could easily become 100 percent with mass vaccination because of the phenomenon known as herd immunity.[1]

---

1. If just about everyone in a population is vaccinated, even if the vaccine isn't 100 percent effective (and none are), the disease can't easily get a foothold—the "herd" becomes immune. People who refuse vaccination undermine herd immunity and thereby risk not just their own lives but those of other people.

In 1955 the first anti-polio mass vaccinations began, with the results described above.

But some scientists thought Salk's method of using dead (deactivated) viruses was the wrong way to go about things. Chief among these was the Russian-American virologist Albert Sabin. He felt a dead-virus vaccine could only ever be a temporary measure, because the dead virus material would be flushed out of the system and the body would eventually wind down its antibody production. He was right: Salk's vaccine required "booster" shots every few years. Sabin's line of approach was to use living viruses that had been artificially weakened (attenuated) to the state they could stimulate antibody production but were too feeble to cause the disease. A major feature of Sabin's vaccine was that it could be taken by mouth (typically on a sugar lump); a big advantage, aside from the obvious, was that the virus then permeated the system much as a real infection would, thus mimicking far better the behavior of the full-fledged virus.

After field-testing, Sabin's attenuated-virus vaccine was introduced into the US in 1962 in place of Salk's, and for a long time it was the preferred technique. By 1979 the annual number of US infections caused by the wild polio virus had dropped to zero. There were, however, still a few annual cases of polio. These were caused, as Salk had warned they might be, by rare examples of viruses that had been insufficiently weakened; usually the person infected wasn't the one who'd been inoculated but someone else in the household who was vulnerable to the disease. HIV sufferers were especially at risk, because of the immunosuppressive drugs they were taking. In recent years, therefore, Salk's vaccine has come once more to be preferred—at least in the developed countries. In many parts of the world people have superstitious or ideological fears of doctors wielding hypodermic syringes, while religious figures can fan those fears for fascistic reasons; sometimes polio vaccinators are lynched by religious mobs. In such instances, an innocuous-looking sugar lump can be the better option.

Salk never made any money out of his vaccine, and he devoted his later life to aiding his fellow humans while showing little interest in personal gain. In 1963, with the backing of the National Foundation for Infantile Paralysis (now called the March of Dimes), he was able to open the Salk Institute for Biological Studies, in San Diego; the institute has produced a number of Nobel laureates. Salk worked there until the end of his life, conducting cancer research and trying (lucklessly) to find a vaccine for AIDS. ■

BUT THERE'S MORE . . .

■ Jeffrey Kluger's *Splendid Solution* (2004) is a highly recommended account of Salk and his work. Also recommended are Richard Carter's *Breakthrough: The Saga of Jonas Salk* (1966) and David M. Oshinsky's *Polio: An American Story* (2005).

■ On October 28, 2014, which would have been Salk's hundredth birthday, he was honored with a Google Doodle, and in 2006 the US Post Office issued a 63¢ stamp commemorating him as well as an 87¢ stamp honoring Sabin; polio vaccination had earlier been commemorated on a 1999 33¢ stamp, on the back of which was an inscription specifically acknowledging Salk's role.

■ Salk's second wife, the artist Françoise Gilot, had been Picasso's mistress and "muse" from 1944 to 1953, having two children with the great artist.

JAMES LOVELOCK
(b. 1919)

The UK inventor and environmentalist whose Gaia hypothesis gave us a whole new way of looking at the planet, and our interactions with it.

Very few scientists have produced a theory that completely changes the way we look at our world. The UK environmentalist James Lovelock's Gaia hypothesis, advanced in the 1970s and refined in its details ever since, tells us we should regard the Earth as a living organism, one made up of countless components that encompass rocks and oceans and air and living creatures (including us), all interacting in enormously complex ways—much as our own bodies operate, in fact. And, just as our bodies tend to self-repair, the living Earth automatically seeks configurations of stability, of balance. If a severe imbalance arises, the world will shift to a new configuration. While each configuration will contain its own eco-system, there's no guarantee that any particular life-form will survive the transition from one ecosystem to the next. In fact, transitions tend to be characterized by mass extinctions of earlier species. In other words, you really don't want to be around during one of those periods of transition.

Although, despite Lovelock's qualifications, the Gaia hypothesis was initially greeted by many commentators as just a sort of hippie-dippie, New Age, feel-good piece of fancy for the tree-hugging community, it's now widely regarded as a theory, in the scientific meaning of that word.

James Ephraim Lovelock was born to a working-class family in Letchworth, about 40 miles (65 km) north of London. From very early he showed an aptitude for science, and his highly intelligent mother, who'd been deprived by circumstances of a proper schooling herself, pushed for him to get the best education he could. Unfortunately, the young Jim didn't get on well with the discipline of school and, even after he'd been persuaded not to play hooky the whole time, still refused to do any homework.

Even so, he eventually gained a degree in chemistry in 1941 from Manchester University and in 1948 a PhD in medicine from the London School of Hygiene and Tropical Medicine. Betweentimes, he worked as an assistant at the National Institute for Medical Research, investigating infectious diseases in wartime London. It was during this period that it began to be brought home to him that everything on Earth is interrelated. Over the years, that initial intuition flowered to become the Gaia hypothesis.

Throughout his life, Lovelock has been a very ingenious gadgeteer. One of his numerous inventions, from 1957, is the electron capture detector, a device used to detect trace quantities of chemicals in gas chromatography. The device played an important part in our discovery that CFCs[1] were lingering in the atmosphere far longer than anticipated and that their breakdown products in the upper atmosphere were damaging the ozone layer.

In the early 1960s Lovelock did consultancy work at NASA's Jet Propulsion Laboratory, where people were trying to devise experiments to detect life on Mars when probes were sent there. Lovelock pointed out that the experiments they were planning might be fine for finding Earth-type life, but there was no reason to believe any hypothetical Martian life was anything like Earth-type.

Asked how we could find life that *wasn't* like ours, he produced several ideas, most importantly that we should be able to tell from a planet's atmosphere whether or not there's much in the way of life there.

Life affects its surroundings. One reason the Earth's atmosphere is such a dynamic system is that the planet is covered with life. Plants exchange carbon dioxide for oxygen. Animals do it the other way round. Organic matter decomposes. Vegetation cover changes the reflectivity of surfaces. And so on. A planet with a very static (high-entropy) atmosphere, by contrast, is very unlikely to harbor significant life. And Mars is such a planet.

So far, Lovelock's diagnosis seems correct, although the tests that probes have done on Mars have necessarily been very limited. It's still possible we'll find some low-level life there, but the prospects aren't good.

Once again, this work contributed to his formulation of the Gaia hypothesis, concerning which he began publishing scientific papers in the early 1970s, culminating in the book *Gaia* (1979). The name Gaia (or Gaea) is that of the Greek mother goddess, the embodiment of the Earth; the novelist William Golding suggested giving the name to Lovelock's hypothesis.

As early as the 1980s, Lovelock was one of the first to raise the alarm about climate change, pointing out that human activities were impeding

---

1.   Chlorofluorocarbons, chemicals that had applications in a wide variety of everyday devices, from aerosol sprays to fridges.

Earth's ability to maintain stable, life-supporting conditions. He envisaged that by the year 2100 the only fertile areas on Earth would be at the poles, areas capable of supporting at most a few million human beings. Since then he's backtracked a little, saying that deleterious effects of greenhouse-gas emissions from fossil fuels are progressing more slowly than he'd expected, so we have more time than he'd thought to take actions to forestall global disaster. Others, like James HANSEN, disagree.

Among the forms of energy Lovelock supports as replacement for fossil fuels is nuclear power, an advocacy that shocks many of his fellow environmentalists. He points out that it's extremely safe by comparison with fossil fuels, which claim millions of lives annually through air pollution alone.

Lovelock has been widely honored within the scientific community; he became a Fellow of the Royal Society in 1974 (the same year as Stephen HAWKING) and received the Wollaston Medal in 2006. Perhaps surprisingly in light of his lifelong socialist views, born from his early Quaker ideals, he accepted a CBE[1] from Margaret Thatcher's government; she had originally trained as a scientist, and although the two were politically at opposite poles, she recognized the importance of his warnings on climate change.

For most of his professional career, Lovelock has worked as an independent scientist, unattached to any commercial organization or academic institution. He's been able to do this because of the proceeds from his many inventions, the royalties from his books, and the hefty cash bonuses that have come with several of his awards. He now lives in rural Devon, in the southwest of England, with his second wife, Sandy, to whom all his books are dedicated. ∎

BUT THERE'S MORE ...

■ Lovelock has written a string of books on the Gaia hypothesis and related matters. He has also written an autobiography, *Homage to Gaia* (2000). *James Lovelock* (2009), by John and Mary Gribbin, is a very entertaining popular biography.

■ You can find lectures by and interviews with Lovelock all over YouTube, as well as attempted takedowns by the likes of Alex Jones. The protagonist of the science-fiction novel *Lovelock* (1994), by Orson Scott Card and Kathryn H. Kidd, is named for him. Lovelock himself cowrote an SF novel with Michael Allaby, *The Greening of Mars* (1984).

---

1. Commander of the British Empire, one of the honors awarded annually by the UK government.

ROSALIND FRANKLIN
(1920–1958)

*The X-ray crystallographer upon whose work Crick and Watson
based their conclusions about the structure of DNA.*

Rosalind Elsie Franklin was just thirty-seven when she died. The cause
of her death was ovarian cancer, and it's believed this was a consequence of her frequent exposure to X-rays during the course of her research. The irony is that her most important and intensive work was
on elucidating the structure of DNA, the complex molecule that's the
chemical building block of life. She died because of her efforts to find
out how life works.

Born in London, she graduated in physical chemistry from Cambridge
University's Newnham College for Women in 1941, by which time
World War II was raging. For some months she did postgraduate studies at Cambridge, also serving as an air-raid warden; she then took a job
at the British Coal Utilisation Research Association doing work that
related to the war effort, since it enabled better designs for the charcoal
filters in gas masks. It also linked to her postgraduate research.

On receiving her PhD in 1945 she went to work in Paris, again on
coal. She was finally lured back to London by a post at King's College,
where she was to work with the New Zealand–born biophysicist Maurice
Wilkins and his assistant Raymond Gosling on attempts to deduce the
structure of the DNA molecule. Unfortunately, there was a bureaucratic
communications failure: Wilkins was led to believe Franklin was to work
under him while Franklin believed she was supposed to be working au-
tonomously. The diffident Wilkins couldn't understand why Franklin
reacted so aggressively to instructions while Franklin assumed Wilkins
was being a chauvinist pig when he tried to boss her around.

What Franklin was doing was taking raw DNA samples that Wilkins
had obtained and trying to analyze them using the techniques of X-ray
crystallography. Wilkins and a couple of colleagues had become reasonably certain that the DNA molecule had a helical structure, but further
than that they couldn't go. Franklin began X-ray photographing DNA

strands in the presence of moisture and discovered that, under high humidities, the molecules stretched out a bit, so their structure became a little more evident.

"A little more" is the key phrase. The problems facing Franklin were that those X-ray crystallography techniques she was using were designed for investigating crystals, not squishy organic molecules, and that interpreting the fuzzy patterns that showed in the photographs was an incredibly finicky business.

Others were in pursuit of DNA's structure. One was Linus Pauling at Caltech. There was also a pair at the Cavendish Laboratory in Cambridge, Francis Crick and James Watson. The rivalry among these three groups was complicated by the fact that Wilkins and Crick were good friends.

By early 1953 Franklin had become sick of the poisonous atmosphere at her King's College workplace, and had accepted a position doing unrelated research at Birkbeck College, also part of the University of London. For reasons that were likely innocent, Wilkins showed Crick and Watson one of Franklin's X-ray photos, perhaps the clearest she'd managed to make. Although the Cambridge pair didn't have the skills to interpret the photo, they knew enough that they could see the molecule's helical structure.

As if that weren't enough, because Franklin was preparing to shift jobs, she was required to produce a report for the Medical Research Council summarizing her work at King's. In this report she included the calculations she'd done of the dimensions of the DNA molecule. One of the committee to whom she submitted this report was the molecular biologist Max Perutz, who just happened to be the head of the Cavendish Laboratory's Molecular Biology Unit, where Crick and Watson were working. Again probably in all innocence, Perutz gave his two colleagues a copy of Franklin's report.

Largely—almost entirely—on the basis of these two contributions from Franklin, passed along not just without her permission but without even her knowledge, Crick and Watson were, by the end of February 1953, able to construct the double-helix model for the DNA molecule that we know so well today. Once the structure had been elucidated, it became clear how the DNA molecule could serve as a "copying mechanism" to transmit information from one generation to the next, and how faults in the copying process could account for the sorts of variations (mutations) that underpinned evolution. The discovery validated not just Darwin's theory that the mechanism for evolution was natural selection but also Mendel's ideas on heredity.

The trouble was that Franklin's role went almost completely unmentioned. When Crick, Watson, and Wilkins received the Nobel Prize in Physiology or Medicine in 1962 for their DNA work, there was no question of Franklin sharing it with them, because by then she was dead and Nobel prizes aren't awarded posthumously. But there's no real reason to believe that her contribution would have been recognized by the Nobel Committee even had she still been alive, so much had she been written out of the story.

In his best-selling book about the discovery, *The Double Helix* (1968), Watson performed a hatchet job on Franklin. He maliciously called her "Rosy," a diminutive she hated, and described her in terms beyond unflattering: "[I]t was quite easy to imagine her the product of an unsatisfied mother who unduly stressed the desirability of professional careers that could save bright girls from marriages to dull men . . . [G]iven her belligerent moods, it would be very difficult for Maurice [Wilkins] to maintain a dominant position that would allow him to think unhindered about DNA . . . The thought could not be avoided that the best home for a feminist was in another person's lab"—and so on.

Partly because the treatment of her in Watson's book was so hateful, interest in Franklin's role grew, and it became evident that she herself had been well on the way to deducing DNA's double-helical structure— that, left alone, she might have got there within a matter of months, even weeks. She was, however, in obedience to her training, working methodically toward that conclusion, whereas Crick and Watson felt free to trust in their intuition and make a leap in the dark.

Franklin was not condemned to remain in the shadows for as long as, for example, Émilie DU CHÂTELET, but her decades-long exile from history is shameful enough. Luckily her pivotal role in elucidating the science of life is now more clearly seen. ■

BUT THERE'S MORE . . .

■ Brenda Maddox's 2002 biography *Rosalind Franklin* is the best book on Franklin I've come across. Jane Polcovar's *Rosalind Franklin and the Structure of Life* (2006), for younger readers, is good too.

■ If you're lucky, your local library may have a DVD of the Nova documentary *DNA: Secret of Photo 51* (2003), narrated by Sigourney Weaver, which is all about Franklin and her work. The play *Photograph 51* by Anna Ziegler, covering similar territory, ran in small theaters in the US before opening in London's West End in September 2015 with Nicole Kidman in the lead role.

STEPHEN HAWKING
(b. 1942)

The UK theoretical cosmologist who's become a household name the world around.

Stephen Hawking is one of science's rare rock stars. Like EINSTEIN decades before him, he has one of the most recognized faces in the world. He features on magazine covers. Movies have been made based on his life—one of them, *The Theory of Everything* (2014), won a stack of Oscar nominations. And, again like Einstein, this is all the more remarkable in that most of the general public can understand little or nothing of the work he's doing.

Stephen William Hawking was born on January 8, 1942—an auspicious date for a cosmologist because it happened to be GALILEO's three hundredth birthday. He grew up a fairly normal boy; although obviously bright, he didn't excel at school. In his final school years he wanted to specialize in math—because that was what all the cool kids were doing—but his father insisted he focus on chemistry instead, on the grounds that there weren't many jobs for mathematicians but industry always wanted chemists.

At least the chemistry course involved a certain amount of math . . . and, surprisingly, that was the last formal training in math that Hawking ever received. All the rest of his math education he picked up as he went along, mainly from books.

He got a scholarship to University College, Oxford, in 1959 and spent the next three years doing as little work as possible. He joined the boating club, and because he was quite young to be at university and anyway fairly slight, was in some demand as a cox.

Armed with a decent degree in physics, in 1962 he went to Cambridge University's Trinity Hall to do postgraduate work. By now his interests had focused on cosmology. It was a time when most other physicists were attracted by quantum mechanics, which seemed to be where all the excitement was happening; Hawking, however, reckoned cosmology was due for a stir of its own, since the ramifications of Einstein's general theory of relativity hadn't yet been properly explored. In particular, having encountered the astrophysicist Jayant Narlikar, he was hoping to work alongside Narlikar's internationally renowned colleague Fred Hoyle.

Largely because so much of his work has since been overturned, it's hard today to realize what a titan of a figure Hoyle was in those days. He was the person who gave the Big Bang theory its name, although he actually did so disparagingly. A wonderful lecturer,[1] he was—along with Herman Bondi and Thomas Gold—one of the major proponents of the steady state theory, which attempted to explain the expansion of the universe not through a major eruption into existence of spacetime, billions of years ago, but through the constant emergence of tiny quantities of new stuff in interstellar space. (That's why the theory is sometimes called continuous creation.) The debate between the Big Bang and steady state theories raged for decades, until the discovery of the cosmic microwave background in 1964 settled the argument in favor of the Big Bang. Later Hoyle, often with Chandra Wickramasinghe, promoted the idea that the seeds of life formed in outer space and were brought to Earth by comets,[2] suggested that *Archaeopteryx* was a fake, and lots more. It's been said of Hoyle that much of the dramatic progress made in mid-twentieth-century astronomy and cosmology came largely from efforts to "prove Fred wrong"!

Hawking was disappointed that, instead of Hoyle, the person he was going to be working with was the brilliant physicist Dennis Sciama. In retrospect he recognized how lucky he was. Not only was Sciama immensely supportive of him, but Hawking soon realized that the steady state theory, with which he'd have been working under Hoyle, couldn't possibly be right. Even so, he regularly attended lectures given at King's College, London, by Hoyle's co-conspirator, Bondi.

A GRIM DIAGNOSIS, BUT WORK CONTINUES

Around this time, Hawking finally went to the doctor about his increasing clumsiness and slurredness of speech. After a barrage of tests, in 1963 he was diagnosed with amyotrophic lateral sclerosis (ALS)[3] and given two years to live. Not long before, he'd met a friend of his sister's, Jane Wilde, and the two had fallen in love. Despite Stephen's gloomy prognosis, they married in July 1965, soon after he'd been accepted for a

---

1. I once saw him lecture, and he held a packed hall absolutely enthralled . . . even though just about everyone there disagreed with what he was saying.

2. The theory is technically called panspermia, and forms of it were proposed long before Hoyle introduced his version.

3. Also known as motor neurone disease and as Lou Gehrig's disease.

research fellowship at Caius College, Cambridge.

In the latter part of the 1960s and into the 1970s, much of Hawking's work was done in collaboration with physicist Roger Penrose. The pair began by looking at the properties of black holes and in particular singularities, the point-size locations where the laws of physics break down and where spacetime is crushed out of existence. Ordinarily a singularity is shielded within the confines of a black hole, but for a while it was thought that under certain circumstances there could be such a thing as a "naked" singularity—that is, one visible to the rest of the universe. Hawking and Penrose disproved this possibility, and showed it was likely the universe was born from a singularity rather than from the hypothetical "cosmic egg" proposed by earlier cosmologists.

Hawking proposed a "law" of black-hole behavior: that a black hole's event horizon (its "outer surface") can never get smaller. He strongly supported the hypothesis that "black holes have no hair"—that all the attributes of whatever goes into a black hole are lost forever, so the complete description of a black hole comprises just its mass, rotation, and electrical charge. By the mid-1970s, however, having been persuaded by Russian colleagues that HEISENBERG's uncertainty principle dictates that rotating black holes must emit particles, Hawking repeated his earlier work and came to the conclusion that indeed, black holes *do* have "hair"; they must emit a steady trickle of radiation that, while small, will eventually, over perhaps billions of years, deplete the black hole until it evaporates entirely. (He'd therefore also disproved his own "law" about event horizons never getting smaller.) There was initially a lot of skepticism over Hawking radiation, as it came to be called, but the consensus is now in its favor.

Hawking was elected a Fellow of the Royal Society in 1974 (the same year as James LOVELOCK). At the time, he was working at Caltech, where he'd accepted a visiting professorship. While there he formed a strong friendship with physicist Kip Thorne that lasts to this day; the wild bets between the two of them (and others) over various physical phenomena have become legendary, as have the prizes—such as a year's subscription to *Penthouse*.

In 1979 Hawking was elected Lucasian Professor in Mathematics at Cambridge, filling the same chair once held by NEWTON.

POPULARIZING SCIENCE

While in Switzerland to visit CERN in 1985, Hawking suffered an attack of pneumonia so severe the doctors suggested switching off life support.

Jane was determined he'd pull through, though, and he was flown home to Cambridge, to Addenbrooke's Hospital. The doctors there eventually decided that to save him they had to perform a tracheotomy. A side effect of this was that Hawking lost the last of his powers of speech. Although his ALS had already reduced his speech to the point that only those who knew him well could work out what he was saying, this was a cruel blow. Since then he's had to rely on various pieces of clever technology in order to form words letter by letter—currently he has a sensor in his spectacles that detects movements of his cheek. Once he has the words complete on his computer screen, he can use similar means to send them to the speech synthesizer that produces the "voice" for which he has now become famous.

This process is of course incredibly laborious; he reckons he can create three words a minute on average, four a minute on a good day. And that's for normal prose. Scientific equations are far more difficult. Here he's helped, though, by the fact that, from quite soon after the onset of the ALS, he got into the habit of thinking of equations pictorially, rather than in written form. (Einstein once said much the same—see page 162.) He still has to go through the toilsome process when communicating those equations to others, but at least he doesn't have to do so when working things out for himself.

He'd decided in 1982 to write a popular book about cosmology—one that might be found in airport terminals rather than in dusty libraries. The result eventually appeared in 1988, and Hawking has widely acknowledged the help of his editor at Bantam, Peter Guzzardi, in helping him craft the final version. This book is *A Brief History of Time*, and it astonished everyone by being a massive best seller. He has written other popular books since, including a concise autobiography.

By now his relationship with Jane was fraying. Around the time of their wedding he'd been given just a couple of years to live. Of course, he's gloriously proved this prognosis awry—by about half a century, and counting—but there was always the sense for Jane that he might pop off at any time, and this grew more acute after the incident at CERN and the subsequent tracheotomy. In the late 1970s she'd become friendly with a church organist, Jonathan Jones, and by the mid-1980s that friendship had considerably warmed. Jane put it to her husband that, should anything happen to him, she'd want to marry Jones, who'd not only be a husband to her but a father to the children. The net result was that Jones moved into the Hawking home.

In due course the situation became intolerable. While Jane's affections swung to Jones, Hawking was becoming fond of Elaine Mason, one of the three nurses who took shifts in giving him round-the-clock care. Hawking moved out of the family home in 1990, and he and Jane were divorced in 1995. A few months later he married Elaine (they've since divorced), while Jane married Jones.

TIME TRAVEL AND OTHER DELIGHTS

All through this period, Hawking had been examining the possibility of time travel. Once again, his interest had been spurred by Kip Thorne, who had suggested time travel might be possible through wormholes.

In ordinary spacetime time travel is impossible; so is faster-than-light travel. However, spacetime isn't a simple flat surface, as envisaged by scientists from EUCLID to Newton and beyond. As Einstein showed, spacetime is a curved surface. It's also quite a complicated one. It's theoretically likely there are structures linking different areas of spacetime that would otherwise be widely separated. This idea is, of course, a wonderful freebie for science-fiction writers and moviemakers, who can send their starships halfway across the universe in a matter of hours.

Such a journey wouldn't violate the laws of physics and the velocity of light. In terms of normal spacetime, however, you've definitely gotten from one place to another far faster than light could have managed the trip, plodding across spacetime. According to relativity, however, if you can travel faster than light (which is what you'd be doing, effectively, by jaunting through a wormhole . . . even though you wouldn't; who said physics was easy to get your head around?), you're also traveling backward in time. If, now, you came *back* through your wormhole, would it be possible to arrive here before you'd left?

The idea's a violation of all common sense, but then so is much of modern physics and cosmology. That doesn't mean they're not right; common sense isn't necessarily the best lens through which to perceive the universe.[1] Hawking spent some time theoretically analyzing the problem. As a science-fiction fan since boyhood, he was perfectly aware of all the paradoxes writers had explored when dealing with time-travel scenarios—like the parent paradox. (If you went back in time and killed one of your parents before you were conceived, how could you now exist to go back in time to kill the parent?)

Hawking realized there were free-will issues involved, too. We think

---

1. The physicist Richard Feynman once said that, if you think you understand quantum mechanics, that's a clear indication you don't.

of everything as moving forward through time, from the past, now over with and thus immutable, to the future, yet to come about and thereby malleable. Again, that matches common sense, but it may not be true. If you look at spacetime as a four-dimensional structure, with time as merely one of those dimensions, then in a very real sense the future has, just like the past, "already happened." It's done and dusted. We just haven't got there yet.

In the end, Hawking concluded that time travel via wormhole couldn't be viable. In practical terms, it wasn't viable anyway. If wormholes exist—as they may well do—they're likely to be of extraordinarily small "diameter." There's not much fun in traveling backward in time if you arrive in the form of a stream of fundamental particles.

Another important component of Hawking's thinking is the so-called Many Worlds hypothesis—which he describes as the "sum over histories." Born from quantum mechanics, the Many Worlds hypothesis reflects the idea that in every instant, in every tiniest cranny of the universe, there are countless "choices" for what might happen next. A uranium atom might decay, or it might not decay. Stephen Hawking might die of pneumonia in 1985, or he might not. But what if all those possible outcomes were realized? In that case, every single instant in the universe's history would spawn a near-infinite number of alternative universes, each equally "real." That means, of course, that there must be a near-infinite number of ever so slightly different *yous*, each reading a copy of this book that's infinitesimally different from the one in the "next" universe!

Hawking's "sum over histories" version of this is actually even more interesting. Rather than envisaging a near-infinite number of possible *futures*, what it's saying is that all the possible *past* histories of the universe are equally valid. If that doesn't blow your mind, nothing will.

Hawking has frequently observed that the universe is a very dangerous place to live, and that our technological civilization brings with it hazards of its own. Among possible species-exterminating dangers he's identified are asteroid impacts (remember what happened to the dinosaurs), artificial intelligence (it may well be that the end point of human evolution is machine "life-forms"), extraterrestrials (if they're more advanced than us and see us as a threat or just a nuisance, well, forget about the heroics in *Independence Day*), and even the Higgs boson.

This last, Hawking said, tongue in cheek, "has the worrisome feature that it might become metastable at energies above 100bn giga-electron-volts." Such instability would cause "vacuum decay" that would spread through the universe; since it would do so at the speed of light, we'd know nothing at all about it until it hit us. To people who were worried that CERN's Large Hadron Collider might trigger such a catastrophe, Hawking pointed out that an accelerator capable of 100bn GEV would be bigger than the planet; such a project, he added wryly, is "unlikely to be funded in the present economic climate."

Hawking's sense of humor is not so much famous as notorious, and it's evident in his writings and TV appearances. Clearly, inside that crumpled body, there beats the eager heart of a ten-year-old. ■

BUT THERE'S MORE . . .

■ There are plenty of books and documentaries about Hawking and his work; consult the catalogue of your local library for a deluge. Of particular interest are *My Brief History* (2013), by the man himself, and two overlapping memoirs by Jane Hawking: *Music to Move the Stars* (1999) and *Travelling to Infinity* (2007). The latter book was famously filmed as the Oscar-winning *The Theory of Everything* (2014), with Eddie Redmayne as Stephen and Felicity Jones as Jane. Another movie based on his life is *Hawking* (2004), which has Benedict Cumberbatch in the title role. *Hawking* (aka *Hawking: A Brief History of Mine*; 2013) is a documentary based on Hawking's memoir.

■ Hawking has written a number of books, of which some are aimed at a general audience. *The Grand Design* (2010), with Leonard Mlodinow, discusses theories of the universe with a particular focus on M-theory; its lucid explanation of the physics of how a universe can emerge from nothing, without any requirement for a creator, generated howls of outrage from the usual sources.

■ Hawking's massive *God Created the Integers* (2005) collects original writings by mathematicians from Euclid to TURING. Some of these can be pretty hard going for those not versed in math, but Hawking's lengthy introductions to the life and work of each mathematician are invaluable (although again often requiring a fair amount of math). His earlier *On the Shoulders of Giants* (2002) performs the same service for COPERNICUS, Galileo, KEPLER, Newton and Einstein.

■ He has also written science-based children's fiction (with daughter Lucy) and a bunch of scholarly works.

■ The asteroid 7672 Hawking was discovered in 1995.

JOCELYN BELL BURNELL
(b. 1943)

The astronomer who made the first discovery of pulsars.

In 1967 a team of Cambridge astronomers began to wonder if they'd picked up signals from an extraterrestrial civilization.

Susan Jocelyn Bell was born in Belfast, Northern Ireland, and raised in Lurgan, County Armagh. Her father had been an architect on the Armagh Observatory, and the staff there encouraged the young Jocelyn's interest in astronomy. In 1965 she went to study for her PhD at New Hall, University of Cambridge, where she worked under the supervision of Professor Antony Hewish. The subject of her PhD was quasars, and she spent her first two years at Cambridge building a highly sensitive radio telescope to detect these enigmatic sources.[1]

One day in July 1967 she noticed an unusual radio source—a piece of "scruff," as she called it—in the charts of the previous night's observations. What was interesting was that it was pulsing rapidly—once every 1.337 seconds—and that it was in the night sky in the direction away from the Sun. She and her team were accustomed to seeing fluctuations in the signals from quasars, but these were caused by the solar wind (the flow of particles from the Sun) and thus were observed in the direction of the Sun, not away from it.

Analyzing the signals from this new source, she at first thought it must be some piece of radio interference from a source either on the Earth or nearby—a communications satellite, perhaps. But it soon became obvious the source was among the stars. One possibility Bell and her team considered was that they'd picked up an artificial signal from an alien civilization—they even dubbed the source LGM–1, the "LGM" standing for "Little Green Men"! For fear of the press going berserk, Bell and Hewish kept their lips buttoned on this.

---

1. They're now known to occur when two galaxies collide. The cores of the galaxies collide too, and form either a vast black hole or a pair of huge black holes in close orbit around each other. Either way, there's an extraordinary release of energy—a quasar is many times brighter than all the stars of our own galaxy put together.

Over the next few months Bell discovered several similar, rapidly pulsing radio sources. It became evident to her and to Hewish that what she'd discovered was a new type of star, which the press immediately dubbed a pulsar.[1] Soon after the announcement of the discovery, US astronomer Thomas Gold demonstrated that what they'd detected were actually rapidly rotating neutron stars, a class of celestial objects first predicted way back in the 1930s by Subrahmanyan CHANDRASEKHAR.

At the ends of their lives, stars of similar size to our Sun collapse to form small, dense stars known as white dwarfs. Stars somewhat larger than our Sun die in a supernova explosion, and their cores may form a white dwarf but more likely will collapse to form a neutron star, in which the matter is so closely crammed together that a mass greater than the Sun's is all packed into a sphere just a few miles across. (The end product of the collapse of even bigger stars is a black hole.)

Just as spinning skaters spin faster when they pull in their arms, neutron stars rotate far more rapidly than the stars that gave birth to them. They also tend to have very strong magnetic fields, and so emit high-energy beams of electromagnetic radiation. If the neutron star happens to be oriented in just the right way, we see rapid pulses of energy. It's rather as if we were watching a lighthouse's beam as the lamp rotates.

Bell's discovery was announced in a paper in *Nature* in February 1968. A few days earlier, Hewish discussed the findings in a public seminar, and the media, as predicted, went wild. Obviously the LGM scenario was given a lot of coverage, even though the scientists involved knew it was a nonstarter. As for Bell herself . . . well, as she later described it,

> I had my photograph taken standing on a bank, sitting on a bank, standing on a bank examining bogus records, sitting on a bank examining bogus records. Meanwhile the journalists were asking relevant questions like was I taller than or not quite as tall as Princess Margaret, and how many boyfriends did I have at the time?

Hewish, as Bell's project supervisor, was listed first among the authors of the paper, with Bell second. This became controversial a few years later, in 1974, when Hewish was awarded the Nobel Physics Prize—shared

---

1.   It's a confusing term, probably born out of the fact that the astronomical cause célèbre at the time was quasars. Quasars and pulsars are entirely different kettles of fish, but tell that to a journalist in search of a cheesy headline.

with another UK astronomer, Sir Martin Ryle—for his work leading up to the discovery of pulsars. Many people, both among the general public and in the astronomical community, felt the prize should have been shared with Bell. She herself, to her great credit, is not one of them, pointing out that, as her supervisor, Hewish was ultimately responsible for the success or failure of her work.

Not long after the announcement of her discovery, she married Martin Burnell and adopted the style Jocelyn Bell Burnell. (They divorced in 1993.)

A lifelong Quaker, Bell Burnell has made spectacular contributions to astrophysics and has racked up a whole scad of distinguished international scientific awards. But she'll always be remembered as the young scientist, then still in her mid-twenties, who discovered the first pulsars and for a few weeks had to live with the possibility that she'd detected the first known radio messages from ET. ■

BUT THERE'S MORE . . .

■ Bell Burnell has coedited (with Maurice Riordan) an anthology of poems inspired by astronomy: *Dark Matter: Poems of Space* (2008). You can download for free a PDF or MP3 of her 2013 James Backhouse Lecture, "A Quaker Astronomer Reflects: Can a Scientist Also Be Religious?," from www.quakers.org.au/page/29/.
■ Asteroid 25275 Jocelynbell is named in her honor.

JAMES HANSEN
(b. 1941)

The US atmospheric scientist who alerted the world to the dangers of climate change.

On June 23, 1988, a rather diffident-seeming scientist, the director of NASA's Goddard Institute for Space Studies (GISS), gave disturbing testimony to the US Senate Committee on Energy and Natural Resources. That scientist was James Hansen, and the news he brought to the committee was grim. NASA had concluded, with 99 percent confidence—about as close as you get to cast-iron certainty in science—that the observed warming of the atmosphere in recent decades was the result of a greenhouse effect created by increased levels of greenhouse gases, notably carbon dioxide and methane, in the atmosphere. The situation was already becoming critical in terms of dangerous climate change, he reported. Those gases were the product of human activity, particularly the burning of fossil fuels. We had a stark choice: change our habits or face disaster.

James Edward Hansen was born in rural Iowa to a farming family. His interest in science was spurred by the launch of Sputnik 1, the first artificial satellite, in 1957. At the University of Iowa he attained, in succession, a BA in physics and math (1963), an MS in astronomy (1965), and a PhD in physics (1967). He was lucky enough to study under the space scientist James Van Allen, the discoverer of the Van Allen belts— belts of charged particles orbiting the Earth.[1] It was Van Allen who got the young Jim Hansen interested in the atmosphere of the planet Venus, and this topic ended up being the subject of Hansen's PhD thesis.

Hansen then joined GISS. Over the next decade or more he continued to study the Venusian atmosphere and, with colleagues, was able

---

1. My favorite Van Allen story concerns microwave ovens. In the early 1970s there was an irrational panic that these ovens might give their users radiation sickness. This was potentially bad news for the manufacturers, one of whom was based in Amana, Iowa. Step forward proud Iowan James Van Allen, who in 1973 told the world that he'd "sit down on my Amana Radarange for a solid year while it is in full operation, with no apprehension as to my safety." He was believed.

to establish that the famous ever-shrouding clouds of the planet were likely to be largely of sulfuric acid in suspension. By then it had become clear that Venus is an inhospitable, implacably hot world—Carl Sagan famously described it as the closest known approximation to Hell—and that the reason is almost certainly that, at some early stage, Venus fell victim to a runaway greenhouse effect. The composition of its atmosphere is over 95 percent carbon dioxide (CO_2), the gas whose presence in our own atmosphere has been known since the late nineteenth century to be the primary reason why the surface of our planet is warmer than can be explained simply by incoming heat from the Sun.

Hansen was responsible for one of the experiments aboard NASA's *Pioneer Venus* probe, but even as the craft made its approach to the planet he decided his research efforts would be better directed toward the state of the atmosphere on our home world, about which he was becoming increasingly concerned. Clearly we were adding CO_2 to the atmosphere at unprecedented rates through burning fossil fuels. Hansen decided it was important to study the effect this could have on the world's climate.

During the 1980s he and colleagues at GISS conducted a succession of analyses of global temperatures, based on records from meteorological stations that went back in some instances as far as 1880. They discovered there was a strong correlation between global surface temperatures and greenhouse-gas emissions. The lower atmosphere—the important bit, because it's the bit we live in—was and is unquestionably getting warmer. Increasingly sophisticated analyses done since then have confirmed that the temperature trend has been relentlessly upward.

Although the transcript was watered down for political reasons, Hansen's 1988 testimony to the US Senate Committee on Energy and Natural Resources put the subject of global warming onto the map of political and popular awareness. Unfortunately, the popular understanding was that climate change would involve just lots of droughts and record temperatures. What wasn't widely understood, despite the efforts of Hansen and Senator Al Gore, is that a warmer atmosphere is more dynamic and holds more water vapor, so we could expect heavier downpours, flooding, more violent hurricanes, and even (when they happened) heavier snowfalls.

After 1989 Hansen concluded that public communication wasn't really his forte, and he decided to stick to science. Over the next decade or so, however, he became increasingly concerned that, even though the sympathetic and science-savvy Gore was now vice president, political deadlock and obstructionism—boosted by corporate-funded campaigns of misinformation on the topic—were ensuring that nothing was actually being done to counter the danger.

In 2001 Hansen gave evidence to the Climate Task Force set up by a new vice president, Dick Cheney, and it was obvious to him that the political mood was in favor of pretending that climate change didn't exist, or wasn't a problem, or that the science wasn't yet settled—anything to avoid the responsibility to take action.

Over the next few years, various government scientists complained that their reports were being edited for political reasons before release to the public. In 2003 a draft report on the environment prepared by the EPA was heavily redacted to remove almost all reference to climate change. In March 2005 Rick Piltz of the US Climate Change Science Program resigned in a storm of protest that the program's reports were being censored by a government lawyer, a former (and future) lobbyist for the petroleum industry. A year or two later Hansen joined the clamor, complaining that, in the wake of a December 2005 address he'd given to the American Geophysical Union, his publications were being revised by political appointees at NASA.

By the end of the decade Hansen was becoming ever more vocal about the dangers of climate change. He has been arrested several times during demonstrations related to increased use of fossil fuels; the lecture he gave on accepting Dickinson College's annual Priestley Award was called "White House Arrest and the Climate Crisis." In April 2013 Hansen retired from GISS in order to concentrate on climate activism and to take up a position as director of the Program on Climate Science, Awareness and Solutions at Columbia University. As he put it in May 2014, "It's time to stop waffling so much."

Hansen has little faith in proposals to decrease greenhouse-gas emissions based on cap-and-trade, whereby corporations and countries have in effect to buy permission to pollute; the idea is that the cost will provide an incentive to drive emissions down. He prefers a fee-and-dividend system, whereby consumers would pay a very heavy levy when purchasing fuel, whether in the gas station or on the electricity bill. This levy would then be returned to consumers in equal dividends every (say) three months, so the person in the gas-guzzler would get the same dividend as the driver with a high-mileage vehicle, or even the cyclist. The problem with such a method is, obviously, that succeeding governments can pervert it; but the same is true of cap-and-trade-based methods.

Because of his activities, Hansen has frequently been accused of having a leftist agenda. In early 2006 he was driven to release a "Statement of Political Inclinations": "These claims are nonsense. Political inclinations should have no impact on scientific analyses . . . I can be accurately described as moderately conservative."

That second sentence is part of what science is all about. ■

BUT THERE'S MORE . . .

- One of the best ways to learn about Hansen's work is through his own book, *Storms of My Grandchildren* (2009); this contains not just a modicum of autobiographical material but a detailed account of his thinking on climate change. Some of the science in the book can seem a bit tough to plow through until you realize that sometimes he uses ordinary words (e.g., "forcing") in quite specific technical meanings.
- He has a website at www.columbia.edu/~jeh1/; there you can sign up for intermittent updates from him about his latest work, research papers, and so on.
- His 2012 TED lecture, "Why I Must Speak Out about Climate Change," can be found on YouTube, as can numerous other talks, interviews, and associated documentaries.

INDEX OF NAMES

Entries in Capitals and small capitals refer to the main essays in this book. Page numbers in **bold** refer to major discussions.

Cicero *(106–43 BCE)* 22
Clairaut, Alexis *(1713–1765)* 79
Clarke, Joan *(1917–1996)* 192
Claudius Ptolemaeus *see* PTOLEMY
Clausius, Rudolf *(1822–1888)* 141
Clement IV *(ca. 1200–1268)*, Pope 45
Clifford, George III *(1685–1760)* 81
Columbus, Christopher *(ca. 1450–1506)* 26–7
Comte, Auguste *(1798–1857)* 176
Constantine the Great *(ca. 272–337)* 30
COPERNICUS, Nicolaus 8, **35–8**, 40, 41, 50, 51, 53, 56, 66
Correns, Carl Erich *(1864–1933)* 127
Crick, Francis *(1916–2004)* 125n, 201, 202, 203
Cromwell, Oliver *(1599–1658)* 63
Curie, Ève *(1904–2007)* 146, 147
CURIE, Marie 8, **143–7**, 149–50
Curie, Paul-Jacques *(1856–1941)* 143
Curie, Pierre *(1859–1906)* **143–5**, 146, 147
Cyril *(ca. 376–444)*, patriarch of Alexandria 30

DALTON, John **99–102**, 155
DARWIN, Charles 8, 82, 87, 88, 104, **110–18**, 125, 125n, 127, 128, 131, 134, 202
Darwin, Emma *(1808–1896)* 113, 117
Darwin, George *(1845–1912)* 118
Darwin, Robert *(1766–1848)* 110
David, Jacques-Louis *(1748–1825)* 96
Davy, Sir Humphry *(1778–1829)* 106–107, 107n
Dawkins, Richard *(b. 1941)* 71–2, 109
de Broglie, Louis *(1892–1987)* 167
de Fourcroy, Antoine *(1755–1809)* 95
de la Rue, Warren *(1815–1889)* 176
Democritus *(ca. 460–370 BCE)* 99
De Morgan, Augustus *(1806–1871)* 120
de Morveau, Guyton *(1737–1816)* 95
Descartes, René *(1596–1650)* 64, 66, 77–8
de Tournefort, Joseph Pitton *(1656–1708)* 80
de Valera, Éamon *(1882–1975)* 169
Devereux, Robert, 2nd Earl of Essex *(1565–1601)* 43

de Vries, Hugo *(1848–1935)* 127–8
Dickens, Charles *(1812–1870)* 120
Diophantus *(ca. 210–ca. 290)* 29
Dirac, Paul *(1902–1984)* 149, 167, 169, 181
Drago, Marco *(fl. 2016)* 160
DU CHÂTELET, Émilie 8, 67, 67n, **77–9**, 141, 203
du Châtelet-Lomont, Marquis Florent-Claude *(fl. 1725)* 77
Duell, Charles H. *(1850–1920)* 148
Dumas, Jean Baptiste André *(1800–1884)* 129
Du Toit, Alexander Logie *(1878–1949)* 164

Earle, Augustus *(ca. 1793–1838)* 111n
Eddington, Arthur *(1882–1944)* 152, 159, 160, 188, 189
Edmonstone, John *(fl. 1830)* 110
Ehret, Georg Dionysius *(1708–1770)* 81
EINSTEIN, Albert 8, 75, 108, 132, 135, 137, 140, 141, 149, **152–62**, 166, 167, 171–2, 181, 188, 190, 204, 207, 208
Einstein, Eduard *(1910–1965)* 158
Einstein, Elsa *(1876–1936)* 158, 160–61, 162
Einstein, Hans Albert *(1904–1973)* 154, 158
Einstein, Lieserl *(b. 1902)* 153
Einstein, Maria "Maja" *(1881–1951)* 162
Einstein, Mileva *(1875–1948)* 153–4, 157–8
Elizabeth (Elizaveta Petrovna) *(1709–1761)*, empress of Russia 85
Elizabeth I *(1533–1603)*, queen of England 43
Enders, John *(1897–1985)* 195
Epicurus *(341–270 BCE)* 99
Eratosthenes *(ca. 276–ca. 195 BCE)* 26
EUCLID OF ALEXANDRIA **17–19**, 28, 29, 64, 136, 158, 208

Fabricius of Aquapendente, Hieronymus *(1537–1619)* 60, 61
FARADAY, Michael **106–109**, 120, 139
Farey, John *(1766–1826)* 104
Fatio de Duillier, Nicolas *(1664–1753)* 69
Fermi, Enrico *(1901–1954)* 149

ACKNOWLEDGMENTS

Many thanks to my editor at Zest, Daniel Harmon, for his continuing encouragement and support, to Pam Scoville, for agenting and so much more, and to Polly Watson, for her astute copyediting. Also, gratitude to Sean Carroll, who kindly gave me permission to quote the extract on page 137 from his article "Thanksgiving." You can (and should!) follow Sean's blog at www.preposterousuniverse.com/blog/.

ABOUT THE AUTHOR

John Grant was born in Aberdeen, Scotland, and now lives in New Jersey. He has written over 70 books, and has won two Hugo awards, a World Fantasy Award and others. His fiction has included novels like *The World* (1992), *The Far-Enough Window* (2002), *The Dragons of Manhattan* (2008) and *Leaving Fortusa* (2008), as well as numerous short stories, some of which have been collected as *Take No Prisoners* (2004) and *Tell No Lies* (2014). He wrote twelve novels with Joe Dever in the series *The Legends of Lone Wolf* between 1989 and 1994. With artist Bob Eggleton he created the two "illustrated fictions" *Dragonhenge* (2002) and *The Stardragons* (2005); the former brought him another Hugo nomination.

His nonfiction has included *The Encyclopedia of Walt Disney's Animated Characters* (three editions: 1987, 1993, 1998), *The Encyclopedia of Fantasy* (1997, with John Clute), *The Chesley Awards* (2003, with Elizabeth Humphrey and Pamela D. Scoville) and a sequence of books on the misuse and misunderstanding of science: *Discarded Science* (2006), *Corrupted Science* (2007), *Bogus Science* (2009) and *Denying Science* (2011). Related to this sequence has been his previous book for Zest, *Debunk It!* (2014). His *A Comprehensive Encyclopedia of Film Noir*, the largest film noir encyclopedia in the English language, was published in October 2013.

He lives with his wife, the animation-art appraiser Pamela D. Scoville, and too many cats.